Analyzing and Mitigating Security Risks in Cloud Computing

Pawan Kumar Goel
Raj Kumar Goel Institute of Technology, India

Hari Mohan Pandey
Bournemouth University, UK

Amit Singhal
Raj Kumar Goel Institute of Technology, India

Sanyam Agarwal
ACE Group of Colleges, India

A volume in the Advances in Information Security, Privacy, and Ethics (AISPE) Book Series

IGI Global
PUBLISHER of TIMELY KNOWLEDGE

Published in the United States of America by
IGI Global
Engineering Science Reference (an imprint of IGI Global)
701 E. Chocolate Avenue
Hershey PA, USA 17033
Tel: 717-533-8845
Fax: 717-533-8661
E-mail: cust@igi-global.com
Web site: http://www.igi-global.com

Library of Congress Cataloging-in-Publication Data

CIP Data in progress

Title: Analyzing and Mitigating Security Risks in Cloud Computing

ISBN: 9798369332498

British Cataloguing in Publication Data
A Cataloguing in Publication record for this book is available from the British Library.

For electronic access to this publication, please contact: eresources@igi-global.com.

Advances in Information Security, Privacy, and Ethics (AISPE) Book Series

ISSN:1948-9730
EISSN:1948-9749

Editor-in-Chief: Manish Gupta, State University of New York, USA

MISSION

As digital technologies become more pervasive in everyday life and the Internet is utilized in ever increasing ways by both private and public entities, concern over digital threats becomes more prevalent.

The **Advances in Information Security, Privacy, & Ethics (AISPE) Book Series** provides cutting-edge research on the protection and misuse of information and technology across various industries and settings. Comprised of scholarly research on topics such as identity management, cryptography, system security, authentication, and data protection, this book series is ideal for reference by IT professionals, academicians, and upper-level students.

COVERAGE

- Cookies
- Device Fingerprinting
- Computer ethics
- Internet Governance
- Global Privacy Concerns
- Cyberethics
- Information Security Standards
- Telecommunications Regulations
- IT Risk
- Electronic Mail Security

IGI Global is currently accepting manuscripts for publication within this series. To submit a proposal for a volume in this series, please contact our Acquisition Editors at Acquisitions@igi-global.com or visit: http://www.igi-global.com/publish/.

The Advances in Information Security, Privacy, and Ethics (AISPE) Book Series (ISSN 1948-9730) is published by IGI Global, 701 E. Chocolate Avenue, Hershey, PA 17033-1240, USA, www.igi-global.com. This series is composed of titles available for purchase individually; each title is edited to be contextually exclusive from any other title within the series. For pricing and ordering information please visit http://www.igi-global.com/book-series/advances-information-security-privacy-ethics/37157. Postmaster: Send all address changes to above address.

Titles in this Series

For a list of additional titles in this series, please visit:
http://www.igi-global.com/book-series/advances-information-security-privacy-ethics/37157

Emerging Technologies and Security in Cloud Computing
D. Lakshmi (VIT Bhopal University, India) and Amit Kumar Tyagi (National Institute of Fashion Technology, New Delhi, India)
Information Science Reference • © 2024 • 400pp • H/C (ISBN: 9798369320815) • US $315.00

Risk Detection and Cyber Security for the Success of Contemporary Computing
Raghvendra Kumar (GIET University, India) and Prasant Kumar Pattnaik (KIIT Univeristy, India)
Information Science Reference • © 2023 • 480pp • H/C (ISBN: 9781668493175) • US $225.00

Privacy Preservation and Secured Data Storage in Cloud Computing
Lakshmi D. (VIT Bhopal University, India) and Amit Kumar Tyagi (National Institute of Fashion Technology, New Delhi, India)
Engineering Science Reference • © 2023 • 516pp • H/C (ISBN: 9798369305935) • US $265.00

Contemporary Challenges for Cyber Security and Data Privacy
Nuno Mateus-Coelho (Lusófona University, Portugal) and Maria Manuela Cruz-Cunha (Polytechnic Institute of Cávado and Ave, Portugal)
Information Science Reference • © 2023 • 308pp • H/C (ISBN: 9798369315286) • US $275.00

For an entire list of titles in this series, please visit:
http://www.igi-global.com/book-series/advances-information-security-privacy-ethics/37157

IGI Global
PUBLISHER of TIMELY KNOWLEDGE

701 East Chocolate Avenue, Hershey, PA 17033, USA
Tel: 717-533-8845 x100 • Fax: 717-533-8661
E-Mail: cust@igi-global.com • www.igi-global.com

Table of Contents

Preface... xv

Chapter 1
Securing the Cloud: Understanding and Mitigating Data Breaches and Insider Attacks in Cloud Computing Environments 1
C. V. Suresh Babu, Hindustan Institute of Technolgy and Science, India
S. Subhash, Hindustan Institute of Technology and Science, India
M. Vignesh, Hindustan Institute of Technology and Science, India
T. Jeyavasan, Hindustan Institute of Technology and Science, India
V. Muthumanikavel, Hindustan Institute of Technology and Science, India

Chapter 2
Security Automation and Orchestration in the Cloud...24
Samridhi Gulati, Raj Kumar Goel Institute of Technology, India
Ayushi Tyagi, Raj Kumar Goel Institute of Technology, India
Pawan Kumar Goel, Raj Kumar Goel Institute of Technology, India

Chapter 3
Quantum Key Distribution and Authentication in the Cloud for Internet of Things 48
Pramod Kumar Sagar, Raj Kumar Goel Institute of Technology, India
Arnika Jain, Sharda School of Engineering and Technology, Sharda University, India

Chapter 4
A Quantitative Study on Cloud Computing in the UAE: Identifying and Addressing Adoption Barriers 66
Muhammad Marakkoottathil, Birla Institute for Technology and Science, UAE
Ramamurthy Venkatesh, Symbiosis International University, India
N. A. Natraj, Symbiosis International University, India

Chapter 5
Fortifying Cloud Storage Using Hash Code 91
N. Ambika, St. Francis College, India

Chapter 6
Impact of Artificial Intelligence (AI) and Machine Learning (ML) on Cloud Security 111
Ruchi Rai, Shri Ram Group of Colleges, India
Ankur Rohilla, Shri Ram Group of Colleges, India
Abhishek Rai, S.D. College of Engineering, India

Chapter 7
Mitigating Phishing Threats in Unmanned Aircraft Systems (UAS) Through Multi-Stage Defense Strategies...125
C. Selvan, REVA University, India
Aravindhan Ragunathan, HCL Technologies Ltd., USA
U. M. Ashwinkumar, REVA University, India

Chapter 8
Threat Modeling and Risk Analysis for Cloud Deployments 163
Prathibha Muraleedhara, Stanley Black & Decker, USA

Chapter 9
Service Level Agreements (SLAs) and Their Role in Establishing Trust 182
Rajeshwari Sissodia, H.N.B. Garhwal University, India
ManMohan Singh Rauthan, H.N.B. Garhwal University, India
Varun Barthwal, H.N.B. Garhwal University, India

Chapter 10
Threat Landscape and Common Security Challenges in Cloud Environments . 194
J. Jeyalakshmi, Amrita VishwaVidhyapeetham, India
S. Gnanavel, Department of Computing Technologies, SRM Institute of Science and Technology-Kattankulathur, India
K. Vijay, Rajalakshmi Engineering College, India
I. Eugene Berna, Bannari Amman Institute of Technology, India

Chapter 11
Strengthening Security, Privacy, and Trust in Artificial Intelligence Drones for Smart Cities 214
R. Sonia, Department of Computer Applications, B.S. Abdur Rahman Crescent Institute of Science and Technology, India
Neha Gupta, Department of Computer Science, ABES Engineering College, India
K. P. Manikandan, Department of CSE (Cyber Security), Madanapalle Institute of Technology and Science, India
R. Hemalatha, Department of Computer Science and Engineering, St. Joseph's College of Engineering, India
M. Jogendra Kumar, Department of Computer Science and Engineering, Koneru Lakshmaiah Education Foundation, India
Sampath Boopathi, Department of Mechanical Engineering, Muthayammal Engineering College, India

Compilation of References 243

About the Contributors 263

Index 268

Detailed Table of Contents

Preface.. xv

Chapter 1
Securing the Cloud: Understanding and Mitigating Data Breaches and Insider Attacks in Cloud Computing Environments 1
C. V. Suresh Babu, Hindustan Institute of Technolgy and Science, India
S. Subhash, Hindustan Institute of Technology and Science, India
M. Vignesh, Hindustan Institute of Technology and Science, India
T. Jeyavasan, Hindustan Institute of Technology and Science, India
V. Muthumanikavel, Hindustan Institute of Technology and Science, India

Cloud computing has emerged as a transformative technology, providing numerous benefits in terms of scalability, cost-efficiency, and accessibility. However, this paradigm shift in data storage and processing also introduces new challenges, particularly concerning security. This chapter explores cloud-specific threats, such as data breaches and insider attacks, within the context of cloud computing. This chapter explores the various dimensions of these threats, discussing the vulnerabilities associated with cloud environments, potential attack vectors, and their impact on data security and privacy. To mitigate these threats, security measures like encryption, access control, and monitoring are examined. Furthermore, this chapter discusses the importance of proactive risk assessment and security strategies to protect sensitive information in the cloud.

Chapter 2
Security Automation and Orchestration in the Cloud..24
Samridhi Gulati, Raj Kumar Goel Institute of Technology, India
Ayushi Tyagi, Raj Kumar Goel Institute of Technology, India
Pawan Kumar Goel, Raj Kumar Goel Institute of Technology, India

As cloud computing evolves, the state of the digital infrastructure and the growth of cloud environments pose unprecedented challenges in protecting critical data and applications. This chapter explores the critical role of security automation orchestration (SAO) in addressing the evolving security requirements of cloud computing. The chapter begins by exploring the basic principles of automation security, providing the benefits and fundamentals that underpin effective automation, followed by the unique security challenges in the cloud in the environment and how automation can be effectively used to mitigate these risks is clear. The comprehensive security framework in cloud environments is presented, showing the integration of security tools and technologies to streamline incident response processes.

Chapter 3
Quantum Key Distribution and Authentication in the Cloud for Internet of Things 48
Pramod Kumar Sagar, Raj Kumar Goel Institute of Technology, India
Arnika Jain, Sharda School of Engineering and Technology, Sharda University, India

Quantum computing is a type of computing that takes advantage of the principles of quantum mechanics to perform certain types of calculations much more efficiently than classical computers. Cloud computing has become the budding engine of the internet of things (IoT) and has become one of the most popular technologies in the last few years. The security of cloud computing is a key issue in the security of IoT. Quantum key distribution (QKD) and quantum authentication methods have been proposed in this chapter. The proposed protocol is able to authenticate the users in cloud using a short, shared key. The QKD is based on a quantum key distribution protocol that consists of two levels, namely, private key distribution and quantum authentication. The first level authentication takes place using shared key distribution. The second level authentication uses a shared key, and the third level authenticates the user in the cloud. The third level authentication is carried out using the quantum key distribution protocol.

Chapter 4
A Quantitative Study on Cloud Computing in the UAE: Identifying and Addressing Adoption Barriers 66
Muhammad Marakkoottathil, Birla Institute for Technology and Science, UAE
Ramamurthy Venkatesh, Symbiosis International University, India
N. A. Natraj, Symbiosis International University, India

Information technology and digitization of the business are the key enablers for success in the current competitive market. Businesses across all industries face many challenges when choosing relevant technology solutions and their platforms. However, adoption of cloud computing among enterprises varies in different countries and global markets. Even in emerging markets such as UAE, adoption of cloud is facing definite barriers as highlighted by some recent studies. This research study is aimed at extending current literature on barriers of cloud adoption in UAE with more fine-grained factors and interpretations with the help of quantitative survey research. Resultant analyses were presented as a model for further validation by select IT experts and professional managers, who reconfirmed the research results are applicable, fit, and valid for UAE market. This study thus enhances the current literature on cloud adoption barriers in general and provides more fine-grained factors specific to UAE IT market perceptions.

Chapter 5
Fortifying Cloud Storage Using Hash Code 91
N. Ambika, St. Francis College, India

The data owner has complete control over it under the previous paradigm. Data owners set smart contracts. In smart contracts, the data owner stores data hash. On data, Ethereum performs encryption. It is also in charge of creating data hashes. The data owner receives a request from the user. The data owner updates information in smart contracts. After that, smart contracts provide access permissions and duration to the data user. After that, users of data can access data stored in the cloud. The recommendation suggests tracing the user and his doings.

Chapter 6
Impact of Artificial Intelligence (AI) and Machine Learning (ML) on Cloud Security 111
Ruchi Rai, Shri Ram Group of Colleges, India
Ankur Rohilla, Shri Ram Group of Colleges, India
Abhishek Rai, S.D. College of Engineering, India

This chapter explores the profound impact of artificial intelligence (AI) and machine learning (ML) on the realm of cloud security. As organizations increasingly migrate their operations and data to cloud environments, ensuring robust security measures becomes paramount. The integration of AI and ML technologies introduces novel ways to enhance threat detection, prevention, and response in the cloud. This chapter delves into various aspects of this synergy, discussing the benefits, challenges, and future prospects of utilizing AI and ML for safeguarding cloud infrastructures. This chapter also presents the benefits, challenges, and future directions. It underscores the transformative potential of AI and ML in fortifying cloud infrastructures and safeguarding sensitive information in the digital age.

Chapter 7
Mitigating Phishing Threats in Unmanned Aircraft Systems (UAS) Through Multi-Stage Defense Strategies 125
C. Selvan, REVA University, India
Aravindhan Ragunathan, HCL Technologies Ltd., USA
U. M. Ashwinkumar, REVA University, India

Phishing attacks, while more commonly associated with targeting individuals or organizations through traditional communication channels like email or social media, pose potential threats to unmanned aircraft systems (UAS) or drones. Although not as prevalent in this domain, there exist scenarios where phishing tactics could compromise UAS operations and data. Attackers might impersonate legitimate UAS entities, crafting emails that appear credible and relevant to UAS operations. A multi-stage approach incorporating natural language processing and machine learning is introduced to combat such threats. This approach employs techniques like conditional random field (CRF) and latent Dirichlet allocation (LDA) to detect phishing attacks and discern manipulated content. A novel web crawler utilizing web ontology language (OWL) is devised, leveraging semantic relationships to filter out fake sites from search results. The experimental results demonstrate the effectiveness of these methods in detecting and preventing phishing attacks across different platforms.

Chapter 8
Threat Modeling and Risk Analysis for Cloud Deployments............................163
Prathibha Muraleedhara, Stanley Black & Decker, USA

Today, most of the solutions and applications are migrated to cloud platforms. All the cloud service providers (CSP) employ a shared responsibility model. This means the cloud providers are responsible for the security "of the cloud" and the customers are responsible for the security "in the cloud." Based on research it is stated that 95% of cloud security breaches are because of user misconfigurations. Cloud security almost entirely depends on the consumers configuring and using the cloud platform. Thus, it is important to understand the threat landscape of cloud implementations, the risks involved, and ways to remediate them. One of the earliest and most important processes is threat modeling. This process helps in analyzing the cloud architecture, identifying security threats, evaluating risks, and prioritizing remediation efforts. This chapter describes how to apply some of the popular threat modeling frameworks to access cloud architectures.

Chapter 9
Service Level Agreements (SLAs) and Their Role in Establishing Trust 182
Rajeshwari Sissodia, H.N.B. Garhwal University, India
ManMohan Singh Rauthan, H.N.B. Garhwal University, India
Varun Barthwal, H.N.B. Garhwal University, India

In the ever-evolving landscape of modern business, the cultivation of trust between service providers and their clients stands as a linchpin for sustainable success. This chapter seeks to explore the pivotal role played by service level agreements (SLAs) in establishing and fortifying this essential trust. In essence, this chapter aims to provide a comprehensive understanding of SLAs as more than contractual obligations, positioning them as instrumental tools for navigating the complex terrain of modern business relationships. Through insightful analyses and practical insights, the chapter will contribute to the discourse on trust-building mechanisms, underscoring the indispensable role of SLAs in shaping the dynamics of contemporary business interactions.

Chapter 10
Threat Landscape and Common Security Challenges in Cloud Environments. 194
J. Jeyalakshmi, Amrita VishwaVidhyapeetham, India
S. Gnanavel, Department of Computing Technologies, SRM Institute of Science and Technology-Kattankulathur, India
K. Vijay, Rajalakshmi Engineering College, India
I. Eugene Berna, Bannari Amman Institute of Technology, India

Because of the proliferation of cloud computing, the security landscape in these settings presents a unique set of difficulties and risks. The benefits and game-changing consequences of cloud apps make them essential in the digital era. The ability to scale up or down helps organizations maximize their time and money commitments. They enable remote work and cooperation by letting users access their data and apps from anywhere. Cloud services save money by reducing hardware, software, and maintenance costs. But the security threats are deterring their performance. Data breaches are caused by, for example, insufficient encryption or slack access controls, interface and API vulnerabilities that can be exploited, insider threats caused by the misuse of privileges, identity and access management flaws, poor configuration and security practices, DoS attacks, shared technology flaws, data privacy and compliance concerns, a lack of oversight and control, and new, unknown threats.

Chapter 11
Strengthening Security, Privacy, and Trust in Artificial Intelligence Drones for Smart Cities 214
R. Sonia, Department of Computer Applications, B.S. Abdur Rahman Crescent Institute of Science and Technology, India
Neha Gupta, Department of Computer Science, ABES Engineering College, India
K. P. Manikandan, Department of CSE (Cyber Security), Madanapalle Institute of Technology and Science, India
R. Hemalatha, Department of Computer Science and Engineering, St. Joseph's College of Engineering, India
M. Jogendra Kumar, Department of Computer Science and Engineering, Koneru Lakshmaiah Education Foundation, India
Sampath Boopathi, Department of Mechanical Engineering, Muthayammal Engineering College, India

Smart cities are transforming by integrating artificial intelligence (AI) drones for various applications, including traffic monitoring, public space management, and surveillance. However, the increasing reliance on AI drones raises concerns about the security, privacy, and trust of both the technology and the data it collects and processes. Ensuring these factors is crucial for the success of these smart cities. The chapter explores the challenges and strategies for improving security, privacy, and trust in AI drones in smart cities. It emphasizes the role of AI drones in urban innovation, the evolving threat landscape, and the importance of robust security measures. Privacy considerations are also discussed, along with transparency, accountability, ethical use, and public engagement. Technical solutions include AI algorithms, secure communication protocols, and trusted hardware and software components. The chapter also explores future trends and emerging technologies in AI drones and the evolving regulatory landscape.

Compilation of References 243

About the Contributors 263

Index 268

Preface

As editors of *Analyzing and Mitigating Security Risks in Cloud Computing*, we are honored to present this comprehensive reference book crafted by Pawan Kumar Goel, Hari Mohan Pandey, Amit Singhal, and Sanyam Agarwhal. In an age defined by digital transformation, the adoption of cloud computing has become a cornerstone in the evolution of technology, reshaping the landscape for businesses and individuals alike. The scalability, accessibility, and cost-efficiency of the cloud have ushered in unparalleled opportunities, but they have also given rise to a complex web of challenges that demand a nuanced understanding and strategic approach.

Our motivation for this book stems from the recognition that the multifaceted issues surrounding cloud computing—particularly in the realms of security, privacy, and trust—require more than a cursory exploration. "Analyzing and Mitigating Security Risks in Cloud Computing" endeavors to be a definitive guide, arming readers with the knowledge, insights, and practical strategies needed to navigate the intricate realm of cloud computing while safeguarding their most valuable assets.

A WORLD OF OPPORTUNITIES, A UNIVERSE OF RISKS

Cloud computing has democratized access to cutting-edge technologies, offering opportunities for innovation, flexibility, and business growth on an unprecedented scale. However, beneath the surface lies a constellation of risks—data breaches, cyberattacks, and unauthorized access—that threaten both the information stored in the cloud and the very operations of organizations. Our preface sets the stage for a deeper exploration, emphasizing the delicate balance between the advantages and risks inherent in cloud adoption.

THE PILLARS OF SECURITY, PRIVACY, AND TRUST

Security, privacy, and trust are the cornerstones of a resilient cloud strategy. In our exploration, we take a holistic approach, recognizing the interdependence of these pillars. Security forms the fortress, privacy ensures the respectful handling of personal information, and trust fosters a relationship grounded in transparency, reliability, and accountability.

NAVIGATING THE CHAPTERS

As readers embark on this multidimensional expedition, they will delve into encryption algorithms, access control mechanisms, compliance and governance intricacies, and real-world case studies. From data encryption techniques to incident response protocols, our goal is to provide practical insights and actionable strategies for IT professionals, security experts, and decision-makers.

Chapter 1 serves as a foundational exploration into the transformative landscape of cloud computing, emphasizing its benefits in scalability, cost-efficiency, and accessibility. However, the paradigm shift in data storage and processing introduces new challenges, with a particular focus on security. The abstract delves into cloud-specific threats, such as data breaches and insider attacks, within the context of cloud computing. Readers can expect an in-depth examination of the vulnerabilities associated with cloud environments, potential attack vectors, and their implications for data security and privacy. Moreover, the chapter provides insights into security measures, including encryption, access control, and monitoring, offering a proactive approach to risk assessment and security strategies to safeguard sensitive information in the cloud.

Chapter 2 addresses the evolving security requirements of cloud computing by exploring the critical role of Security Automation Orchestration (SAO). Beginning with an exploration of the basic principles of automation security, the chapter outlines the benefits and fundamentals that underpin effective automation. It delves into unique security challenges in cloud environments and demonstrates how automation can be effectively utilized to mitigate these risks. Readers can anticipate a comprehensive framework that integrates security tools and technologies, streamlining incident response processes in cloud environments.

As quantum computing emerges as a powerful force in computation, Chapter 3 explores its impact on cloud security, particularly in the context of the Internet of Things (IoT). Focusing on the budding engine of IoT, the chapter introduces Quantum Key Distribution (QKD) and quantum authentication methods as crucial elements for securing cloud computing. Readers can expect an examination of a proposed protocol utilizing shared keys and multi-level authentication, illustrating how QKD can enhance security in the cloud. The chapter provides valuable insights into the evolving landscape of quantum technologies and their application in preserving data privacy in cloud environments.

This research-driven chapter delves into the dynamics of cloud adoption among enterprises, with a specific focus on the challenges faced in the UAE market. Building on existing literature, Chapter 4 aims to extend the understanding of barriers to cloud adoption by presenting fine-grained factors and interpretations. Readers can anticipate a quantitative survey research approach, the presentation of resultant analyses, and a model validated by IT experts and professional managers. The chapter contributes to the broader literature on cloud adoption barriers, offering market-specific insights that enhance our understanding of perceptions in the UAE IT market.

Chapter 5 explores a paradigm shift in data control, moving from the previous owner-centric model to a blockchain-enabled approach using smart contracts. Readers can expect an exploration of how smart contracts, powered by blockchain technology, redefine data ownership and access permissions in the cloud. The chapter outlines the processes where the data owner sets smart contracts, updates information, and provides access permissions to users. Additionally, recommendations for tracing user activities are presented, showcasing the potential of blockchain in enhancing data control in cloud computing.

Chapter 6 delves into the transformative impact of Artificial Intelligence (AI) and Machine Learning (ML) on cloud security. With organizations increasingly migrating operations to the cloud, ensuring robust security measures becomes paramount. Readers can expect an exploration of various aspects of this synergy, discussing benefits, challenges, and future prospects of utilizing AI and ML for safeguarding cloud infrastructures. The chapter highlights the transformative potential of these technologies in fortifying cloud infrastructures and safeguarding sensitive information in the digital age.

Chapter 7 addresses a unique but critical threat landscape – phishing attacks on Unmanned Aircraft Systems (UAS) or drones. While less prevalent, such attacks could compromise UAS operations and data. Readers can anticipate a multi-stage approach incorporating Natural Language Processing (NLP) and Machine Learning (ML) to detect and prevent phishing attacks. The chapter introduces techniques like Conditional Random Field (CRF) and Latent Dirichlet Allocation (LDA) and a novel web crawler utilizing Web Ontology Language (OWL) to filter out fake sites. Experimental results demonstrate the effectiveness of these methods across different platforms.

Chapter 8 focuses on the shared responsibility model in cloud computing, emphasizing the critical role of threat modeling in analyzing cloud architectures. Readers can expect insights into the threat landscape of cloud implementations, risks involved, and ways to remediate them. The chapter particularly addresses the prevalence of user misconfigurations as a significant contributor to cloud security breaches. Practical guidance on applying popular threat modeling frameworks to assess cloud architectures is provided, offering a foundational understanding of effective threat management in cloud environments.

Chapter 9 delves into the pivotal role played by Service Level Agreements (SLAs) in establishing and fortifying trust between service providers and clients. Readers can anticipate a comprehensive understanding of SLAs beyond contractual obligations, positioning them as instrumental tools for navigating the complex terrain of modern business relationships. Through insightful analyses and practical insights, the chapter aims to contribute to the discourse on trust-building mechanisms, emphasizing the indispensable role of SLAs in shaping the dynamics of contemporary business interactions.

Chapter 10 provides a comprehensive overview of the security threats and challenges in cloud computing. Readers can expect an exploration of the benefits and game-changing consequences of cloud applications, coupled with an in-depth analysis of security threats deterring their performance. The chapter covers a spectrum of security threats, including data breaches, insider threats, identity and access management flaws, and more. It highlights the need for a robust security posture in the face of evolving threats, emphasizing the importance of oversight, control, and proactive security practices.

As smart cities integrate AI drones for various applications, Chapter 11 explores the challenges and strategies for improving security, privacy, and trust in AI drones. Readers can expect an examination of the role of AI drones in urban innovation, the evolving threat landscape, and the importance of robust security measures. Privacy considerations, transparency, accountability, ethical use, and public engagement are discussed, providing a holistic view of the security landscape in the context of AI drones. Technical solutions, including AI algorithms and secure communication protocols, are presented, along with insights into future trends and emerging technologies in AI drones and the regulatory landscape.

EMBARKING ON A TRANSFORMATIVE ODYSSEY

Our transformative odyssey invites readers to uncover the secrets of fortifying cloud environments against threats, embrace privacy-enhancing technologies, and forge unbreakable bonds of trust. The challenges are significant, but the rewards are equally substantial. By enhancing security, privacy, and trust in cloud computing, we collectively chart a course toward a safer, more resilient digital future.

OBJECTIVES OF THE BOOK

The primary objective of *Analyzing and Mitigating Security Risks in Cloud Computing* is to provide a comprehensive and authoritative guide that addresses the multifaceted challenges of security, privacy, and trust in the context of cloud computing. The book aims to achieve the following specific objectives:

- Offer readers a clear and in-depth understanding of the complex interplay between security, privacy, and trust in cloud computing. The book demystifies technical jargon and concepts, making them accessible to a wide range of audiences.
- Present a holistic coverage of topics related to cloud security, privacy, and trust. Cover various aspects including encryption, access controls, compliance, incident response, data governance, and emerging technologies impacting cloud security.
- Provide practical insights into industry best practices for securing cloud environments. This includes detailed guidance on implementing security measures, privacy-enhancing technologies, and fostering a culture of trust in cloud operations.
- Explore real-world case studies and examples of both successful cloud security implementations and notable breaches. These scenarios will offer practical lessons and illustrate the potential consequences of inadequate security measures.
- Demonstrate the applicability of Artificial Intelligence (AI) and Machine Learning (ML) in safeguarding cloud infrastructure, detect and prevent phishing attacks and suggest mechanism to mitigate with future challenges.

By addressing this diverse audience, "Analyzing and Mitigating Security Risks in Cloud Computing" aims to empower professionals at various levels to effectively tackle the security, privacy, and trust challenges associated with cloud computing.

Pawan Kumar Goel
Raj Kumar Goel Institute of Technology, India

Hari Mohan Pandey
Bournemouth University, UK

Amit Singhal
Raj Kumar Goel Institute of Technology, India

Sanyam Agarwal
ACE Group of Colleges, India

Chapter 1

Securing the Cloud:
Understanding and Mitigating Data Breaches and Insider Attacks in Cloud Computing Environments

C. V. Suresh Babu
https://orcid.org/0000-0002-8474-2882
Hindustan Institute of Technolgy and Science, India

S. Subhash
Hindustan Institute of Technology and Science, India

M. Vignesh
Hindustan Institute of Technology and Science, India

T. Jeyavasan
Hindustan Institute of Technology and Science, India

V. Muthumanikavel
Hindustan Institute of Technology and Science, India

ABSTRACT

Cloud computing has emerged as a transformative technology, providing numerous benefits in terms of scalability, cost-efficiency, and accessibility. However, this paradigm shift in data storage and processing also introduces new challenges, particularly concerning security. This chapter explores cloud-specific threats, such as data breaches and insider attacks, within the context of cloud computing. This chapter explores the various dimensions of these threats, discussing the vulnerabilities associated with cloud environments, potential attack vectors, and their impact on data security and privacy. To mitigate these threats, security measures like encryption, access control, and monitoring are examined. Furthermore, this chapter discusses the importance of proactive risk assessment and security strategies to protect sensitive information in the cloud.

DOI: 10.4018/979-8-3693-3249-8.ch001

1. INTRODUCTION TO CLOUD COMPUTING AND ITS SIGNIFICANCE

Cloud computing is a revolutionary technology that enables the delivery of a variety of IT services, including storage, computing power, and applications, over the Internet (Suresh Babu, 2023). Due to its versatility, flexibility and cost-effectiveness, it has gained great importance in today's digital landscape. Cloud computing eliminates the need for organizations to maintain and invest in extensive infrastructure, allowing access to resources on a pay-as-you-go basis that can be scaled up or down quickly to meet changing demands. Armbrust et al. (2010), cloud computing offers powerful computing resources and the democratization of data storage, benefiting a variety of industries from start-ups to large enterprises. According to Raj and Srinivasan (2019, p. 72), insider threats are a major security concern for cloud computing environments.

Cloud computing has become the pinnacle of the digital age, a ground-breaking technological innovation that has dramatically changed the way individuals and organizations access, use, and manage their computing resources, data, and applications. This transformation goes beyond simplicity to the core of how businesses and individuals operate in the interconnected world of the 21st century. The importance of cloud computing is demonstrated by its versatile capabilities, including on-demand self-service, ubiquitous networking, resource pooling, rapid agility, and scalable services. This feature allows users to find optimal computing resources from almost anywhere and dynamically scale their resources in response to changing demands, providing unparalleled flexibility. The importance of cloud computing is increasing with different deployment models. custom solutions for a variety of requirements. Public clouds are available to the public and are often used for web-based email services, data storage, and application hosting. Private clouds, on the other hand, are dedicated to organizations that provide enhanced control over data and resources while maintaining cloud-like characteristics. According to Smith (2018, p. 17), "cloud computing introduces new security risks, such as data breaches, account hijacking, and denial-of-service attacks. Community clouds, designed for a specific group of users with common problems, provide an environment where organizations can collaborate and share resources while following common policies and requirements. Cloud computing environments are vulnerable to a variety of security threats, including data breaches, denial-of-service attacks, and insider attacks, Goyal, Kakkar, and Kumar (2020, p. 1).

Another measure of the impact of cloud computing is in the service model. Among them Infrastructure as a Service (IaaS), Platform as a Service (PaaS), and Software as a Service (SaaS). IaaS provides virtualized computing resources over the Internet by providing additional infrastructure elements such as virtual machines, storage, and networks. PaaS provides a platform for developers to build, deploy, and manage applications without having to deal with existing infrastructure. Finally, SaaS delivers software over the Internet, eliminating the need to install and maintain software on users' local devices. This service-based approach simplifies software delivery and maintenance, reducing the administrative burden for users and IT teams. The continued importance of cloud computing is the basis of many innovations and disruptions. Cloud services rely on the infrastructure of countless applications, from data storage and processing to advanced technologies. It enables organizations to embrace digital transformation and respond quickly to changing market conditions, as infrastructure management challenges are outsourced to cloud providers. The scalable and cost-effective nature of the cloud has become the core of modern business processes, allowing businesses to focus on value-added activities and remain flexible in the face of the ever-evolving technological landscape and market.

This technology has become an important element in today's digital age, enabling innovation and agility while reducing capital costs and becoming a pillar of the modern enterprise and technology ecosystem.

1.1 A Brief Introduction to Cloud Computing and Its Growing Importance in Today's Digital Landscape

Cloud computing has become the core of the modern digital landscape, offering a revolutionary approach to providing computing services (Mell & Grace, 2011). Infrastructure works by providing platforms and software, eliminating the need for local infrastructure (Armbrust et al., 2010). Key concepts in cloud computing such as Infrastructure as a Service (IaaS), Platform as a Service (PaaS), and Software as a Service (SaaS) have brought scalability, cost savings, and access to the fore (Mell & Grace, 2011). Deployment models, including public, private, and hybrid clouds, meet different organizational requirements (NIST, 2011). The cloud supports infrastructure deployment (Amazon Web Services, Microsoft Azure, Google Cloud Platform), software development (Hofmann et al., 2019), and big data analytics power (Marz & Warren, 2015). The growing importance is in cost effectiveness, innovation, flexibility and fostering a sustainable form of disaster recovery (Leimeister et al., 2018). With its global reach and 24/7 access, cloud computing has become an integral part of the digital landscape, enabling businesses and organizations to thrive in today's fast-paced digital world.

Cloud computing, a transformative technology paradigm, has changed the way individuals and organizations access, manage and use their digital resources. According to Babu and Srisakthi (2023, p. 104), cyber-physical systems (CPS) are becoming increasingly widespread in a variety of industries, including healthcare, transportation, and manufacturing. Computing services, storage, processing, networking, etc. provide via the internet. Cloud computing has become a staple of the modern digital landscape, shaping our relationship with technology and data. In the digital era, its great importance and great importance is evident in its wide spread in various industries. According to Jha and Buyya (2013, p. 389), cloud computing environments are vulnerable to a variety of security threats, including data breaches, denial-of-service attacks, and insider attacks.

One of the key features of cloud computing is the on-demand self-service capability, where users can access computing resources as needed. According to Hu and Liu (2016, p. 50), cloud computing environments are vulnerable to a variety of security threats, including data breaches, denial-of-service attacks, and insider attacks. This flexibility is complemented by ubiquitous network access that allows users to connect to cloud services from anywhere with an Internet connection. Cloud resources are pooled, enabling efficient use and dynamic distribution, allowing organizations to scale up or down in response to changing demands. This growth is further enhanced by its rapid flexibility, which enables rapid and automated deployment. Cloud resource consumption is accurately measured, following a "pay-as-you-go" model where users are billed for resources consumed.

Cloud services are divided into three main service models: Infrastructure as a Service (IaaS), Platform as a Service (PaaS), and Software as a Service (SaaS). IaaS virtual machines provide virtualized computing resources over the Internet, including storage and network components. PaaS provides a platform for developers to build, deploy, and manage applications by abstracting the underlying infrastructure management. SaaS provides software over the Internet, eliminating the need to install and maintain software on users' local devices.

The growing importance of cloud computing in the digital landscape is illustrated by its key role in enabling digital transformation. The cloud has become the backbone of digital services, from data storage and processing to advanced technologies such as artificial intelligence, machine learning and the Internet of Things. Its scalable and cost-effective nature allows organizations to focus on innovation and flexibility in the face of evolving market conditions. In an era characterized by rapid technological development and interdependence, cloud computing is not just a trend; is a key enabler of digital innovation and business success.

1.2 Highlighting the Benefits and Advantages of Cloud Computing for Organizations

Cloud computing offers many advantages and benefits to organizations. It greatly improves cost efficiency by eliminating the need for large investments and allowing premium pricing (Armbrust et al., 2010). Scalability is a feature as cloud services can seamlessly adapt to changing workloads and seasonal requirements, ensuring optimal use of resources. Accessibility and mobility are facilitated, allowing the workforce to access information and applications from anywhere with an Internet connection (Buya et al., 2009). Cloud computing fuels innovation and agility, and providers continue to offer new services for organizations to improve their competitiveness in a dynamic market. Its flexibility means services can be quickly tailored to meet specific business needs and as requirements change. Reliable disaster recovery options increase resilience and global scale of cloud providers facilitates international expansion (Armbrust et al., 2010). Although security remains a concern, many cloud providers invest heavily in security measures (Mell & Grace, 2011). In addition, cloud data center resource efficiency can reduce the environmental impact of the organization (Marz & Warren, 2015). These advantages make cloud computing an attractive and strategic option for optimizing operations and driving growth in organizations of all sizes.

Cloud computing has become an important asset for organizations in today's digital landscape with many benefits. One of the main benefits is cost efficiency. Cloud computing eliminates the need for organizations to make significant investments in on-premise infrastructure, including servers, data centers and IT staff. Instead, they can choose a subscription or a paid model, where they only pay for the computing resources they use. This will significantly reduce the cost of capital, allowing efforts to allocate resources more efficiently and invest in other areas that are important for their growth (Gupta et al., 2016).

Scalability is an attractive benefit of cloud computing. Cloud services offer unparalleled flexibility in providing resources. Organizations can quickly and easily adjust computing power, storage and services to meet changing workloads. This flexibility is especially important for businesses with seasonal or unpredictable demand patterns. This ensures that they can effectively manage peak periods, optimizing resource utilization and savings without overprovisioning during leaner periods (Mell & Grace, 2011).

The solution lies in cloud computing through multiple service models. Organizations can define Infrastructure as a Service (IaaS), Platform as a Service (PaaS), and Software as a Service (SaaS). IaaS provides virtual computing resources, PaaS provides a development and deployment platform, and SaaS provides software over the Internet. This flexibility allows organizations to choose the most suitable cloud service for running applications, hosting websites, or managing data storage for their unique needs (Mell & Grace, 2011).

Accessibility is an important advantage in an era of increasingly common remote work and global collaboration. Cloud services can be accessed from anywhere with an internet connection, which allows employees to work from different locations and devices. This availability has proven to be important as it ensures business continuity and smooth operations, especially in recent times due to disruptions such as the COVID-19 pandemic (Marr, 2021).

Cloud computing also relieves organizations of the burden of maintenance and upgrades. Cloud service providers are responsible for managing and providing infrastructure and software. This means that the organization does not need to spend time and resources on routine maintenance, reducing the burden on the IT department and ensuring that they are always up to date with the latest software versions and security updates (Mell & Grace, 2011).

Security is a major concern for businesses and cloud computing does not disappoint in this regard. Cloud providers invest heavily in security measures, often beyond what most organizations can achieve on their own. They implement strong security protocols, encryption, access control and identity management to protect data and resources. Data redundancy and backup services improve disaster recovery capabilities by ensuring data is safe and available (Marr, 2021).

In addition, cloud-based collaboration tools and productivity suites such as Google Workspace and Microsoft 365 improve collaboration and communication. These tools facilitate seamless document sharing, communication, and project management, allowing employees to work efficiently and access their work from different devices (Marr, 2021).

The global scale of cloud computing is an invaluable asset. With data centers located around the world, cloud providers offer low-latency access to services, ensuring minimal delays to users. This makes it easier for organizations to expand into international markets and attract a global audience, improving user experience and enabling business growth (Bogate, 2018).

The analytical potential of cloud computing is enormous. Computing power and extensive storage capabilities are essential for data analytics, which enable organizations to extract valuable insights from large databases. This is especially important for decision-making and gaining competitiveness in a data-driven world (Bogate, 2018).

Importantly, cloud computing can benefit the environment. Cloud service providers often operate data centers that are more energy efficient and environmentally friendly than traditional in-house data centers. By sharing resources and optimizing data center operations, cloud providers reduce the carbon footprint associated with computing operations and contribute to environmental sustainability (Marr, 2021).

2. CLOUD-SPECIFIC THREATS

2.1 An In-Depth Exploration of the Security Challenges Unique to the Cloud Environment

Security challenges in cloud environments are varied and distinct due to the dynamic, public, and abstract nature of cloud computing. The distribution of data in several, possibly international, data centers complicates data privacy and data privacy (Ristenpart et al., 2009). While cloud providers offer encryption, managing encryption keys and ensuring data privacy remain critical issues (Gentry, 2009). Access control and identity management are complex in multi-tenant cloud environments, often resulting in misconfiguration and data breaches (Almorsy et al., 2016). Ensuring compliance with regulatory requirements such as GDPR or HIPAA can be complex because cloud providers share responsibilities, but compliance responsibility ultimately rests with the organization (Katsaros et al., 2018). Network security is becoming increasingly difficult due to the risk of shared infrastructure and DDoS attacks (Sharma & Squicciarini, 2018). Incident response and litigation is hampered by the limited visibility of cloud infrastructure (Louridas, 2017). To overcome these challenges, organizations must adopt strong security practices and continuously adapt to emerging threats in the evolving cloud landscape.

2.2 Discussion of How Cloud-Specific Threats Differ From Traditional Cybersecurity Concerns

In the field of cybersecurity, cloud-specific threats present special challenges compared to traditional problems, mainly due to fundamental differences in cloud computing. According to Babu and Yadav (2023, p. 131), cyber-physical systems (CPS) are becoming increasingly interconnected with the cloud, which poses new security challenges. A shared responsibility model where cloud service providers (CSPs) and customers define security roles can lead to misunderstandings and gaps if not managed effectively (Ristenpart et al., 2009). Virtualization and multi-tenancy expose vulnerabilities such as hypervisor compromise that can affect multiple virtual machines (Göktas, 2017). Data localization and jurisdictional complexity in cloud environments can affect data privacy and compliance (Katsaros et al., 2018). The rapid growth and flexibility of cloud services require real-time adaptation of security measures, which is a challenge for traditional security practices. API dependencies and service dependencies can lead to data breaches and unauthorized access if not properly secured (Armbrust et al., 2010). Frequent misconfigurations can expose sensitive information. The complexity of IAM is more evident in multi-cloud environments (Almorsy et al., 2016) and the dependence on third parties creates supply chain risks (Sharma & Squicciarini, 2018). These cloud-related challenges require a new approach to security to effectively protect data, applications, and infrastructure in a cloud environment.

3. DATA BREACHES IN THE CLOUD

3.1 A Thorough Examination of Data Breaches, One of the Most Prevalent and Impactful Cloud Threats

Data breaches in cloud computing have high consequences for organizations and have significant consequences. The shared responsibility model inherent in cloud environments can lead to security gaps and misunderstandings about the definition of responsibility, which can open the door to data breaches (Ristenpart et al., 2009). Misconfiguration of cloud resources is often the cause, and cloud clients inadvertently expose public data due to misconfiguration access control or repositories (Almorsy et al., 2016). Insider threats and security risks are more severe in the cloud and require strong security measures to detect and prevent unauthorized access (Sharma & Squicciarini, 2018). Poor encryption and supply chain vulnerabilities contribute to the risk landscape (Gentry, 2009). In addition, the rapid growth of resources can create unexpected vulnerabilities if not managed effectively. Successful mitigation involves not only preventing disruptions, but also responding quickly with specific incident responses and remediation plans (Louridas, 2017). As the adoption of cloud computing increases, understanding and managing these risks is a top priority for organizations of all sizes.

3.2 Analysis of the Factors Contributing to Data Breaches in Cloud Environments

Data breaches in cloud environments are caused by a number of factors, each of which contributes to increased risk. Misconfiguration of cloud resources appears as the main source of disruption, such as inadequately secure storage or access control (Almorsy et al., 2016). A shared responsibility model that defines security responsibilities between cloud service providers (CSPs) and customers can lead to confusion and gaps if not managed effectively (Ristenpart et al., 2009). Insider threats, whether due to malicious intent or negligence, pose a significant risk in the cloud, requiring vigilant oversight and robust monitoring controls (Sharma & Squicciarini, 2018). Privilege compromise is often the result of weak password policies and phishing attacks, which offer unauthorized access to attackers, underscoring the need for multi-factor authentication and strong password policies. Dependence on third parties exposes supply chain vulnerabilities that can be exploited by attackers (Gentry, 2009). Inadequate encryption practices and the complexity of data protection contribute to the breach landscape. In addition, the rapid growth of resources and the lack of effective logging and monitoring can delay the detection and response of breaches. Developing a comprehensive incident response strategy is critical to managing the impact of a data breach (Louridas, 2017). As cloud adoption increases, understanding and proactively addressing these contributing factors is critical to data security in cloud environments.

3.3 Real-World Examples and Case Studies of Data Breaches in the Cloud

Actual studies of data breaches in cloud environments clearly show the vulnerabilities and potential risks associated with cloud computing. In 2019, Amazon One, a former employee of Amazon Web Services, experienced a major breach using a web application firewall that did not compromise the personal information of more than 100 million customers (Armer, 2020). The massive Equifax breach in 2017 exposed the sensitive data of 143 million people due to unpatched vulnerabilities (Gross, 2019). The 2017 Verizon breach involved an Amazon S3 bucket that was not modified by a third-party vendor, while Dow Jones and Accenture experienced similar incidents of misconfigured S3 buckets (Stearns, 2017). Time Warner Cable's exposure to four million subscriber records demonstrates the importance of cloud configuration (Muncaster, 2017). These cases highlight the critical importance of robust cloud security practices, continuous monitoring, and effective incident response measures to mitigate the multifaceted and growing risk of data misuse in cloud environments.

4. INSIDER ATTACKS IN THE CLOUD

4.1 An Exploration of Insider Attacks, Including Their Motives and Potential Consequences

Insider attacks, an important cyber security issue, are initiated by privileged individuals within an organization, and the causes can be very different (Suresh Babu, C. V., Andrew Simon, P., et. al. 2023). Some insiders are motivated by financial gain, intending to use sensitive financial information for personal gain, while others may use their knowledge to harm their employers and retaliate against injustice (Anderson, 2020). Internalization represents another reason why insiders act as insiders for external organizations or competitors by distorting sensitive information for strategic purposes (Cappelli et al., 2012). Curiosity or random actions can lead to insider threats, and employees can cause intentional security breaches (Krombholz et al., 2015). The consequences of insider attacks are profound and multifaceted, including data breaches that compromise sensitive data, financial losses, reputational damage, performance disruptions, business disruption, intellectual property loss, and legal and regulatory consequences (CERT, 2016). To counter these threats, organizations use proactive security measures and strong incident response plans, along with technical and non-technical measures, including access controls, user monitoring, security awareness training, and implementing strong security policies (CERT, 2016).

4.2 Discussion of the Techniques Used by Insiders to Compromise Cloud Security

Insiders with special access to the organization's cloud resources use a variety of techniques that create significant opportunities to compromise cloud security. They can be involved in data theft, directly stealing sensitive data stored in the cloud, or intentionally weakening access controls and exploiting misconfigurations that allow unauthorized access. Data exfiltration techniques are common, with insiders transferring data via e-mail, USB drives, or personal cloud storage accounts to avoid detection. Abuse and identity theft can lead to unauthorized actions and legitimate user identities. Insiders can spread malware in the cloud environment, manipulate data, gain privileges, or simply gain access and access. Social engineering tactics allow insiders to manipulate employees or cloud service providers to obtain sensitive information (CERT, 2016). Mitigation of this insider threat in the cloud requires secure monitoring and continuous monitoring, as well as non-technical approaches such as security awareness training, user behavior analysis and special access management. An effective incident plan is critical to detect, respond to, and recover from internal security incidents (CERT, 2016).

4.3 Strategies for Detecting and Mitigating Insider Threats in the Cloud

Effectively detecting and mitigating insider threats in the cloud requires a multi-pronged approach that includes a variety of strategies. Secure access controls and least privilege principles should be followed to limit unauthorized access (CERT, 2016). User and Entity Behavior (UEBA) tools can monitor and identify unusual behavior, while Data Loss Prevention (DLP) solutions help prevent unauthorized access to sensitive data. For cloud environments, specific internal threat detection tools play an important role in detecting anomalous behavior, and logging and monitoring, along with Security and Event Management (SIEM) solutions, provide insight into suspicious activity (NIST, 2020). Security awareness training, awareness programs, and good incident response plans foster a security-aware culture and facilitate early threat detection (CERT, 2016). Regular security checks, a zero-trust model, and encrypted data storage and transmission improve the overall security posture. Insider threat policies and consistent monitoring of user activity and strategic access permissions contribute to a comprehensive approach to insider threat mitigation (NIST, 2020).

5. THE INTERSECTION OF CLOUD COMPUTING AND IOT

5.1 Examining the Challenges Posed by the Integration of IoT Devices Into Cloud Environments

The integration of Internet of Things (IoT) devices into cloud environments presents many challenges stemming from the variety and diversity of IoT devices. Due to the often limited security features in IoT devices, security and privacy issues that may expose sensitive data are greater (Sharma et al., 2020). The large amount of data generated by IoT devices can expand network bandwidth and cause significant storage costs, while real-time processing requirements can be hampered by delays introduced during data transfer and cloud processing (Han et al., 2018). Ensuring compatibility between different devices and manufacturers and communication protocols poses another hurdle. Understandably, robustness in harsh environments and effective data analysis are important considerations (Mazhelis et al., 2019). Security updates and patch management can be difficult, compliance and data management are issues, and cost management is a constant focus. The growing role of energy efficiency and edge computing in IoT-cloud integration further complicates the challenge (Han et al., 2018). Overcoming these challenges requires a comprehensive strategy that includes security, data management, efficient resource allocation, and adaptation to the evolving IoT landscape (Sharma et al., 2020).

5.2 Analyzing How IoT Devices Can Become Vectors for Cloud-Related Attacks

IoT devices can be vectors for cloud-related attacks due to their vulnerabilities, making them attractive targets for exploitation (Al-Fuqaha et al., 2015). Trusted IoT devices can be used to launch widespread denial-of-service (DDoS) attacks against cloud services, causing service disruptions and cloud resources to be unavailable to legitimate users. In addition, attackers can use compromised IoT devices as channels for data exfiltration, identity and identity theft, leverage, and malware distribution in cloud environments (Suresh Babu. C.V., Akshayah N. S., et. al. 2023). These compromised devices can also create proxies to launch attacks against cloud services, hiding the attacker's identity. To mitigate this risk, organizations should strengthen security for IoT devices and cloud environments using, among other measures, regular device updates, access control, behavioral monitoring, intrusion detection systems, and threat intelligence. Network segmentation is important to isolate IoT devices from critical cloud resources (Etang et al., 2019).

5.3 Strategies for Securing IoT Devices and Data in the Cloud

Securing IoT devices and data in the cloud requires a multi-pronged approach to protect against potential threats and vulnerabilities. Implementing strong device recognition, authorization, and encryption mechanisms (Roman et al., 2013) ensures that only authorized devices can access cloud resources, protecting data in transit and at rest. Regular software updates are important to address known vulnerabilities and improve security features (Etang et al., 2019), while secure boot processes and hardware-based security solutions further strengthen IoT devices. Network segmentation helps isolate IoT devices from critical cloud resources to limit the impact of potential compromises, and intrusion detection and monitoring systems continuously analyze network traffic and device behavior to detect anomalies (Aarts et al., 2016). Availability control, data lifecycle management, compliance and governance, threat detection and response, user education, and vendor and supply chain security all contribute to a security strategy. Adherence to cloud security best practices and native cloud security tools further strengthen the overall security posture (Etang et al., 2019).

6. SOLUTIONS AND BEST PRACTICES

6.1 A Comprehensive Review of Best Practices and Security Measures to Mitigate Cloud-Specific Threats

Mitigating cloud-specific threats is essential in the evolving digital landscape, and a set of best practices and security measures are required to secure cloud environments. Secure identity and access management (IAM) strategies such as MFA and RBAC control user access, while encryption ensures data privacy at rest and in transit. Security Groups and Network ACLs provide granular control over network traffic, limiting exposure to potential threats. Cloud Security Posture Management (CSPM) tools continuously assess the cloud for configuration errors, vulnerabilities, and performance issues, improving threat detection (Han et al., 2018). Rigorous logging and monitoring, along with incident response planning, is essential to detect and respond to security incidents. Consistent patch management, data backup and recovery, and secure API usage minimize vulnerabilities. Authorization and auditing, security integration into DevOps processes, and threat-based security measures strengthen security measures. Utilizing cloud service provider (CSP) security features and disaster recovery planning ensure resilience (Etang et al., 2019). Maintaining cloud security requires constant adaptation and vigilance against evolving threats.

6.2 Discussion of the Role of IoT technology in Enhancing Cloud Security

IoT technology plays an important role in improving cloud security by introducing innovative strategies and mechanisms. The synergy between IoT and cloud technologies opens up new ways to strengthen security in the digital landscape. An important contribution of IoT to cloud security is in identity and access management (IAM). IoT devices can strengthen security protocols and have additional authentication factors. For example, biometric data from IoT sensors, such as fingerprints or facial recognition, can be integrated into multi-factor authentication systems, making unauthorized access to cloud resources more difficult. This authentication layer improves the overall security posture by ensuring that only authorized users and devices have access (An, Q., Zhang, K., Wang, J., Ma, J., & Yu, S., 2018).Continuous monitoring is another key advantage that IoT devices bring to cloud security. Equipped with various sensors, IoT devices constantly monitor their physical environment. From a cloud security perspective, this means IoT devices can detect anomalies and generate alerts in response to unauthorized access or environmental disturbances. This real-time monitoring capability improves security by providing immediate notification of potential threats or breaches. For example, environmental sensors can detect changes in temperature, humidity, or even physical intrusion, allowing for quick incident response and risk mitigation (Zhangang, J., Zhangang, Y.., Siong, N. N., & Mao, Y., 2019) .

In addition, IoT technology can facilitate remote access to cloud resources, reducing the need for physical access that can pose security risks. For example, remote maintenance and management of IoT devices can be done securely over encrypted channels, reducing the need for technicians to be physically present. This not only improves security by reducing physical access points, but also offers convenience and cost savings. By limiting physical access and using secure remote access mechanisms, the attack surface is significantly reduced and the potential for security breaches is reduced (Romawi, R., Lopez, J., & Mambo, M., 2013). In addition, IoT technology contributes to improving physical security in data centers and other cloud infrastructure facilities. IoT devices, such as surveillance cameras and access control systems, increase physical security measures, making it more difficult for unauthorized persons to gain access to critical infrastructure. By monitoring access points, recording video, and providing access control, IoT devices offer an additional layer of security to the physical environment, ensuring cloud infrastructure is protected from cyber and physical threats (Mazhelis, O., Suomi, H., & Tyrväinen, P., 2019).

Effective management of IoT devices is essential to realizing IoT's potential to improve cloud security. This includes secure shipping, regular updates and proper shipping procedures. Ensuring that only authorized and secure devices are connected to the network reduces the attack surface and reduces security risks. It is important to have an accurate inventory of IoT devices, regularly update software to address vulnerabilities, and safely retire obsolete devices. Effective device management is a key aspect of IoT security in the cloud (Tannian, R., Byers, S., & Wu, Y., 2020).

6.3 Guidance on Building a Robust Cloud Security Strategy

In today's digital landscape, creating a strong cloud security strategy is essential. To begin with, organizations should have a solid understanding of the cloud environment by introducing a shared responsibility model that defines security responsibilities among cloud service providers (CSPs). Risk assessment is important to identify specific threats and vulnerabilities, taking into account industry specific requirements (Duncan, 2020). Establishing clear security policies and standards is the foundation for a secure cloud environment, including data protection, access control, encryption, and incident response. It is important to implement access control, the principle of least privilege, and use multi-factor authentication (MFA) for enhanced security (Kushida et al., 2020). Continuous monitoring and surveillance is required to detect and respond to suspicious activity in real time. Implementing a robust incident response plan, data backup and recovery strategy, and keeping patches up-to-date contribute to resiliency. It fosters a safety-conscious culture, including employee training, regular safety assessments and intervention testing (Zhangang et al., 2019). Using cloud-native security tools and integrating security into DevOps processes is essential for comprehensive protection. Consequently, it is important to constantly review and adapt your cloud security strategy against evolving threats and technologies.

7. CASE STUDIES AND USE CASES

Case Study 1: Equifax Data Breach

In 2017, Equifax, a major credit reporting agency, experienced a data breach that affected over 147 million people. The breach was caused by a vulnerability in Equifax's website that allowed attackers to access and steal customer data. The data that was stolen included names, Social Security numbers, dates of birth, and addresses. "The Equifax data breach was a preventable cybersecurity disaster." (House of Representatives Committee on Oversight and Government Reform, 2018, p. 1).

The Equifax data breach is a classic example of a data breach that can occur in a cloud environment. The breach was caused by a vulnerability in Equifax's website, which is hosted in the cloud. Additionally, the data that was stolen was stored in the cloud.

Use case:

A company uses a cloud-based customer relationship management (CRM) system to store customer data. The company does not implement strong security controls to protect the CRM system, such as encryption and access controls. As a result, an attacker is able to gain access to the CRM system and steal customer data. The attacker then sells the stolen data on the dark web.

Case Study 2: Marriott Insider Attack

In 2020, Marriott International, a major hotel chain, experienced an insider attack that affected over 5 million guests. "The Marriott insider attack was a sophisticated and damaging attack that highlights the risks of insider threats." (CSA, 2023, p. 1). The attack was carried out by a former employee of Marriott who had access to the company's reservation system. The employee used their access to steal customer data, including names, passport numbers, and credit card numbers.

"Insider threats are a serious cybersecurity threat for organizations of all sizes. By implementing a layered security posture and monitoring employee behavior, organizations can reduce their risk of being victimized by an insider attack." (NIST, 2023, p. 1). The Marriott insider attack is an example of a threat that can occur in any organization, regardless of whether it uses cloud computing or not. However, cloud computing can make insider attacks more difficult to detect and prevent. This is because cloud environments are often complex and distributed, making it difficult to track and monitor user activity.

Use case:

An employee of a company that uses a cloud-based ERP system has access to the company's financial data. The employee steals the financial data and sells it to a competitor. The competitor then uses the data to gain an unfair advantage in the market.

Data breaches and insider attacks can have a significant impact on organizations, both financially and reputationally. Financial losses can result from the cost of investigating the breach, notifying affected customers, and remediating the damage. Reputational damage can lead to lost customers and revenue.

There are a number of best practices that organizations can follow to mitigate cloud-specific threats, such as:

- Implementing strong security controls, such as encryption, access controls, and data loss prevention systems.
- Educating employees about security best practices.
- Monitoring for and responding to suspicious activity.
- Maintaining a secure cloud infrastructure.

Case Study 3: Capital One Data Breach

"The Capital One data breach was a complex attack that exposed the vulnerabilities of cloud computing environments." (ACM, 2020, p. 1). In 2019, Capital One Financial Corporation, a major bank, experienced a data breach that affected over 100 million customers. The breach was caused by a vulnerability in Capital One's cloud-based infrastructure that allowed an attacker to access and steal customer data. The data that was stolen included names, Social Security numbers, dates of birth, and addresses. "The Capital One data breach was a reminder that even the largest and most sophisticated organizations are vulnerable to cyberattacks." (Zscaler, 2021, p. 1).

Use case:

A company uses a cloud-based database to store sensitive customer information, such as credit card numbers and Social Security numbers. The company does not implement strong security controls to protect the database, such as encryption and access controls. As a result, an attacker is able to gain access to the database and steal customer data. The attacker then uses the stolen data to commit fraud.

Case Study 4: Cathay Pacific Insider Attack

In 2018, Cathay Pacific, a Hong Kong-based airline, experienced an insider attack that affected over 9.4 million passengers. "The Cathay Pacific insider attack was a wake-up call for organizations of all sizes to the dangers of insider threats." (HKITF, 2022, p. 1) . The attack was carried out by a former employee of Cathay Pacific who had access to the company's passenger database. The employee used their access to steal passenger data, including names, passport numbers, and credit card numbers.

Use case:

An employee of a company that uses a cloud-based HR system has access to the company's employee data. The employee steals the employee data and sells it to a third-party recruiter. The third-party recruiter then uses the data to spam employees with job offers.

Cloud providers play an important role in mitigating cloud-specific threats. Cloud providers offer a variety of security controls and services that organizations can use to protect their data and systems. Additionally, cloud providers have a responsibility to maintain a secure cloud infrastructure.

In summary, combating data breaches and insider attacks is important in cloud computing environments as organizations increasingly rely on the cloud for data storage and processing. The discussion explores the complex challenges posed by these threats and outlines mitigation strategies from encryption and access control to threat detection and robust incident response plans. In addition, the integration of IoT technology as an additional security layer has been explored, showing the potential to improve cloud security through innovative authentication mechanisms and continuous monitoring.

Future trends in this domain show AI and machine learning for smarter threat detection, widespread adoption of Zero Trust Architecture for continuous authentication of users and devices, and privacy-preserving technologies to protect sensitive data in multi-party cloud scenarios. Regulatory issues, supply chain security and threat intelligence from the cloud will also be focused on. In addition, the growth of hybrid and multi-cloud environments requires the development of strategies and tools to efficiently provide different cloud architectures. Due to its ever-evolving role in cloud security, IoT security is important to keep up. Ultimately, organizations must adapt and be proactive in combating these growing threats to protect the data and integrity of their cloud resources and ensure a stable and secure cloud security landscape (Duncan, 2020).

8. SUMMARIZING THE KEY TAKEAWAYS FROM THE CHAPTER

In the realm of cloud computing security, the chapter on "Understanding and Mitigating Data Breaches and Insider Attacks in Cloud Computing Environments" provides critical insights and actionable strategies for organizations navigating the complex digital landscape. It underscores the profound significance of data breaches and insider attacks, elucidating their potential ramifications, which encompass data loss, financial repercussions, and damage to an organization's reputation. The chapter highlights the multifaceted nature of cloud security, elucidating the intricate interplay of shared responsibility, remote accessibility, and the vast scalability of cloud resources. It emphasizes that while the cloud presents opportunities, it also poses formidable security challenges. Cloud computing environments are vulnerable to a variety of cyberattacks, including data breaches, denial-of-service attacks, and insider attacks. Bhattacharjee and Siwa (2016, p. 97). The core takeaway lies in the strategies to mitigate data breaches, which entail a comprehensive approach encompassing encryption, stringent access controls, continuous monitoring, and the development of robust incident response plans. Resilience in security hinges on a three-pronged approach, involving the detection, prevention, and remediation of threats. Notably, the chapter illuminates the role of IoT technology in bolstering cloud security, introducing innovative solutions such as enhanced authentication, continuous monitoring, and refined access control.

Moreover, the chapter underlines the multifaceted challenges posed by insider attacks, regardless of whether they are intentional or inadvertent. It accentuates the importance of user training, behavior monitoring, and privilege management in mitigating these threats. To create a robust cloud security strategy, the chapter advocates embracing identity and access management, encryption, threat intelligence, and the utilization of cloud-native security tools. As the digital landscape evolves, the chapter posits future directions in cloud security that encompass the application of AI and machine learning for advanced threat detection, the widespread adoption of the Zero Trust Architecture, the deployment of privacy-preserving technologies, and an emphasis on regulatory compliance and supply chain security. The enduring relevance of IoT security is highlighted, underscoring the need for continuous improvement as IoT technology evolves. Ultimately, the chapter stresses the necessity of adaptability and proactivity in addressing evolving threats, thereby ensuring the resilience and effectiveness of cloud security in a dynamic and ever-changing environment.

8.1 Exploring Future Trends and Developments in Cloud Security

The future of cloud security is poised for significant advancements as technology advances and security threats become more complex. One of the most notable areas is the adoption of Zero Trust Architecture (ZTA), which challenges traditional perimeter-based security models. ZTA supports continuous authentication and reliable assessment of users and devices accessing cloud resources regardless of location, thereby reducing insider threats and data breaches (Kindervag, 2010). Artificial Intelligence (AI) and Machine Learning (ML) significantly improve threat detection and incident response by offering the ability to analyze large databases for anomaly detection, threat prediction, and automated response (Vemuri et al.,

2021). Cloud-based security solutions are becoming more common as organizations adopt cloud technologies and serverless computing. These solutions are designed to seamlessly integrate with cloud services that provide real-time monitoring, threat detection and response capabilities (Marin et al., 2019).

Container security is an important area of growth with the rise of containerization and orchestration platforms such as Kubernetes. Tools to secure containerized applications, including vulnerability scanning and runtime protection, will play an important role in securing cloud workloads. As cloud adoption expands, identity-centric security will continue to evolve with an emphasis on strong authentication, adaptive access control, and continuous identity verification. In addition, data security and privacy measures will be strengthened due to the increase in data and the need to protect sensitive data. Technologies such as cryptographic computing and data loss prevention will play an important role in data protection (Goyal et al., 2020). With supply chain security, organizations will focus on securing the entire supply chain, from third-party vendors to software components, ensuring the integrity and security of all elements in the cloud environment. With these trends, the future of cloud security is poised to meet the challenges of the digital landscape.

REFERENCES

Aarts, J., Hannink, J., & Olde Keizer, M. (2016). The Internet of Things in Industry: A Survey. *IEEE Transactions on Industrial Informatics*, *12*(6), 2233–2243.

Aljawarneh, S., Aldwairi, M., & Seassein, M. B. (2019). Secure data sharing in the cloud: a systematic literature review. *IEEE Introduction, 7*, 1003-1012.

Armbrust, M., Fox, A., Griffith, R., Joseph, A. D., Katz, R., Konwinski, A., Lee, G., Patterson, D., Rabkin, A., Stoica, I., & Zaharia, M. (2010). A view of cloud computing. *Communications of the ACM*, *53*(4), 50–58. doi:10.1145/1721654.1721672

Awad, A., & Ali, M. (2015). Cloud Computing: A Survey. *Journal of Grid Computing*, *13*(3), 331–355.

Babu, C. V., & Srisakthi, S. (2023). Cyber Physical Systems and Network Security: The Present Scenarios and Its Applications. In R. Thanigaivelan, S. Kaliappan, & C. Jegadheesan (Eds.), Cyber-Physical Systems and Supporting Technologies for Industrial Automation (pp. 104–130). Academic Press.

Babu, C. V., & Yadav, S. (2023). Cyber Physical Systems Design Challenges in the Areas of Mobility, Healthcare, Energy, and Manufacturing. In R. Thanigaivelan, S. Kaliappan, & C. Jegadheesan (Eds.), Cyber-Physical Systems and Supporting Technologies for Industrial Automation (pp. 131–151). Academic Press.

Beloglazov, A., & Buya, R. (2010). Energy-efficient resource management in virtualized cloud data centers. In *2010 10th IEEE/ACM International Conference on Cluster, Cloud and Grid Computing* (pp. 826-831). IEEE. 10.1109/CCGRID.2010.46

Bhattacharjee, R., & Siwa, S. (2016). Internet of Life: Securing the Cloud. In *IoT and big data technologies for next generation healthcare* (pp. 97–112). Springer.

Chen, M., Ma, Y., Song, J., Lai, C. F., & Hu, B. (2019). Edge computing in the Internet of Things. In *Internet of Things* (pp. 1–16). Springer.

Chow, R., Golle, P., Jakobsson, M., Shi, E., Staddon, J., Masuoka, R., ... Devadas, S. (2009). Controlling data in the cloud: outsourcing computation without outsourcing control. In *Proceedings of the 2009 ACM workshop on Cloud computing security* (pp. 85-90). 10.1145/1655008.1655020

DiPetro, J. (2014). Cloud computing security. *Journal of Computer Information Systems*, *54*(1), 1–10.

Duncan, D. B. (2020). *Certified Cloud Security Professional (CCSP)*. All-in-One Exam Guide. McGraw-Hill Education.

Goyal, D., Kakkar, P., & Kumar, N. (2020). Information Security in Cloud Computing: Issues, Challenges, and Solutions. In Recent Trends and Future Technologies in Cloud Computing (pp. 1-14). Springer.

Gu, Y., Zhang, Y., Han, Q., Li, B., & Shu, L. (2019). *Fog Computing in the Internet of Things: A Survey*. Raja Saud University-Journal of Computer and Information Science.

Hashizume, K., Rosado, D. G., Fernandez-Medina, E., & Fernandez, E. B. (2013). Analysis of security issues for cloud computing. *Journal of Internet Services and Applications*, *4*(1), 5. doi:10.1186/1869-0238-4-5

Hu, C., & Liu, X. (2016). Cloud computing security: A survey. *Security and Privacy*, *14*(3), 5.

Huth, A., & Cebula, J. (2013). Basics of cloud computing. Academic Press.

Jansen, W., & Grace, T. (2011). Guidelines for security and privacy in public cloud computing. *NIST Special Publications*, *800*(144), 800–145. doi:10.6028/NIST.SP.800-144

Jha, D., & Buyya, R. (2013). Cloud security: A survey of challenges and solutions. *Journal of Network and Computer Applications*, *36*(1), 388–405.

Jhaveri, R. H., & Patel, R. B. (2017). Objects and Cloud Computing: A Study. In *2017 International Conference on Computing and Communication Methods (ICCMC)* (pp. 1076-1080). IEEE.

Kandias, M., & Gritzalis, D. (2012). Cloud insiders: The threat within. *Computer*, *45*(8), 49–55.

Kshetri, N. (2017). Will Blockchain Power the Internet of Things? *IT Professional*, *19*(4), 68–72. doi:10.1109/MITP.2017.3051335

Kushida, M., O'Leary, D., Le, T., & Paliwal, A. (2020). *Advanced cloud security and application security*. Springer.

Mather, T., Kumaraswamy, S., & Latif, S. (2009). *Cloud Security and Privacy: An Enterprise Perspective on Risks and Compliance*. O'Reilly Media.

One, Q., Zhang, K., Wang, J., Ma, J., & Yu, S. (2018). Edge computing in the Internet of Things: A new architecture for efficient and real-time data processing. *IEEE Journal of Internet of Things*, *5*(1), 396–405.

Prasanna, R. (2017). Basics of cloud computing. In *Big data analytics and cloud computing* (pp. 3–11). Springer.

Raj, P., & Srinivasan, A. (2019). A Survey of Insider Threats in Cloud Computing. In *2019 International Conference on Machine Learning and Cyber Security (ICMLCS)* (pp. 72-77). IEEE.

Rios, A., Muppala, J. K., & Van Dijk, M. (2013). Survey of Cloud Computing Security Management. *Journal of Cloud Computing: Advances, Systems, and Applications*, *2*(1), 1–17.

Ristenpart, T., Tromer, E., Shacham, H., & Savage, S. (2009). Hey, You, Get Off of My Cloud: Exploring Information Leakage in Third-Party Compute Clouds. In *Proceedings of the 16th ACM Conference on Computer and Communications Security (CCS '09)* (pp. 199-212). 10.1145/1653662.1653687

Rittinghouse, J. W., & Ransome, J. F. (2016). *Cloud Computing: Implementation, Management, and Security*. CRC Press.

Rizomiliotis, P., Maniatakos, M., & Karatza, H. (2017). Cloud forensic analysis based on virtual machine research. *Next Generation Computer Systems*, *76*, 237–250.

Roman, R., Lopez, J., & Mambo, M. (2013). Mobile Edge Computing, Fog, and More: Overview and Analysis of Security Threats and Challenges. *Future Generation Computer Systems*, *78*, 680–698. doi:10.1016/j.future.2016.11.009

Smith, J. (2018). Cloud Computing Security: Threats and Solutions. *International Journal of Computer Applications*, *181*(8), 17–21.

Spathoulas, P., Bravos, G., Samoladas, I., & Votis, K. (2016). Cloud litigation overview and key dimensions of cloud litigation preparation. *International Journal of Cloud Computing and Services Science (IJ-CLOSER)*, *5*(1), 38-55.

Subashini, S., & Kavitha, V. (2011). A survey of security issues in the cloud computing service delivery model. *Journal of Computer Networks and Applications*, *34*(1), 1–11. doi:10.1016/j.jnca.2010.07.006

Suresh Babu, C.V., Akshayah, N. S., Maclin Vinola, P., & Janapriyan, R. (2023). IoT-Based Smart Accident Detection and Alert System. In P. Swarnalatha & S. Prabu (Eds.), Handbook of Research on Deep Learning Techniques for Cloud-Based Industrial IoT (pp. 322-337). IGI Global. doi:10.4018/978-1-6684-8098-4.ch019

Suresh Babu, C.V. (n.d.). *Introduction to Cloud Computing*. Anniyappa Publications.

Suresh Babu, C. V., Andrew Simon, P., & Barath Kumar, S. (2023). The Future of Cyber Security Starts Today, Not Tomorrow. In S. Shiva Darshan, M. Manoj Kumar, B. Prashanth, & Y. Vishnu Srinivasa Murthy (Eds.), *Malware Analysis and Intrusion Detection in Cyber-Physical Systems* (pp. 348–375). IGI Global. doi:10.4018/978-1-6684-8666-5.ch016

Vaquero, L. M., Rodero-Merino, L., Caceres, J., & Lindner, M. (2011). Disruption in the Cloud: Towards a Cloud Definition. *ACM SIGCOMM Computer Communications Review*, *39*(1), 50–55. doi:10.1145/1496091.1496100

Verma, S., & Shisodia, P. (2017). Security Threats, Connectivity and Countermeasures in IoT: A Survey. In *2017 International Conference on I-SMAC (IoT in Social, Mobile, Analytics and Cloud) (I-SMAC)* (pp. 790-794). IEEE.

Wu, J., Mao, Z., Zhang, M., Li, J., & Li, J. (2010). Planning in cloud computing: Research challenges and opportunities. In *Proceedings of the 6th International Conference on Grid and Pervasive Computing (GPC'11)* (pp. 1-10). Springer.

Zhang, J., Zhang, Y., Xiong, N. N., & Mao, Y. (2019). Internet of Things (IoT) Security: Current Status, Challenges, and Future Solutions. *IEEE Journal of Internet of Things*, *6*(2), 1993–2002.

Chapter 2
Security Automation and Orchestration in the Cloud

Samridhi Gulati
Raj Kumar Goel Institute of Technology, India

Ayushi Tyagi
Raj Kumar Goel Institute of Technology, India

Pawan Kumar Goel
https://orcid.org/0000-0003-3601-102X
Raj Kumar Goel Institute of Technology, India

ABSTRACT

As cloud computing evolves, the state of the digital infrastructure and the growth of cloud environments pose unprecedented challenges in protecting critical data and applications. This chapter explores the critical role of security automation orchestration (SAO) in addressing the evolving security requirements of cloud computing. The chapter begins by exploring the basic principles of automation security, providing the benefits and fundamentals that underpin effective automation, followed by the unique security challenges in the cloud in the environment and how automation can be effectively used to mitigate these risks is clear. The comprehensive security framework in cloud environments is presented, showing the integration of security tools and technologies to streamline incident response processes.

DOI: 10.4018/979-8-3693-3249-8.ch002

1. INTRODUCTION

In the ever-expanding landscape of cloud computing, organizations face a growing array of opportunities and challenges. While the cloud offers unprecedented scalability and flexibility, the complexity of securing a dynamic multi-layered environment has made it central need for robust security management and it is transformative This chapter begins by examining a transformative process in cloud security—security automation and orchestration (SAO) (Lauwers & Tamburri, n.d.). With the digitization of business operations and the proliferation of cloud services, the availability of attacks for malicious actors has increased dramatically Traditional security methods, which rely on manual processes and isolated sets of tools, struggle to navigate is coupled with the dynamic nature of the cloud ecosystem. Security automation and orchestration is emerging as a mainstream strategy, providing a proactive framework (Jaeger, 2008) for strengthening security, effectively managing threats, and adopting a cloud security environment.

1.1 Foundations of Security Automation: To understand the importance of SAO, we start by examining its basic principles. Key automation includes mechanization of routine safety tasks, speeding up response times to reduce the burden on human operators .This section examines the key features of safety automation and allows for a more nuanced analysis of its integration in cloud environments

1.2 Navigating Cloud Security Challenges: Identifies many cloud security challenges—from data breaches to compliance concerns. Here we delve into the unique risks associated with cloud computing and explain how automation is a powerful ally in addressing these challenges. By aligning security policies with the dynamic nature of the cloud, organizations can proactively prevent threats and increase their resilience.

1.3 Security planning in cloud environments: A key component of SAO is orchestra-based—integrating security tools (Wang et al., 2010) and technologies in a cooperative manner. This section provides for integrated incident response in the cloud is clear, and demonstrates how security systems integration can improve security measures.

Device architecture and technology: The diversity of the cloud environment requires a tailored approach to strategic security. We go through different automation orchestration tools (Wang et al., 2010), compare their performance, and provide insights into choosing tools that are compatible with complex cloud systems.

2. FUNDAMENTALS OF SECURITY AUTOMATION IN CLOUD COMPUTING

In the dynamic landscape of cloud computing, where agility and scalability are paramount, Security Automation emerges as a critical component for safeguarding digital assets and ensuring robust cyber security. This section delves into the fundamental principles that define Security Automation in the context of cloud computing, elucidating its role, benefits, and key components.

2.1. Definition and Significance: Security Automation in cloud computing refers to the systematic use of automated processes and tools to enhance the security posture of cloud environments. The significance of Security Automation in the cloud lies in its ability to adapt to the dynamic nature of these environments, where resources are provisioned and de-provisioned on-demand and security must keep pace with the rapid scale and change.

2.2. Benefits of Security Automation in the Cloud: The adoption of Security Automation (Armbrust et al., 2009) in the cloud offers a multitude of advantages that align with the unique characteristics of cloud computing:

- **Scalability:** Automation allows security measures to scale seamlessly with the dynamic nature of cloud environments, ensuring consistent protection as workloads fluctuate.
- **Speed and Efficiency:** Automated processes respond swiftly to security incidents, reducing response times and minimizing potential damage.
- **Consistency:** Security policies are consistently applied across diverse and distributed cloud resources, mitigating the risk of misconfigurations.

2.3. Key Features of Cloud Security Automation: A robust cloud security automation system includes key features designed for the cloud environment:

- **Cloud-native APIs:** When combined with cloud provider APIs, provide seamless connection and interaction with cloud services.
- **Infrastructure as code (IaC):** Automating security configurations by code, allowing for consistent and repeatable deployment of secure infrastructure.
- **Continuous monitoring**: Automated tools for real-time monitoring of cloud infrastructure, to quickly detect and respond to security incidents.

2.4. Issues in Cloud Security Automation: Security automation in the cloud looks at applications that have different functionalities that are required to maintain a secure cloud environment:

- **Automated Threat Identification:** Using machine learning and analytics to detect and respond to abnormal activities in real time.
- **Auto-scaling security policy:** Modify dynamic security controls based on changes in workload and supply.
- **Automated Incident Response:** Streamlining incident response workflows, from detection to containment and remediation.

Figure 1. Fundamentals of security automation

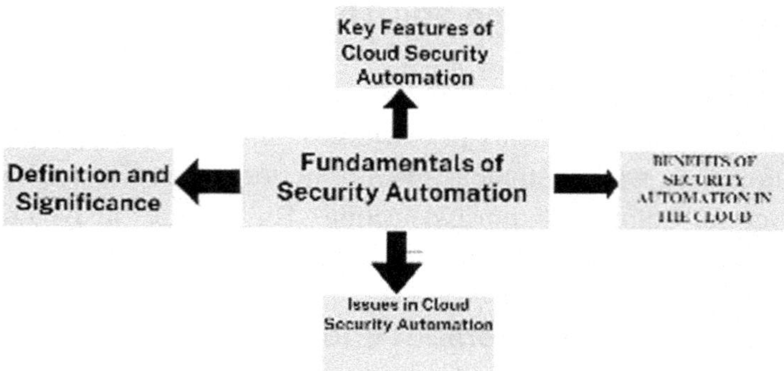

3. CLOUD SECURITY CHALLENGES ADDRESSED BY AUTOMATION

The dynamic landscape of cloud computing (Chen, 2009) abounds in security challenges stemming from the inherent challenges of high tenancy environments, speed, and the evolving threat landscape This section explores how strategic security is workload acts as a way to mitigate and address these challenges, increasing resilience cloud infrastructure.

3.1. Security Automation

Challenge: Security automation ensures that security policies are documented and implemented consistently using Infrastructure as Code (IaC) (Cai, 2009) principles, allowing for automated and rapid deployment of secure systems when deployed things for or exchange it.

3.2. Complex Multi-Cloud Environments

Challenge: Organizations are increasingly adopting multi-cloud strategies, resulting in different and complex infrastructures across different cloud service providers

Automation Response: Automation tools (Wang et al., 2010) designed for multi-cloud compatibility streamline security management, which provides centralized policy capabilities for command, threat detection and incident response across multiple cloud environments.

3.3. Continuous Monitoring and Threat Detection

Challenge: The dynamic cloud environment requires continuous monitoring to detect and respond to security incidents in real time. Automation Response: Integrates security automation with continuous monitoring tools and uses machine learning and analytics for automated threat detection. This ensures a dynamic security environment, reacting quickly to abnormal activities without manual intervention.

3.4. Configuration Management and Compliance

Challenge: Infrastructure (IaC) as a code enables the automation of security measures, reduces the risk of misconfiguration, and ensures consistent compliance.

3.5. Speed and Consistency

Challenge: Manual incident responses are time-consuming and may lack accuracy, delaying risk mitigation. Automation Response: Security automation streamlines incident response operations, and automates routine tasks such as containment, detection, and correction. This not only accelerates response times but also provides a consistent, systematic approach to security incidents.

3.6. Resource Scaling and Auto-Scaling Security Management

Challenge: Workloads change frequently in a cloud environment (Dillon, 2010), requiring complex dynamic scaling of resources and corresponding changes related to security management.

Automation response: Automatic scaling of security controls, which generally auto-scale security that said, it ensures that security measures smoothly adapt to changes in workload, and drive appropriate and effective security levels.

3.7. Data Encryption and Key Management

Challenge: Strong encryption and key management techniques are required to protect sensitive data in transit and at rest. Automation response: Security automation (Ranjan et al., 2015) makes it easier to deploy and maintain the encryption protocols, and ensures that data remains secure without causing operational complications significant changes and policy implementations can also be implemented in a way that it operates to improve security.

Figure 2. Challenges in cloud security

4. Security Orchestration in Cloud Environments

The complexity and dynamic nature of cloud environments requires a unified and integrated approach to security management. Security architecture emerges as the dominant approach, seamlessly integrating security tools and technologies to plan and execute incident response operations. This section explores the principles, features and applications of security architecture in the cloud circumstances.

4.1. Definition of Security Systems: Security systems are strategic planning and automation of security systems, using a centralized system to integrate and facilitate the functionality of various security tools in cloud environments, somewhere with agility being key, a security plan ensures that security incidents and challenges are handled in a harmonized manner.

4.2. Integration Points in Cloud Security Orchestration: Security orchestration (Tomarchio et al., 2020) relies on integration points to communicate and interact with security appliances, ensuring a cohesive security ecosystem.

In cloud environments these integration points are:

- **Cloud-native APIs:** Use APIs provided by cloud service providers to integrate and manage with security controls.
- **Security Information and Event Management (SIEM) systems**: Hybrid SIEM platforms provide centralized logging, analysis, and communication of security incidents.
- **Threat Intelligence Feeds**: Include threat intelligence feeds to enhance incident detection and response.
- **Incident response forums**: Coordinate incident response activities through centralized forums that facilitate collaboration and automation.

4.3. Applications for security planning in cloud environments: Security planning in the cloud requires applications in different use cases, making security operations more efficient and effective:

- **Incident Response Automation**: Design an end-to-end incident response process from detection to containment, mitigation, and recovery.
- **Vulnerability Management**: Automates the scanning, assessment and repair of vulnerabilities in cloud resources.
- **Threat Hunt**: Link various sources of security information and set up proactive threat hunting activities.
- **Policy Implementation and Compliance**: Automate security controls and ensure compliance with regulatory requirements at all times.

4.4. Cloud Security Orchestration Framework Components: A robust cloud security infrastructure architecture includes key elements required for seamless integration and automation:

- **Orchestration Engine**: Central hub that manages and automates security processes, ensuring simultaneous reactions to incidents.
- **Playbooks and business plans**: A series of prescribed steps that define how to develop security measures in response to specific events.
- **Automation connectors**: Interfaces that allow integration with security equipment, enabling two-way communication.
- **Centralized dashboard**: User interface that provides visibility into security events, ongoing orchestration activities and performance metrics.

4.5. Benefits of cloud security orchestration: Adopting security orchestration (Tomarchio et al., 2020) across cloud environments offers several benefits:

- **Improved response time**: Automated synchronization accelerates incident response time, reducing the impact of security incidents.
- **Consistent enforcement**: Ensures that security measures are applied consistently across various cloud resources.
- **Improved collaboration:** Facilitates collaboration between security teams, enterprises, and other stakeholders through centralized meetings.

4.6. Challenges and considerations: While a security orchestration offers great benefits, challenges must be overcome, ex.

- **Strong integration**: Developing various security tools requires a careful integration plan to ensure compatibility.
- **Human oversight**: While automation is a powerful ally, human oversight is crucial, especially in complex decision-making.

5. AUTOMATION AND ORCHESTRATION TOOLS

Automation and orchestration are important aspects of cloud computing that help simplify and streamline various processes, increase efficiency and scalability. These tools (Wang et al., 2010) play an important role in consuming and provisioning resources, consuming applications role, ensuring cloud environments health and overall performance of Automation orchestration available resources.

5.1. AWS Cloud Formation

- **Provider:** Amazon Web Services (AWS)
- **Description:** AWS Cloud Formation allows users to define and deliver AWS configuration as code. It uses templates written in JSON or YAML to describe objects, enabling you to automate the creation and management of AWS objects.

5.2. Azure Resource Management (ARM)

- Provider: Microsoft Azure

- **Description:** Azure Resource Manager is an orchestration service in Azure that allows users to use declarative templates and manage resources. ARM templates are written in JSON and describe the resources required for the application, their dependencies, and various deployment options.

5.3. Google Cloud Deployment Manager

- Provider: Google Cloud Platform (GCP).
- Description: Google Cloud Deployment Manager allows users to define, deploy, and manage GCP objects using templates written in YAML or Python. It helps in the automation of supply chains and services.

5.4. Terraform

- Provider: HashiCorp
- Description: Terraform as a code tool is an open-source infrastructure that supports multiple cloud providers including AWS, Azure, GCP, and more. It uses a declarative configuration language (HCL) to define and provision the infrastructure, making it a versatile option for multi cloud environments.

5.5. Ancil

- **Provider:** Red Hat (now IBM).
- **Description:** Ancil is an open-source automation tool that can be used for system management, application deployment, and task automation. It uses a YAML script called a playbook to define automation tasks, making it agentless and easy to use for provisioning and managing cloud resources.

5.6. Jenkins: 2016-09-19

- **Provider:** Jenkins (Local)
- **Description:** Jenkins is an open-source automation server commonly used to develop, test, and deploy applications. It supports the creation of continuous integration and deployment (CI/CD) pipelines, making it a valuable tool for creating responsive software development processes in the cloud.

5.7. Kubernetes (K8s)

- **Provider:** Cloud-agnostic (typically applied to cloud types);
- **Description:** Although Kubernetes is primarily known as a container orchestration platform, it also plays a role in automating the deployment, scaling, and management of containerized applications in the cloud Kubernetes can be used to manage containerized workloads across different cloud providers.

These tools help organizations access infrastructure as a code (IaC) product, enabling automation of common tasks, reducing human error, improving overall performance in cloud environments Choosing a specific tool often depends on the cloud provider, infrastructure complexity, development and operations team discretion.

Figure 3. Automation and orchestration tools

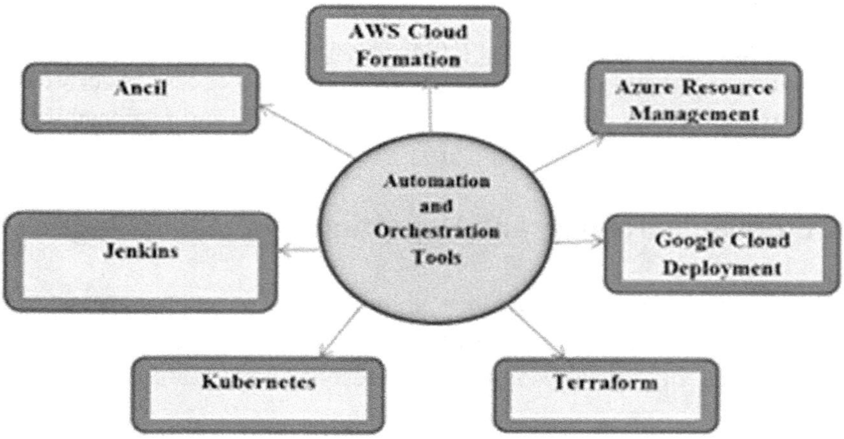

6. COMMON USE CASES FOR SECURITY AUTOMATION IN THE CLOUD

Security in the cloud is critical for addressing today's dynamic and often complex cyber security threats. Here are some common terms for security automation in cloud environments.

6.1. Incident Response Automation

- **Use Case:** Automatically detects and responds to security incidents, such as unauthorized access or data breaches, by triggering a predefined incident response playbook. This may include isolation, notification of relevant stakeholders, and initiation of forensic investigations.

6.2. Vulnerability Management

- **Use Case**: Have vulnerabilities detected and fixed in the cloud infrastructure. This includes finding vulnerabilities, prioritizing risk-based measures, and actually applying patches or system changes to fix identified vulnerabilities.

6.3. Identity Management (IAM)

- **Use Case:** Use automation to manage user privileges and access. This includes automating user setup, authorization, and access checks to ensure that users have the proper access based on their role and responsibilities.

6.4. Compliance Review and Reporting

- **Use Case:** Automatically address compliance assessments against industry standards or regulatory requirements. Conduct regular reports on the compliance of cloud resources, and resolve any non-compliant systems yourself.

6.5. Security Policy Enforcement

- **Use Case:** Define and implement consistent security policies in a cloud environment. Automate network security, encryption, and data protection policies to maintain a secure and compliant system.

6.6. Log Management and Analysis

- **Use Case:** Automatically collect, store, and analyze log data from various cloud services. Use automation to identify and alert to suspicious activity, such as multiple failed login attempts or unusual data access.

6.7. Security Measures for Multi-Cloud Environments

- **Use Case:** Deploy security automation across multi-cloud environments to ensure a consistent and unified level of security. This includes integrating security tools and coordinating scope responses from different cloud providers.

6.8. Phishing and Email Security

- **Use Case:** Operate the investigation and response to phishing emails or malicious attachments. This can include automatically blocking malicious emails, changing email filtering rules, and notifying users of potential threats.

6.9. Endpoint Security Automation

- **Use Case:** Integrate endpoint security solutions with cloud environments to enable threat detection and prevention of endpoints. This may include isolating faulty devices, initiating a scan, and implementing security measures.

6.10. Security Awareness Training

- Use Case: Self-provide end-user security training. Schedule and follow up on training sessions, and automate appropriate security briefings to keep users up to date on current threats and best practices.

6.11. Cloud Security Posture Management (CSPM)

- Use Case: Perform ongoing monitoring of cloud infrastructure for misconfigurations and security risks. Manage misconfiguration yourself to ensure a secure and compliant cloud environment.

Leveraging security measures in these contexts not only makes security operations (Hilley, 2009) more efficient but also helps companies react faster to emerging threats and maintain a proactive security posture at in the ever-changing landscape of cloud computing.

7. BEST PRACTICES FOR IMPLEMENTING SECURITY AUTOMATION IN THE CLOUD

7.1. General Safety Policy

- **Practice:** Integrate security automation into a comprehensive cloud security strategy including prevention, detection, response, and recovery.
- **Rationale:** A holistic approach ensures that security automation is aligned with broad security objectives, creating a unified and consistent level of security.

7.2. Integrating Cloud-Native Security Tools

- **Practice**: Use cloud-native security tools and APIs for seamless integration with security automation frameworks.
- **Rationale:** Cloud-based devices are designed to operate efficiently in a cloud environment, increasing interoperability and reducing integration complexity.

7.3. Ongoing Training and Skill Development

- **Practice:** Invest in training and skills development for security IT teams to understand and effectively use security automation tools.
- **Rationale:** Educated and skilled employees are needed to maximize the benefits of security automation and adapt to evolving security challenges.

7.4. Infrastructure (IaC) Security as a Rule

- **Practice:** Enter security policies into infrastructure (IaC) templates as code to ensure automatic and consistent deployment of secure infrastructure.
- **Rationale:** IaC encourages the development of security best practices, and facilitates the creation and maintenance of secure automated cloud infrastructure.

7.5. Threat Reporting Integration

- **Practice:** Integrate threat notification feeds to increase security automation's ability to detect and respond to emerging threats.
- **Rationale:** Real-time threat intelligence ensures that security automation is prepared to address the latest cyber security threats and vulnerabilities.

7.6. Joint Ventures

- **Practice:** Encourage collaboration between security, operations, and development teams to ensure automated security measures align with organizational objectives.
- **Rationale:** Interdisciplinary collaboration ensures consistent implementation of security automation across teams and processes.

7.7. Safe DevOps Practices

- **Practice:** Integrate security automation into DevOps processes and ensure that it is a core part of the security development lifecycle.
- **Rationale:** By integrating security early in the development process, organizations can better identify and address security issues.

By adhering to these best practices, organizations can lay a solid foundation for security automation in the cloud, giving them the ability to manage security issues managing incidents, maintaining compliance, and safely navigating the dynamics of cloud computing.

8. CHALLENGES AND LIMITATIONS

Cloud computing offers many advantages (Armbrust et al., 2010), such as scalability, flexibility and cost savings, but it also comes with its own set of challenges and limitations and addressing these issues is essential for organizations to make the most of their cloud infrastructure. Below are some of the major challenges and limitations associated with cloud computing.

8.1. Security Concern

- **Challenge:** Since most cloud environments are multitenant, security in the cloud is the main concern. Organizations worry about unauthorized access, data breaches, and compliance issues.
- **Limitations:** While cloud service providers implement robust security measures, the organization is ultimately responsible for the security of data and applications Shared responsibility models and encryption are important but cannot eliminate all security risks.

8.2. Data Privacy and Compliance

- **Challenge:** Getting organizations to navigate a complex regulatory process to ensure compliance with data protection laws and industry regulations.
- **Limitations:** Cloud providers may have data centers in multiple locations, making it difficult to ensure compliance with industry-specific regulations. Organizations should carefully select providers with appropriate credentials and compliance mechanisms.

8.3. Break Time and Availability

- **Challenge:** Cloud services often interrupt work, creating potential uptime for organizations.
- **Limitations:** Even with high availability guarantees from cloud providers, service interruptions can still occur. Organizations should implement disaster recovery plans for layoffs to mitigate the impact of power outages.

8.4. Integration Challenges

- **Challenge:** Moving existing applications and data to the cloud and integrating with on-premise systems can be difficult.
- **Limitations:** Legacy systems may not integrate well with cloud services, requiring significant migration and integration efforts. Organizations may face compatibility issues between different cloud providers or services.

8.5. Network Performance and Latency

- **Challenge:** Network latency can affect the performance of cloud-based applications (Rizvi et al., n.d.), especially for data-intensive workloads.
- **Limitations:** Some applications may require low-latency connections, and the distance between the user and the cloud data center may affect performance. Edge computing is emerging as a solution to solve latency problems.

8. 6. Limited Flexibility and Control

- **Challenge:** Cloud services provide customized solutions, limiting the ability to scale the infrastructure and services.
- **Limitation:** Organizations may face constraints in developing products to meet specific requirements. This limitation can be a concern for businesses with unique and specialized computing needs.

8.7. Vendor Lock In

- **Challenge:** Vendors may be locked into accepting the services of a particular cloud provider, making it difficult to switch providers.
- **Limitations:** Switching between cloud providers can be difficult and expensive due to differences in architecture, APIs, and service offerings. Organizations need to carefully consider the long-term implications of their vendor choices.

8.8. Examples of Costs

- **Challenge:** Cloud costs can be unpredictable, and organizations can struggle with budget overruns.
- **Limitations:** While the pay-as-you-go system offers flexibility, it requires careful management and control to deal with unexpected costs. Cloud cost management tools and processes are critical for cost control.

8.9. Data Migration Challenges

- **Challenge:** Uploading and downloading large amounts of data to the cloud can be time-consuming.
- **Limitations:** Bandwidth constraints can slow down data transfers, affecting the speed at which large amounts of data are migrated to or fetched from the cloud when needed.

8.10. Edge Visibility and Monitoring

- **Challenge:** Organizations can experience uncertainty in the underlying infrastructure (Liu et al., 2015) of cloud service.
- **Limitations:** Cloud providers eliminate much of the infrastructure, making it difficult for organizations to have granular control over certain parts. This can be a concern for businesses with specific regulatory or compliance requirements.

Navigating these challenges and limitations requires careful planning; a thorough understanding of the chosen cloud environment, and ongoing monitoring and optimization Organizations that proactively address these issues the role is well positioned to use cloud computing to mitigate the possibility of error.

Figure 4. Challenges and limitations

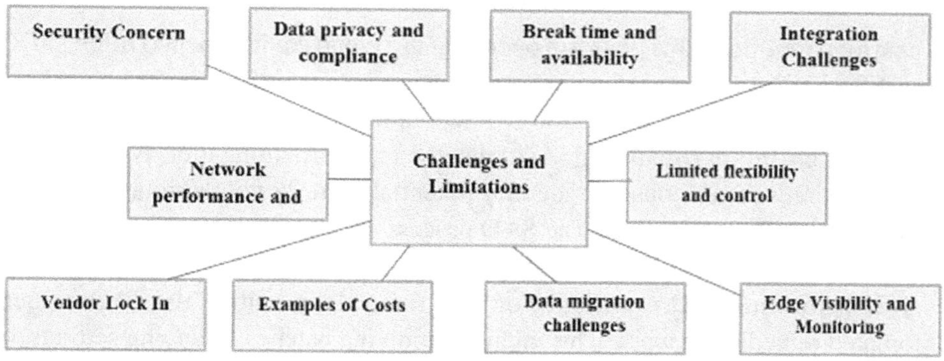

9. CASE STUDIES IN SECURITY AUTOMATION AND ORCHESTRATION IN THE CLOUD

9.1. Incident Response Automation

Scenario: A multinational company relies on cloud services for its business-critical applications and data. The organization uses SAO (Lauwers & Tamburri, n.d.) to automate incident response systems.

When a security incident occurs, such as malware detected in a cloud hosted application, the SAO system triggers an automatic playback response:

9.1.1. Detection: Security tools identify abnormal behaviors that indicate the presence of malware in the cloud.

9.1.2. Isolation: The SAO system automatically isolates the affected application or virtual machine to prevent further spread.

9.1.3. Forensic analysis: The automated tools perform a preliminary forensic analysis to understand the nature and scope of the case.

9.1.4. Prevention: Based on the analysis, the SAO system initiates automatic prevention measures, such as removing bad files and flushing and restoring backups.

9.1.5. Reports: Participants receive an automated report with information about the incident, actions taken and recommended follow-up steps.

This proactive incident response reduces response time, limits the impact of the incident, and ensures a consistent and documented approach to managing security incidents in the cloud processing.

9.2. Vulnerability Management Automation

Scenario: An e-commerce platform operating in a cloud environment (Dillon, 2010) faces the challenge of managing and securing a dynamic infrastructure.

The organization is adopting SAO in order to automate vulnerability management:

9.2.1. Continuous Scanning: Automated security scanning tools typically scan cloud resources continuously to identify potential security vulnerabilities.

9.2.2. Risk Prioritization: The SAO process assesses the severity of identified vulnerabilities and prioritizes them based on risk.

9.2.3. Automated Prevention: For high-risk vulnerabilities, the SAO triggers automated remediation work. This includes applying patches, changing settings, or isolating vulnerabilities.

9.2.4. Validation: Automated validation tests confirm that the corrective actions were successful with unintended consequences.

9.2.5. Reports: The SAO (Bellendorf & Mann, 2018) is an automated report that summarizes vulnerabilities, corrective actions, and ongoing risk assessments.

This strategic approach ensures that an organization can proactively address vulnerabilities in its cloud infrastructure, minimizing attacks and increasing overall security.

9.3. Cloud Security Orchestration for Compliance

Scenario: A bank that operates in multiple clouds must meet strict compliance standards (Böhm & Wirtz, 2022). The organization uses SAO for compliance automation:

9.3.1. Policy Implementation: The SAO establishes the security policies that will be implemented across multiple cloud platforms to ensure compliance with regulatory requirements.

9.3.2. Automated audits: The system performs automated audits of cloud configurations and activities, and provides detailed compliance reports.

9.3.3. Alerting and Reporting: The SAO monitors comprehensive compliance and triggers automatic alerts when non-compliance is detected.

9.3.4. Automatic Remediation: In the event of non-compliance, the SAO system (Alien4Cloud, 2020) initiates automatic remediation actions to restore the environment to compliance.

9.3.5. Documentation: Documentation of compliance activities, including amendments made and corrections made is prepared for audit purposes.

This approach streamlines the compliance process, reduces the risk of breaches, and provides a consistent and automated audit trail. This hypothesis highlights how organizations can use security products and infrastructure to enhance security, respond to incidents, address vulnerabilities, and maintain compliance in a cloud environment Real-world applications require choices and develop specific tools based on an organization's needs and policies.

10. FUTURE TRENDS IN SECURITY AUTOMATION AND ORCHESTRATION IN CLOUD

The field of security automation orchestration (SAO) (Lynn et al., 2020) in cloud computing is rapidly evolving to address emerging threats and the dynamic nature of cloud environments and it is expected that in the future more features will shape the SAO landscape in the cloud.

10.1. Integration of Artifacts and Machine Learning

- **Trends:** The integration of artificial intelligence (AI) and machine learning (ML) into SAO tools is expected to increase. This technology will enhance the ability to analyze large amounts of security data, identify patterns, and automate decision-making processes. AI-powered threat detection, behavior analysis and anomaly detection will be an integral part of the SAO solution.

10.2. Zero Trust Security Models

- **Trends:** As organizations embrace the trustless security framework, the SAO plays a key role in implementing and implementing these principles. Ensuring that users, devices and applications are consistently reliable will benefit from automation, ensuring that access points are flexible and responsive it is about the context.

10.3. Cloud-Native Security Solutions

- **Trends:** With the increasing adoption of cloud-native technologies such as containers and server less computing, SAO solutions will evolve to provide key support to secure these areas. Automation will be designed to meet the unique challenges of designing security in cloud-native architectures.

10.4. Extended Ecology

- **Trends:** SAO tools (Wang et al., 2010) will become more integrated with the broader ecosystem of security solutions, creating a unified security fabric. This includes seamless integration with identity management systems, endpoint protection platforms, threat notification feeds, and other security technologies to provide comprehensive, structured protection against evolving threats.

10.5. API-Driven Security Automation

- **Trends:** Using APIs to communicate with integration between security tools will become more common. SAO solutions will use APIs to communicate with cloud services, security platforms, and other tools, making automation workflows much more agile and flexible.

10.6. Self-Healing Safety Systems

- **Trends:** SAO will move towards a self-healing capability, where operating systems can not only identify and respond to security incidents but also correct vulnerabilities and incorrect security policies. This proactive approach aims to reduce reliance on human intervention for routine security tasks.

10.7. DevOps Integration

- **Trends:** Integrating security automation into DevOps (Santos et al., 2009) practices becomes seamless. SAO tools will fit into the DevOps pipeline, making security an integral part of the software development lifecycle. Automation will make it easier to continuously test, monitor and control security controls in the cloud.

10.8. Behavior Analysis and User Enterprise Behavior Analysis (UEBA)

- **Trends:** SAO solutions will increasingly include behavioral analysis and UEBA (Amazon, 2020) to identify unusual patterns in user activity.

Automation can be used in response to abnormal behavior, such as isolating corrupted accounts or enforcing new methods of authentication.

10.9. Quantum-Secure Security Automation

- **Trends:** As the advent of quantum computing poses a potential threat to existing cryptographic algorithms, SAO solutions will be developed to incorporate quantum-safe security measures Automation in the transition to quantum-resistant cryptographic protocols and in secure cryptographic keys. It will help in business.

10.10. Privacy-Focused Security

- **Trends:** With increasing emphasis on data privacy regulations, SAO tools will evolve for features that incorporate privacy management priorities and automation. It includes automated data classification, encryption and access control to ensure compliance with evolving privacy standards.

These future trends in automated and orchestral security highlight the importance of continuing to recognize technological advances and evolve security strategies to meet the evolving challenges of cloud computing emphasize the role of the. As organizations continue to embrace cloud services, SAO's role in delivering flexible, intelligent, automated security solutions will become increasingly important.

CONCLUSION

In conclusion, the exploration of Security Automation and Orchestration in the Cloud has unveiled a transformative landscape where traditional security approaches are being redefined as organizations increasingly migrate their infrastructure and applications to the cloud, the imperative to fortify defenses while maintaining operational efficiency becomes paramount. This chapter has delved into the pivotal role that automation and orchestration play in achieving this delicate balance. The marriage of security with automation not only accelerates response times to potential threats but also ensures a proactive defense strategy. By leveraging the power of automation, security teams can streamline routine tasks, allowing them to focus on more complex and strategic aspects of threat detection and mitigation. Furthermore, the orchestration of security processes ensures seamless collaboration between disparate security tools, creating a cohesive and integrated defense ecosystem. The cloud environment, with its dynamic nature, demands an agile security posture. This chapter has underscored the adaptability and scalability that automation and orchestration bring to the table, aligning security practices with the pace of cloud infrastructure changes. From incident detection to response, the integration of automated workflows and orchestrated playbooks offers a comprehensive approach that is not only efficient but also resilient in the face of evolving threats. While the benefits are clear, it is crucial to acknowledge the challenges and considerations that come with Security Automation and Orchestration in the Cloud. Striking the right balance between automation and human intervention, ensuring interoperability among diverse security tools, and addressing compliance concerns.

REFERENCES

Alien4Cloud. (2020). https://alien4cloud.github.io/

Amazon. (2020). *Aws cloudformation: Speed up cloud provisioning with infrastructure as code*. https://aws.amazon.com/cloudformation/

Armbrust, M., Fox, A., Griffith, R., Joseph, A. D., Katz, R., Konwinski, A., Lee, G., Patterson, D., Rabkin, A., Stoica, I., & Zaharia, M. (2010). A view of cloud computing. *Communications of the ACM*, *53*(4), 50–58. doi:10.1145/1721654.1721672

Armbrust, M., Fox, A., Griffith, R., Joseph, A. D., Katz, R. H., Konwinski, A., Lee, G., Patterson, D. A., Rabkin, A., Stoica, I., & Zaharia, M. (2009). *Above the clouds: A berkeley view of cloud computing*. Technical Report UCB/EECS-2009-28.

Bellendorf, J., & Mann, Z. Á. (2018). Cloud topology and orchestration using TOSCA: A systematic literature review. In: Lecture Notes in Computer Science (including subseries Lecture Notes in Artificial Intelligence and Lecture Notes in Bioinformatics). doi:10.1007/978-3-319-99819-0_16

Böhm, S., & Wirtz, G. (2022). Cloud-edge orchestration for smart cities: A review of kubernetes-based orchestration architectures. *EAI Endorsed Trans Smart Cities*, *6*(18), e2–e2. doi:10.4108/eetsc.v6i18.1197

Cai. (2009). *Customer Centric Cloud Service Model and a Case Study on Commerce as a Service*. Academic Press.

Chen. (2009). *What's New About Cloud Computing Security?* Academic Press.

Dillon. (2010). *Cloud Computing: Issues and Challenges*. Academic Press.

Hilley. (2009). *Cloud Computing: A Taxonomy of Platform and Infrastructure-level Offerings*. Academic Press.

Jaeger, P. T. (2008). Cloud computing and information policy: Computing in a policy cloud? *Journal of Information Technology & Politics*, *5*, 269–283.

Lauwers, C., & Tamburri, D. (n.d.). *OASIS Topology and Orchestration Specification for Cloud Applications*. www.oasis-open.org/committees/tosca

Liu, J., Zhao, T., Zhou, S., Yu, C., & Niu, Z. (2015). CONCERT: A Cloud-based Architecture for Next-Generation Cellular Systems. *IEEE Wireless Communications*, 21.

Ranjan, R., Benatallah, B., Dustdar, S., & Papazoglou, M. P. (2015). Cloud Resource Orchestration Programming: Overview, Issues, and Directions. *IEEE Internet Computing*, *19*(5), 46–56. doi:10.1109/MIC.2015.20

Rizvi, S., Ryoo, J., Kissell, J., & Aiken, B. (n.d.). A stakeholder-oriented assessment index for cloud security auditing. *Proceedings of the 9th International Conference on Ubiquitous Information Management and Communication*, 1-7. 10.1145/2701126.2701226

Santos, N., Gummadi, K. P., & Rodrigues, R. (2009). Towards trusted cloud computing. USENIX Hot Cloud.

Svorobej, S., Bendechache, M., Griesinger, F., & Domaschka, J. (2020). Orchestration from the Cloud to the Edge. In T. Lynn, J. G. Mooney, B. Lee, & P. T. Endo (Eds.), *The Cloud-to-Thing Continuum: Opportunities and Challenges in Cloud, Fog and Edge Computing* (pp. 61–77). Springer International Publishing. doi:10.1007/978-3-030-41110-7_4

Tomarchio, O., Calcaterra, D., & Modica, G. D. (2020). Cloud resource orchestration in the multi-cloud landscape: A systematic review of existing frameworks. *Journal of Cloud Computing (Heidelberg, Germany)*, *9*(1), 49. Advance online publication. doi:10.118613677-020-00194-7

Wang, C., Ren, K., Lou, W., & Li, J. (2010). Toward publicly auditable secure cloud data storage services. *IEEE Network*, *24*(4), 19–24. doi:10.1109/MNET.2010.5510914

Chapter 3
Quantum Key Distribution and Authentication in the Cloud for Internet of Things

Pramod Kumar Sagar
Raj Kumar Goel Institute of Technology, India

Arnika Jain
Sharda School of Engineering and Technology, Sharda University, India

ABSTRACT

Quantum computing is a type of computing that takes advantage of the principles of quantum mechanics to perform certain types of calculations much more efficiently than classical computers. Cloud computing has become the budding engine of the internet of things (IoT) and has become one of the most popular technologies in the last few years. The security of cloud computing is a key issue in the security of IoT. Quantum key distribution (QKD) and quantum authentication methods have been proposed in this chapter. The proposed protocol is able to authenticate the users in cloud using a short, shared key. The QKD is based on a quantum key distribution protocol that consists of two levels, namely, private key distribution and quantum authentication. The first level authentication takes place using shared key distribution. The second level authentication uses a shared key, and the third level authenticates the user in the cloud. The third level authentication is carried out using the quantum key distribution protocol.

DOI: 10.4018/979-8-3693-3249-8.ch003

1. INTRODUCTION

In the rapidly evolving landscape of modern technology, cloud computing stands as a transformative force, revolutionizing the way organizations store, process, and manage data. This section provides an essential foundation by defining cloud computing and elucidating its profound significance in today's digital era. Additionally, a brief exploration of the historical evolution of cloud computing sets the stage for understanding its current prominence.

1.1 Definition of Cloud Computing

Cloud computing can be succinctly defined as a paradigm that involves the delivery of computing services, including storage, processing power, and applications, over the internet. Unlike traditional computing models that rely on localized servers and dedicated infrastructure, cloud computing facilitates on-demand access to a shared pool of computing resources. This model allows users to leverage scalable and flexible services without the need for extensive on-premises hardware (Qian, 2009).

At its core, cloud computing is characterized by five key attributes:

On-Demand Self-Service: Users can provision and manage computing resources as needed, without requiring human intervention from the service provider.

Broad Network Access: Services are accessible over the network and can be accessed by various devices, such as laptops, smartphones, and tablets.

Resource Pooling: Computing resources are pooled and shared among multiple users, enabling efficient utilization and optimization of resources.

Rapid Elasticity: Resources can be quickly scaled up or down based on demand, providing flexibility and cost-efficiency.

Measured Service: Cloud computing resources are metered, and users are billed based on their usage, fostering transparency and cost control.

1.2 Brief History of Cloud Computing Evolution

The roots of cloud computing can be traced back to the 1960s, with the concept of time-sharing on mainframe computers. However, the term "cloud computing" gained prominence in the early 21st century. A pivotal moment occurred with the introduction of Amazon Web Services (AWS) in 2002, marking the commercialization of cloud services. AWS played a pivotal role in popularizing Infrastructure as a Service (IaaS) and paved the way for subsequent cloud providers.

In 2006, Google launched Google App Engine, contributing to the development of Platform as a Service (PaaS). Soon after, in 2009, Salesforce.com introduced Force.com, showcasing the potential of Software as a Service (SaaS) in the cloud.

The evolution continued with Microsoft Azure's entry in 2010, solidifying the competition among major cloud providers. Since then, the cloud computing landscape has expanded rapidly, witnessing the emergence of various services and deployment models. Today, cloud computing is integral to the operations of businesses, governments, and individuals worldwide, providing a dynamic and scalable infrastructure for the digital age.

As we delve deeper into the facets of cloud computing, it becomes apparent that its significance extends far beyond technological convenience, influencing organizational strategies, innovation, and the very fabric of the digital ecosystem.

2. KEY CONCEPTS OF CLOUD COMPUTING

Understanding the key concepts of cloud computing is crucial for navigating the diverse landscape of cloud services. This section delves into fundamental concepts, including Infrastructure as a Service (IaaS), Platform as a Service (PaaS), and Software as a Service (SaaS). Additionally, the principles of virtualization and resource pooling are explained to illuminate the underlying technologies that empower the cloud computing paradigm.

2.1 Infrastructure as a Service (IaaS)

IaaS represents a cloud computing service model where virtualized computing resources, including servers, storage, and networking, are provided over the internet. IaaS allows users to rent infrastructure on a pay-as-you-go basis, providing the flexibility to scale resources based on demand (Jadeja & Modi, 2012; Qian, 2009).

Key Characteristics:

1. Virtualization: IaaS relies heavily on virtualization technologies to create virtual instances of physical hardware. This enables the abstraction of resources from underlying physical infrastructure.
2. Scalability: Users can scale computing resources up or down based on their requirements, offering cost-effective solutions for varying workloads.
3. Self-Service: IaaS platforms typically offer self-service interfaces, empowering users to provision and manage resources without direct intervention from the service provider.

2.2 Platform as a Service (PaaS)

PaaS is a cloud computing service model that provides a platform allowing customers to develop, run, and manage applications without dealing with the complexities of underlying infrastructure. PaaS offerings include development frameworks, databases, and runtime environments (Rimal & Choi, 2009).

Key Characteristics:

1. Development Tools: PaaS provides integrated development tools, libraries, and frameworks, streamlining the application development process.
2. Automated Deployment: PaaS platforms often automate deployment processes, reducing the burden on developers and facilitating rapid application delivery.
3. Managed Services: The platform manages underlying infrastructure components, allowing developers to focus on coding and application logic.

2.3 Software as a Service (SaaS)

SaaS is a cloud computing service model where software applications are delivered over the internet on a subscription basis. Users can access these applications through web browsers, eliminating the need for local installations and maintenance.

Key Characteristics:

1. Accessibility: SaaS applications are accessible from any device with an internet connection and a web browser, providing flexibility and mobility.
2. Automatic Updates: SaaS providers handle software updates, ensuring users always have access to the latest features and security patches.
3. Scalability: SaaS offerings are scalable, allowing organizations to adjust their subscription levels based on user requirements.

2.4 Principles of Virtualization and Resource Pooling

Virtualization:

Virtualization is a foundational technology in cloud computing that involves creating virtual instances of computing resources, such as servers, storage, and networks.

Abstraction: Virtualization abstracts physical resources, allowing multiple virtual instances to run on a single physical machine. This abstraction enhances flexibility and resource utilization.

Isolation: Virtualization provides isolation between different virtual instances, ensuring that activities on one instance do not impact others. This isolation is critical for security and performance.

Resource Pooling:

Resource pooling is a fundamental concept in cloud computing that involves aggregating computing resources from multiple servers or data centers to serve multiple customers (Rodriguez & Guillemin, 2016).

Dynamic Allocation: Resources are dynamically allocated based on demand. This means that users can scale their resources up or down as needed, and the pooled resources are efficiently shared among multiple customers.

Optimization: Resource pooling optimizes resource utilization, ensuring that the available computing capacity is used efficiently, leading to cost savings and improved performance.

Understanding these key concepts lays the groundwork for exploring the multifaceted nature of cloud computing services, highlighting the flexibility, efficiency, and scalability that define this transformative technology.

3. CLOUD COMPUTING ARCHITECTURE

The architecture of cloud computing is a complex and dynamic system designed to provide scalable and on-demand computing resources. This section elucidates the fundamental components of cloud computing architecture, encompassing both front-end and back-end systems. Additionally, it explores the pivotal roles played by hypervisors, orchestration, and management layers in orchestrating and managing the diverse elements within the cloud infrastructure (Odun-Ayo, 2018).

3.1 Fundamental Components of Cloud Computing Architecture

Front-End Systems:

User Interface (UI): The front-end interface is the user's point of interaction with the cloud system. It includes graphical interfaces, command-line interfaces, and APIs (Application Programming Interfaces) that allow users to access and manage cloud resources.

Client Devices: These are the end-user devices, such as laptops, smartphones, or tablets, through which users interact with the cloud services. The front-end systems enable users to initiate requests, configure settings, and access applications hosted in the cloud.

Back-End Systems:

Cloud Infrastructure: The back-end comprises the physical infrastructure that includes servers, storage devices, and networking components. This infrastructure is responsible for executing the requested tasks and delivering services to users.

Cloud Services: Back-end systems host a variety of services, such as IaaS, PaaS, and SaaS, each providing different levels of abstraction and management for users.

Data Storage: The back-end includes storage systems that store and manage the data generated by cloud applications. This can involve distributed storage solutions, databases, and other data management components.

Security Mechanisms: Security components, including firewalls, encryption tools, and authentication systems, are crucial back-end elements to ensure the confidentiality and integrity of data.

3.2 Role of Hypervisors

Hypervisors, also known as Virtual Machine Monitors (VMMs), are critical components in cloud computing that enable the virtualization of computing resources. They allow multiple virtual machines (VMs) to run on a single physical server (Graniszewski & Arciszewski, 2016).

Abstraction Layer: Hypervisors create an abstraction layer between the physical hardware and the virtual machines. This abstraction enables the isolation and independent operation of multiple VMs on the same hardware.

Resource Allocation: Hypervisors manage the allocation of physical resources to virtual machines, ensuring efficient utilization of computing power, memory, and storage.

3.3 Orchestration and Management Layers

Orchestration: Orchestration involves the coordination and automation of various cloud services and resources to deliver end-to-end solutions. It manages the deployment, configuration, and operation of complex applications (Saadon et al., 2019).

Automation Tools: Orchestration tools automate tasks such as provisioning virtual machines, configuring networks, and scaling resources based on demand. Common orchestration tools include Kubernetes, Docker Swarm, and Apache Mesos.

Management Layer: The management layer oversees the entire cloud infrastructure and ensures its proper functioning. It includes components for monitoring, logging, and optimizing resource usage.

Resource Scaling: The management layer is responsible for dynamically scaling resources based on demand. This involves adding or removing virtual machines and adjusting the allocation of resources to meet performance requirements.

Understanding the interplay between front-end and back-end systems, coupled with the pivotal roles played by hypervisors, orchestration, and management layers, provides a holistic view of the architecture that powers cloud computing. This architecture enables the flexibility, scalability, and efficiency that characterize the modern cloud computing paradigm.

4. QUANTUM KEY DISTRIBUTION (QKD) IN CLOUD COMPUTING

Cloud computing, with its ever-growing importance in modern information technology, demands robust security measures to protect sensitive data transmitted and stored in the cloud.

Figure 1. Quantum key distribution (QKD) in cloud computing

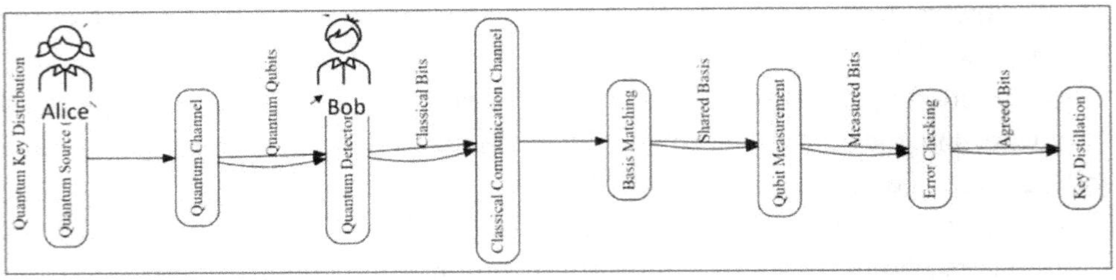

Quantum Key Distribution (QKD) emerges as a cutting-edge technology poised to revolutionize the security landscape of cloud computing. This section delves into the principles of QKD and explores its potential applications and impact within the cloud computing paradigm (Lo & Lütkenhaus, 2007).

Quantum Key Distribution is a cryptographic technique that utilizes principles from quantum mechanics to secure communication channels by enabling the generation of a secret key between two parties. Unlike classical cryptographic methods, which rely on the complexity of mathematical algorithms, QKD leverages the fundamental principles of quantum mechanics, roviding a level of security that is theoretically unbreakable (Matsumoto, 2007).

4.1 Principles of QKD

Quantum Superposition: QKD exploits the principle of superposition, allowing quantum bits or qubits to exist in multiple states simultaneously. This property enables the creation of quantum states that represent binary information.

Quantum Entanglement: Quantum entanglement is a phenomenon where two or more qubits become correlated in such a way that the state of one qubit is dependent on the state of another, regardless of the physical distance between them. QKD utilizes entangled qubits to create a shared secret key between communicating parties.

Quantum Measurement: The act of measuring a quantum state collapses it into one of the possible outcomes. In QKD, any attempt to eavesdrop on the quantum communication would inevitably disturb the quantum states, providing a detectable indication of unauthorized access (Knights, 2007).

4.2. Applications of QKD in Cloud Computing

4.2.1 Quantum-Safe Communication

As cloud computing relies heavily on secure communication channels, integrating QKD into cloud architectures ensures a level of security that withstands the potential threats posed by quantum computers. With the ability to detect any interception attempts, QKD offers a future-proof solution, especially considering the looming threat of quantum computers breaking widely used encryption algorithms.

4.2.2 Securing Cloud Data Centers

QKD can be employed to secure the communication links within and between cloud data centers. As data travels between servers, it can be vulnerable to interception. QKD provides a means to establish secure communication links, mitigating the risk of data breaches and unauthorized access (Chen & Zhao, 2012).

4.2.3 Enhancing Multi-Party Secure Computation

In scenarios where multiple parties collaborate in the cloud, QKD facilitates secure multi-party computation. It enables the creation of shared secret keys among participants, ensuring the confidentiality and integrity of collaborative processes without the risk of information leakage.

4.3. Challenges and Considerations

1. While QKD holds great promise for enhancing the security of cloud computing, practical implementation faces challenges. Factors such as the limited range of current QKD systems and the need for specialized hardware present obstacles to widespread adoption. Additionally, the cost and complexity of deploying QKD in large-scale cloud infrastructures need to be carefully considered.

5. QUANTUM KEY DISTRIBUTION (QKD) PROTOCOL

In the ever-evolving landscape of cybersecurity, the Quantum Key Distribution (QKD) protocol has emerged as a pioneering solution, leveraging the principles of quantum mechanics to secure communication channels. This essay delves into the intricacies of the QKD protocol, elucidating its multilevel approach, which encompasses private key distribution, quantum authentication, and user authentication in the cloud (Buhari et al., 2012; Nielsen & Chuang, 2001). The integration of these levels aims to fortify the security of digital communication in the quantum era.

5.1. Private Key Distribution

The foundation of the QKD protocol lies in private key distribution, where two communicating parties, typically denoted as Alice and Bob, aim to establish a secret cryptographic key. This initial level sets the stage for secure communication by leveraging the principles of quantum mechanics to exchange cryptographic keys without the risk of interception.

The process involves the transmission of quantum bits or qubits, which are quantum analogs of classical bits. The unique properties of qubits, such as superposition and entanglement, enable the creation of a shared secret key between Alice and Bob. The use of entangled qubits enhances the security of the key exchange, as any attempt to eavesdrop on the quantum communication would disrupt the delicate entanglement, serving as a detectable indicator of unauthorized access.

The cornerstone of the Quantum Key Distribution (QKD) protocol lies in the meticulous process of private key distribution, an initial and crucial level that establishes the foundation for secure communication between two parties—Alice and Bob. This level employs the principles of quantum mechanics to facilitate the exchange of cryptographic keys, ensuring a robust and tamper-resistant method of key generation.

Quantum Bits (Qubits) Transmission

At the heart of private key distribution is the transmission of quantum bits, or qubits. Unlike classical bits that represent information as 0s and 1s, qubits harness the principles of quantum mechanics, embodying a state of superposition where they can exist in multiple states simultaneously. This inherent property of superposition allows for a more nuanced representation of information, enabling the creation of a shared secret key between Alice and Bob.

Exploiting Quantum Properties: Superposition and Entanglement

The uniqueness of qubits stems from their ability to exist in a superposition of states. This means that a qubit can be in a state of 0, 1, or any combination of both, opening up possibilities for diverse information representation. Leveraging this superposition, the private key distribution process enables a richer and more secure encoding of information.

Furthermore, the concept of entanglement adds an extra layer of security to the key exchange. Entanglement involves the correlation of quantum states between particles, in this case, qubits. When qubits are entangled, the state of one qubit directly influences the state of the other, regardless of the physical separation between them. Exploiting entanglement in the private key distribution enhances the security of the exchanged keys. Any attempt to eavesdrop on the quantum communication would disturb the delicate entanglement, serving as a reliable indicator of unauthorized access.

Detecting Unauthorized Access

The use of entangled qubits not only enhances security but also provides a built-in mechanism for detecting unauthorized access. The delicate nature of entanglement means that any attempt to intercept or measure the quantum states during transmission would disrupt the entanglement, altering the quantum states in a detectable manner. This inherent feature ensures the integrity of the private key distribution process, making it resilient against potential eavesdropping attempts.

Advancing Quantum Secure Communication

In summary, private key distribution in the QKD protocol marks the initiation of secure communication between Alice and Bob. By leveraging the unique properties of qubits—superposition and entanglement—the protocol creates a shared secret key that forms the basis for subsequent authentication and communication levels. The quantum nature of the key distribution process not only enhances security but also introduces a level of detection, reinforcing the protocol against potential threats. As quantum technologies continue to evolve, private key distribution remains a pivotal component in the arsenal of quantum secure communication methodologies.

5.2 Quantum Authentication

5.2.1 First Level Authentication: Shared Key Distribution

Within the Quantum Key Distribution (QKD) protocol, the journey of authentication begins with the first level—Shared Key Distribution. Following the successful establishment of a secret key in the private key distribution phase, this shared key assumes a dual role as a cryptographic token. It becomes the cornerstone for authenticating the communication between the principal entities, Alice and Bob.

The shared key, having originated from the quantum entanglement and superposition during private key distribution, serves as a trusted identifier. In the realm of QKD, it acts as a robust cryptographic token that validates the identities of both Alice and Bob. This shared secret becomes the linchpin for ensuring the integrity of the transmitted information. Any attempt to compromise the communication by an unauthorized entity would be thwarted, as the absence of the shared key would render decryption unfeasible (Wegman & Lawrence Carter, 1981).

5.2.2 Second Level Authentication: Quantum Key Distribution

As the QKD protocol unfolds, the second level of authentication delves into the intricate realm of Quantum Key Distribution. Building upon the shared key obtained from the private key distribution phase, this level of authentication adds a layer of sophistication to the security framework (Bennett & Brassard, 2014).

The shared key, having proven its mettle in the first level, is now harnessed to authenticate the quantum communication itself. Quantum states, those delicate manifestations of superposition and entanglement, are exchanged between Alice and Bob. In this nuanced dance of quantum information, the shared key acts as a sentinel, verifying the legitimacy of the quantum states exchanged.

The quantum states, serving as unique identifiers, carry the distinctive imprints of the shared key. This combination creates a robust authentication mechanism, where the quantum nature of the communication serves as both the means of information exchange and a secure method of authentication. The shared key not only validates the authenticity of the parties involved but also acts as a shield against potential risks of quantum interception.

5.3 User Authentication in the Cloud

5.3.1 Third Level Authentication: Quantum Key Distribution in the Cloud

In response to the evolving digital landscape where cloud environments play a central role, the Quantum Key Distribution (QKD) protocol introduces a pivotal third level of authentication. This level is meticulously crafted to address the unique challenges posed by cloud-based interactions, emphasizing the critical necessity for robust user authentication (Khalid et al., 2013).

5.3.2 Quantum Key Distribution in the Cloud

Extending Security Paradigm

The third level of authentication within the QKD protocol marks a significant advancement in the security paradigm, acknowledging the prevalence of digital interactions within cloud environments (Zhou et al., 2018). Cloud services have become integral to modern computing, offering scalability, flexibility, and accessibility. However, with the increasing reliance on cloud-based services, ensuring the security and privacy of user interactions becomes a paramount concern.

Figure 2. Quantum key distribution in the cloud

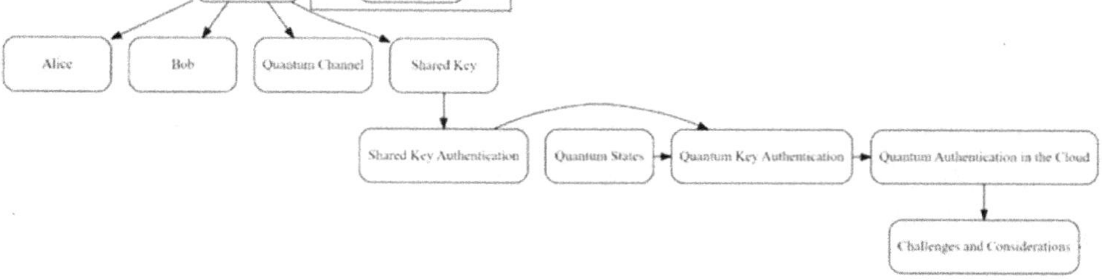

The Need for Robust User Authentication

As digital interactions migrate to cloud environments, the importance of robust user authentication cannot be overstated. Traditional authentication methods face challenges related to scalability, susceptibility to various attacks, and the potential vulnerabilities introduced by centralized systems. In this context, the QKD protocol introduces a quantum-infused approach to user authentication, leveraging the principles of quantum key distribution.

Applying Quantum Key Distribution to Authenticate Users

In this third level of authentication, the principles of quantum key distribution are harnessed to authenticate users accessing cloud services. The shared key, previously established through private key distribution and utilized for quantum authentication, assumes a pivotal role in this phase (Alléaume et al., 2014). As users interact with cloud services, the QKD protocol ensures that their identities are securely verified through the quantum-infused authentication process.

Enhancing Security Through Quantum Measures

Quantum key distribution adds an extra layer of security to user authentication in the cloud. The quantum states exchanged during the authentication process serve as unique identifiers, further fortifying the verification of user identities. The inherent properties of quantum mechanics, such as the no-cloning theorem and the sensitivity to measurement, contribute to the robustness of the authentication process (O'Brien et al., 2009).

Addressing Challenges of Traditional Methods

The quantum approach to user authentication in the cloud addresses challenges posed by traditional methods. The susceptibility of classical cryptographic systems to attacks like quantum computing-based threats is mitigated by the quantum-infused security measures. The distributed and quantum-resistant nature of the QKD protocol aligns with the decentralized and scalable requirements of cloud-based authentication.

5.4 QKD Protocol Steps

5.4.1 Key Generation

- **Quantum Transmission:** Alice prepares a stream of qubits, often in one of two possible states (0 or 1), and sends them to Bob over a quantum channel. The transmission can occur through various quantum carriers, such as photons.
- **Basis Choice:** At the receiving end, Bob randomly chooses a basis (a set of rules for measurements) for each incoming qubit. This basis selection is kept private.
- **Quantum Measurement:** Bob measures each qubit based on his chosen basis. Due to quantum superposition, the qubits are in a combination of states until measured, at which point they collapse into definite states.

- **Public Discussion:** Alice and Bob publicly disclose their basis choices but not the measurement outcomes. This allows them to determine which qubits were measured using the same basis.

5.4.2 Error Checking

- **Comparison:** Alice and Bob compare a subset of their measured qubits to ensure they used the same basis. Any discrepancies may indicate potential eavesdropping.

6. QUANTUM AUTHENTICATION METHODS: A QUANTUM LEAP IN SECURITY

In the rapidly advancing landscape of cybersecurity, traditional authentication methods face unprecedented challenges from the potential advent of quantum computers. Quantum authentication methods emerge as a groundbreaking solution that leverages the principles of quantum mechanics to provide unprecedented security for information exchange and user verification (Curty & Santos, 2001; Sikeridis et al., 2020). This essay explores the foundational concepts, key principles, and potential applications of quantum authentication, shedding light on its transformative role in securing digital communication.

Foundations of Quantum Authentication

6.1 Quantum Key Distribution (QKD)

One of the fundamental pillars of quantum authentication is Quantum Key Distribution (QKD).

Figure 3. Quantum key distribution

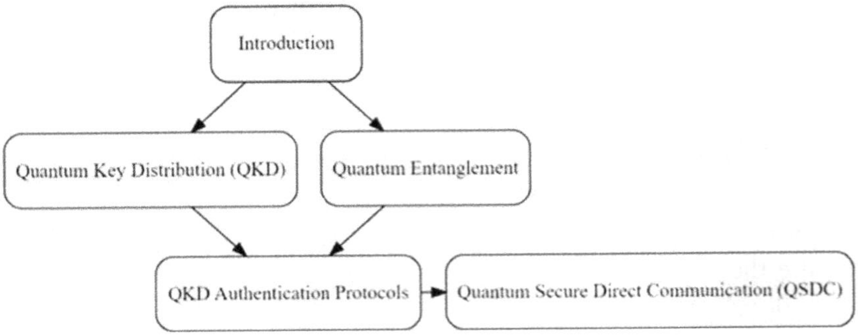

QKD enables secure key exchange between two parties over an insecure communication channel. The process leverages the principles of quantum superposition and entanglement, ensuring that any attempt to intercept or measure the quantum states during transmission is detectable. The keys generated through QKD serve as the foundation for secure authentication, offering a level of security unattainable by classical cryptographic methods.

6.2 Quantum Entanglement in Authentication

Quantum entanglement, a phenomenon where quantum particles become correlated regardless of distance, plays a pivotal role in enhancing the security of quantum authentication. The entangled states can be utilized in authentication protocols to create a unique and secure link between entities. The intricate relationship established through entanglement adds an additional layer of complexity, making it exceedingly difficult for malicious actors to compromise the authentication process.

6.3 Quantum Key Distribution Authentication Protocol

Quantum Key Distribution Authentication Protocols combine the principles of QKD with classical cryptographic techniques to establish secure authentication processes. These protocols ensure that the keys exchanged through quantum channels are used effectively to verify the identity of communicating parties. The integration of quantum-resistant cryptographic primitives further fortifies the authentication mechanisms, making them resilient against potential quantum attacks (Hwang et al., 2007).

6.4 Quantum Secure Direct Communication (QSDC)

While not directly an authentication method, Quantum Secure Direct Communication (QSDC) contributes to the overall secure communication infrastructure. QSDC allows direct communication between two parties with unconditional security, eliminating the need for cryptographic keys exchanged over potentially vulnerable channels. When integrated into authentication processes, QSDC can enhance the overall security of communication and information exchange.

REFERENCES

Alléaume, R., Branciard, C., Bouda, J., Debuisschert, T., Dianati, M., Gisin, N., Godfrey, M., Grangier, P., Länger, T., Lütkenhaus, N., Monyk, C., Painchault, P., Peev, M., Poppe, A., Pornin, T., Rarity, J., Renner, R., Ribordy, G., Riguidel, M., ... Zeilinger, A. (2014). Using quantum key distribution for cryptographic purposes: A survey. *Theoretical Computer Science*, *560*, 62–81. doi:10.1016/j.tcs.2014.09.018

Bennett, C. H., & Brassard, G. (2014). Quantum cryptography: Public key distribution and coin tossing. *Theoretical Computer Science*, *560*, 7–11. doi:10.1016/j.tcs.2014.05.025

Buhari, A., Zukarnain, Z. A., Subramaniam, S. K., Zainuddin, H., & Saharudin, S. (2012). A Quantum Based Challenge Response User authentication Scheme Over Noiseless. *International Journal of Network Security & its Applications*, *4*(6), 67–79. doi:10.5121/ijnsa.2012.4605

Chen, D., & Zhao, H. (2012). Data Security and Privacy Protection Issues in Cloud Computing. *International Conference on Computer Science and Electronics Engineering*, 647-651. 10.1109/ICCSEE.2012.193

Curty & Santos. (2001). Quantum authentication of classical messages. *Physical Review A, 64*(6).

Graniszewski & Arciszewski. (2016). Performance analysis of selected hypervisors (virtual machine monitors-vmms). *International Journal of Electronics and Telecommunications, 62*.

Hwang, T., Lee, K.-C., & Li, C.-M. (2007). Provably secure three-party authenticated quantum key distribution protocols. *IEEE Transactions on Dependable and Secure Computing*, *4*(1), 71–80. doi:10.1109/TDSC.2007.13

Jadeja, Y., & Modi, K. (2012). *Cloud computing-concepts, architecture and challenges. In 2012 international conference on computing, electronics and electrical technologies (ICCEET)*. IEEE.

Khalid, U., Ghafoor, A., Irum, M., & Shibli, M. A. (2013). Cloud based secure and privacy enhanced authentication & authorization protocol. *Procedia Computer Science*, *22*, 680–688. doi:10.1016/j.procs.2013.09.149

Knights, M. (2007). The art of quantum computing. *Engineering and Technology, IEEE*, *2*(1), 30–34. doi:10.1049/et:20070103

Lo, H., & Lütkenhaus, N. (2007). *Quantum cryptography: from theory to practice*. arXiv preprint quant-ph/0702202.

Matsumoto, R. (2007). *Quantum multiparty key distribution protocol without use of entanglement*. arXiv preprint arXiv:0708.0902.

Nielsen & Chuang. (2001). Quantum computation and quantum information. *Phys. Today, 54*(2).

O'Brien, J. L., Furusawa, A., & Vučković, J. (2009). Photonic quantum technologies. *Nature Photonics*, *3*(12), 687–695. doi:10.1038/nphoton.2009.229

Odun-Ayo, I. (2018). Cloud computing architecture: A critical analysis. In *2018 18th international conference on computational science and applications (ICCSA)*. IEEE. 10.1109/ICCSA.2018.8439638

Qian, L. (2009). Cloud computing: An overview. *Cloud Computing: First International Conference, CloudCom 2009, Beijing, China, December 1-4, 2009. Proceedings 1*.

Rimal, B. P., & Choi, E. (2009). A taxonomy and survey of cloud computing systems. In *Fifth International Joint Conference on INC, IMS and IDC*. IEEE Computer Society. 10.1109/NCM.2009.218

Rodriguez, V. K. Q., & Guillemin, F. (2016). Performance analysis of resource pooling for network function virtualization. In *2016 17th International Telecommunications Network Strategy and Planning Symposium (Networks)*. IEEE.

Saadon, G., Haddad, Y., & Simoni, N. (2019). A survey of application orchestration and OSS in next-generation network management. *Computer Standards & Interfaces*, *62*, 17–31. doi:10.1016/j.csi.2018.07.003

Sikeridis, Kampanakis, & Devetsikiotis. (2020). Post-quantum authentication in TLS 1.3: a performance study. *Cryptology ePrint Archive*.

Wegman, M. N., & Lawrence Carter, J. (1981). New hash functions and their use in authentication and set equality. *Journal of Computer and System Sciences*, *22*(3), 265–279. doi:10.1016/0022-0000(81)90033-7

Zhou, L., Wang, Q., Sun, X., Kulicki, P., & Castiglione, A. (2018). Quantum technique for access control in cloud computing II: Encryption and key distribution. *Journal of Network and Computer Applications*, *103*, 178–184. doi:10.1016/j.jnca.2017.11.012

Chapter 4
A Quantitative Study on Cloud Computing in the UAE:
Identifying and Addressing Adoption Barriers

Muhammad Marakkoottathil
Birla Institute for Technology and Science, UAE

Ramamurthy Venkatesh
https://orcid.org/0000-0003-1482-4417
Symbiosis International University, India

N. A. Natraj
https://orcid.org/0000-0002-8726-5284
Symbiosis International University, India

ABSTRACT

Information technology and digitization of the business are the key enablers for success in the current competitive market. Businesses across all industries face many challenges when choosing relevant technology solutions and their platforms. However, adoption of cloud computing among enterprises varies in different countries and global markets. Even in emerging markets such as UAE, adoption of cloud is facing definite barriers as highlighted by some recent studies. This research study is aimed at extending current literature on barriers of cloud adoption in UAE with more fine-grained factors and interpretations with the help of quantitative survey research. Resultant analyses were presented as a model for further validation by select IT experts and professional managers, who reconfirmed the research results are applicable, fit, and valid for UAE market. This study thus enhances the current literature on cloud adoption barriers in general and provides more fine-grained factors specific to UAE IT market perceptions.

DOI: 10.4018/979-8-3693-3249-8.ch004

1. INTRODUCTION

Public cloud computing has gained widespread acceptance as a computing model that offers on-demand services, minimal initial investment, and ease of adoption for businesses, etc. Business organizations across the globe are actively taking advantage of the benefits of cloud computing such as reliable services, cost-effectiveness optimized IT operations. By adopting cloud-based solutions, enterprises could avoid major hardware investments, initial setup costs, time consuming IT project durations and routine maintenance (Alsafi, T.& Fan, I.-S, 2020; Kushwaha, 2021). In other words, cloud computing enables relatively small initial investment with p pay-as-you-go models, on-demand services, and lower IT labour costs (Avram, 2014; Fisher, C. 2018).

Despite the considerable technological advantages associated with cloud computing, the actual deployment of this technology in organisations situated in the United Arab Emirates has not aligned with the anticipated benefits. The limited uptake can be attributed to several factors, including: 1) A prevailing perception among UAE organisations that cloud computing is still in its nascent phase of evolution, and 2) A significant number of companies are still in the process of acquiring knowledge and understanding of cloud computing. Two factors that contribute to the reluctance to adopt a new solution are a lack of awareness and understanding, as well as hesitation. In contrast, numerous firms operating in diverse worldwide marketplaces have enhanced their productivity and competitiveness through the use of cloud computing services (Ross & Blumenstein, 2015). Nevertheless, it is important to note that the determinants influencing the adoption of cloud services may not always lend themselves to easy generalisation (El Gazzar, 2014). In order to comprehensively investigate the adoption of cloud computing, it is imperative to incorporate context-based analysis that considers technological, organisational, and environmental circumstances. This is crucial since each unique setting may possess distinct drivers that influence the adoption process. The utilisation of public cloud services by an organisation is contingent upon a multitude of elements that are influenced by market conditions and industry-specific obstacles. These elements have the ability to either facilitate effective adoption or result in minimal or negligible utilisation. The determinants of public cloud adoption may be influenced by various internal and external elements within the organisation, including but not limited to the cost of the solution provided, technological preparedness, and the availability of experienced people. Numerous extant theories and models elucidate the process of organisational adoption of technology and innovation, which can be extrapolated to encompass cloud-related enterprises. The primary objective of this research study is to enhance the existing body of literature on the obstacles to cloud adoption in the United Arab Emirates (UAE). This will be achieved by examining more detailed aspects and providing nuanced interpretations through the utilisation of quantitative survey research methods. In order to fulfil the objective, an extensive literature review was conducted to identify the most suitable model for this study, as described in the literature review section. The Technology Organisation Environment (TOE) model is widely regarded as the most suitable framework for this study. Subsequently, the research design and analysis were conducted based on this model, as elaborated in the following sections.

2. LITERATURE REVIEW

This section explores the validation of various aspects of cloud computing, including characteristics, pricing models, benefits, concerns, various relevant theoretical frameworks, and model selection.

2.1 Contemporary Challenges in Cloud Computing Adoption

The nature of the business challenge and its appropriate technology solution constitutes the various factors for the reach and acceptance of cloud computing solutions. Five characteristics should exist to consider it as a cloud computing solution. These characteristics are used to measure the difference between traditional and cloud computing systems. Summary of the characteristics are tabulated in Table 1.

Table 1. Cloud computing characteristics

Characteristics	Description	Author
On-demand self-service	Ability to provision IT services whenever needed. It allows customers to automate required computing, storage, or database services, etc. Not required to set up hardware resources	Mell & Grance, 2011
Broad network access	Availability of the services over the network across heterogeneous systems such as laptops, mobiles, tablets, workstations, etc.	Mell & Grance, 2011
Resource pooling	Mechanism in which the resources such as computing, network, and storage, etc. resources are shared between customers from a common resource pool. Clients are often hidden from system complexity and only exposed to the resources they consume	Mell & Grance, 2011
Rapid elasticity	Refers to the ability of the cloud provider to scale up and scale down the resources depending on the demand. From the customer perspective, the resource often appears as unlimited and appropriate for their use any point in time	Erl et al., 2013
Measured service	The ability of cloud services to demonstrate usage and allow optimization by providing corrective action and alerting systems	Erl et al., 2013

2.2 Current Pricing Model

Cloud computing has the potential to allow the smaller companies to rise in the market, it allows the companies to avoid setup cost and use the service in a pay-as-you-go model. The cloud-based services are relatively less expensive as cloud providers make use of the economies of scale model, meaning the greater number of users use the services, the lesser unit cost is. The classification of cloud service pricing primarily categorizes as static/fixed pricing or dynamic pricing. (Kamra, Sonawane, & Alappanavar 2012). First model, namely Static Pricing mode is easier to realize and simpler to use. With this model, resources will have a fixed price. It supports assurance for buyers and also allows them to know how much they will pay, more consistent estimation, lessens risk and makes profit estimation easy. However, the drawback is sometimes it is unfair for consumers because it does not take the supply and demand into consideration. It does not change even if the usage goes more or less. In contrast, the second model namely dynamic pricing model takes usage into account. The price of the resources is determined according to demand and supply or based on the mechanism used by the cloud provider. For dynamic pricing a firm delays its pricing decisions until discovering the market condition. so that it can fit the price accordingly. When demand is ample, set a high price, and when demand is weak, it sets a low price.

2.3 Factors Influencing Cloud Computing Adoption

Following table.2 shows some of the critical advantages of cloud-based services derived from literature research.

Table 2. Benefits of cloud computing

Benefits	Description	Author
Reduced cost	Optimal use of hardware and software is possible through resource pooling. It helps with consumers sharing the resources and only paying for what they use and helps in reducing the cost of maintaining the ICT infrastructure	Fujistu 2011
Setup time	There is no purchase of hardware and setup of compute, or storage hardware devices leading to very less time for hosting business applications	Fujistu 2011
Simplicity	Much easier to use as most of the required hardware resources are already pre-provisioned by the cloud service provider	Fujistu 2011
Affordability	Pay-as-you-go-model followed by the cloud services makes it less capital intensive and hence affordable	Sultan, 2010
Convenience and improved accessibility	Most of the services are accessible from anywhere, the key requirement is to have connectivity or reachability to the cloud provider locations	Fujistu 2011

2.4 Concerns of Cloud Computing

The table.3 displays the typical well-known concerns around cloud adoption.

Table 3. Concerns of cloud computing

Concerns	Description	Author
Information security and privacy	There are more privacy concerns due to shared resources between clients. For example, due to shared resources, company sensitive information such as email and financial accounting could be potentially exposed to others.	Fujistu 2011
Data residency and legal jurisdiction	The cloud could be storing confidential or public or government-related data over its accessibility outside of the geographical border of the country - It poses concern over the legal jurisdiction of the data	El-Gazzer 2014
Regulatory compliance	Enterprises need to maintain data to some sort of compliance requirement, which can be a challenge for cloud adoption	El-Gazzar 2014
Vendor lock-in	Impact of supplier, availability, or service termination	Kumar 2016
Business continuity	How to recover and failover of infrastructure if a provider has connectivity issues	Wilson 2015

3. PUBLIC CLOUD IN UAE CONTEXT

The United Arab Emirates (UAE) acknowledges the potential to establish itself as a prominent centre for cloud computing and data centre operations within the Middle East and North Africa (MENA) region, as stated by the Federal Authority for Telecommunications and Regulation (TRA) in 2018. The ICT development forum was initiated by the TRA in December 2015, recognising the significant role of cloud computing in advancing the digital transformation agenda of the UAE. The United Arab Emirates (UAE) has embraced a cloud-first economy, drawing inspiration from its Vision 2021, national innovation policy, and the Telecommunications Regulatory Authority (TRA). The use of cloud computing in both the public and private sectors in the United Arab Emirates (UAE) has exhibited a favourable trend. The rationale behind the use of cloud computing encompasses several factors, including the potential to decrease capital expenditures, the ability to adapt to fluctuating demand, and the opportunity to prioritise the delivery of essential services. The UAE government acknowledges the advantages of the economy of scale characteristic of cloud computing and the importance of providing firms with access to cloud-based computing resources. According to the Federal Authority for Transport and Road (TRA, 2018). The United Arab Emirates (UAE) hosts several cloud solution providers, encompassing both domestic private managed service providers and international Hyperscalers like Microsoft Azure, Oracle Cloud, G42cloud, Alibaba Cloud (Ali cloud), and others.

The Table 4 provides information on the presence of some Hyperscalers.

Table 4. Cloud solutions providers in UAE

Cloud Providers	Details	Citation
Oracle OCI	The company possesses two data centre facilities in the United Arab Emirates, specifically situated in Abu Dhabi and Dubai.	Oracle, 2022
Microsoft Azure	Microsoft Azure offers two cloud DC centres in the UAE: one in Abu Dhabi for northern clients' disaster recovery solutions and one in Dubai for all customers and partners.	Microsoft, 2019
AWS	It already has cloud edge locations locally in the country and cloud DC centers of AWS in the UAE is also opened in August 2022	AWS, 2022

Cloud computing enables and motivates UAE's, key identified ICT initiatives such as big data, robotics, the internet of things, AI, mobility, and virtual reality. Cloud computing growth in UAE identified to be affected by following key barriers/ challenges 1) Network access/latency solutions, 2) Skill scarcity, 4) Cultural change opposition 5) Data security issues 6 and 7: Delayed savings in costs and workforce change (TRA-Federal Authority 2018).

Resident nation regulation is crucial for cloud adoption. UAE public cloud adoption regulations should follow these. 1) The UAE's Information Assurance Regulations (IAR) set minimum cybersecurity standards for important areas like energy, government, finance and insurance, health services, food and agriculture, ICT, electric and water, and transportation (TRA, 2020). 2) Abu Dhabi government, entities, contractors, and third parties must follow ADISS. 3) UAE Federal Health Data Law-compliant healthcare data storage and processing 4) The UAE DESC CSP Security standard guides information security practise development and implementation.

3.1 Research Significance

In 2019, UAE government ICT funding was $9.9 billion and predicted to reach $23 billion by 2024. The UAE public cloud service market grew 40.9% in 2020 (IDC, 2021) and is expected to expand 38.2% between 2020 and 2027.In 2019, clouding spending was estimated at 1.1 billion dollars. It will reach 1.8 billion in 2022 (UAE ministry of the economy, IDC, Dubai chamber of commerce, Fitch connect, 2021). Cloud computing is crucial to UAE's economic growth, hence cloud adoption research is crucial. The UAE was picked because it is one of the most mature and fastest-growing economies in the Middle East (IT Index 2019 and Network Readiness Index 2021).

3.2 Research Gaps and Proposal

Cloud appears to be efficacious in enhancing an organization's IT, however no research currently exists in the UAE context to understand the factors influencing public cloud adoption decisions. Aiming at this research gap, this paper proposes a research model based on the TOE framework and additionally data was collected from 56 tech influencers and decision-makers from UAE enterprises to assess influencing factors. Thus, this study contributes to scientific knowledge with a holistic analysis to the determinants of cloud computing adoption. There are two key objectives of this study 1) To understand current adoption details of the public cloud-based services in UAE and 2) To analyze the key factors affecting the determinant of cloud adoption in UAE. The study focuses on key elements identified in the TOE framework (Wikipedia, 2021).

4. THEORETICAL MODEL SELECTION

The research method consists of reviewing the literature on the subject and selecting the best theory as a basis for the research according to the objectives. The table below presents the theoretical analysis and its applicability to this study.

Theories that explain technology adoption in terms of individual analysis are not well suited for this study. Both DOI and TOE frameworks fit because they explain the adoption of technology and innovation at an organizational level. However, the model best suited for this study is the TOE framework. It is because the TOE Framework looks at several factors that are both internal and external to the organization along the three dimensions of the organization. The table.5 explores the existing theories ans model details.

Table 5. Theories and model details

Theory/Model	Description	Level of Analysis	Author
TAM	Technological acceptance models aim to study how consumers accept and make use of technology.	Individual	Davis (1989)
Diffusion of Innovation (DOI)	Innovation diffusion theory states that early adopters evaluate innovations based on their relative advantages, compatibility, complexity, trialability, and observability.	Organization or Market	Rogers (1995)
UTAUT	Unified theory of acceptance and use of technology models explains an individual's intention to use an information system, and the user's subsequent behavior based on three contributing factor 1) performance expectation 2) social influence and 3) effort expectation and facilitating conditions.	Individual	Venkatesh (2003)
Technology Organization Environment (TOE)	Three key factors influence an organization's adoption of technological innovations. 1) Technological factors (various characteristics such as complexity, and compatibility of technologies), 2) Organizational factors (a firm's characteristics and resources such as leadership support, firm size etc.), and 3) Environmental factors (Regulation, Competition, etc.).	Organization	Tornatzky and Mitchell Fleischer (1990)

4.1 Cloud Adoption TOE Factors

Various studies have attempted to identify factors influencing public cloud adoption. The following table.6 uses key factors on the basis of TOE framework.

Table 6. TOE factors and their sources

Construct	Factor	Sources
Technology (TC)	Relative Advantage (RA)	Rogers (2003)
	Compatibility (CO)	Rogers (2003)
	Complexity (CX)	Rogers (2003
	Security and Accessibility (SA)	Tehrani (2013); Oguntala et al. (2017)
Organization (OG)	Firm size (FS)	Rogers (2003)
	Technological Readiness (TR)	Gutierrez and Lumsden (2014)
	Top Management Support (TM)	Young and Jordan (2008); Ahmad and Siddiqui (2014)
Environment (EN)	Regulations (RG)	Wilson, Khazaei, and Hirsch (2015)
	Competition Intensity (CI)	Ahmad and Siddiqui (2014)
	Trading Partner Pressure (TP)	Oliveira and Martins (2011)
	Vendor Readiness (VR)	Trivedi (2013)

Relative advantage: Relative advantage: Is defined "as the degree to which an innovation is perceived as being better than the idea it supersedes'' (Rogers 2003). In this study, the innovation is referred to as public cloud computing, and it superseded other computing solutions. This attribute of the innovation is important as it relates to the benefits cloud computing in terms of facilitating the computing process easier, faster, and more efficiently. It also helps create profitability by improving productivity and performance. Some of the relative advantages to look at includes better customer care, efficient communication, robust integration and coordination, lesser capital costs, flexibility in capacity, implementation agility, reliability, and compatibility (Leavitt 2009) hence, therefore, using cloud computing will provide a relative advantage over other alternative systems.

Compatibility: According to Wang-2010 research, it is a key factor in innovation adoption. It is about the degree to which an innovation is perceived as consistent with the experiences, existing values and needs of potential adopters" (Rogers 2003). When new technology is compatible with the existing system, the adoption of the technology is more likely to happen. It is applicable for cloud computing as well.

Complexity: It refers to the "degree to which technology is perceived as relatively difficult to understand and use" (Rogers 2003). It's more about the perception of technological complexity, and the likelihood of perception's impact on adoption. Adopting new technologies may present challenges in terms of process changes, while factors such as ease of use may increase adoption (Lopez 2016)

Security and accessibility: These are related in which expectation is data should be secure and private, however, the data should be accessible whenever needed and these have been deemed as key considerations in the adoption of public cloud by SMEs (Tehrani, 2013). Accessibility also plays a role in cloud service adoption if a business doesn't necessarily have the internet it needs, or the equipment used to access the cloud service may not be particularly useful. It is determined that one of the main barriers to the use of cloud-based services is the security concerns that users have especially in relation to data breaches, outages, and loss (Oguntala et al., 2017).

Company size: The larger the company, the more resources it has to incentivize the adoption of the latest innovations (Dewar and Dutton 1986). Small companies are often financially constrained by lack of expertise, operate in a competitive environment, etc. The researchers also observed that large firms have potential advantages in skills specialization and use of information systems compared to smaller firms. (Hart and Lenihan 2014). In short, the study shows the size of the firm is one of the key reasons of IT adoption

Technology readiness: The degree to which a company has the willingness and ability to embrace and use relevant new technology assets based on previous experience (Vize, Coughlan, Kennedy, and Ellis-Chadwick 2013). Users who already have IT experience using similar services may be more inclined to adopt cloud services and conversely, without sufficient skill levels, the SME may opt to go for the easiest solution, which may or may not be cloud-based (Gutierrez & Lumsden 2014).

Top Management Support: Pan and Jan - 2008 and Zhu - 2004 in their research found a positive relationship between the acceptance of new technologies and management support. Management support is critical to adopting new technologies for two key reasons. 1) It provides adequate resources for adoption and 2) It offer necessary aid for innovation, reinvention, and process changes. (Wang 2010)

Regulations: Refers to government, industry, or market regulations that a business may have to comply with in the environment in which it operates. Researchers such as Wilson, found that regulations largely affected the adoption of cloud computing by SMEs (Wilson, Khazaei, & Hirsch 2015). Regulations may cover government-related, industry-related, or internal policies established by an organization.

Competitive Intensity: Refers to the pressure on a business to perform in a certain way based on other competitors. In the case of cloud computing, SMEs may be forced to adopt cloud-based services due to intense competition (Ahmad & Siddiqui 2014). For example, other businesses and services that are already using cloud services will certainly also influence cloud adoption, and companies can adopt cloud computing to gain the same benefits as their competitors.

Trading partner pressure: This implies to the fact that supplier activities can significantly affect the likelihood of innovation being adopted (Frambach, Barkema, Nooteboom, & Wedel 1998). Trading partner pressure has been identified as a key driver of innovation adoption by firms (Oliveira & Martins 2011). Organizations can be driven to adopt cloud-based services in cases where suppliers, customers, or other trading partners need to use specific cloud-based services. It in turn could lead to the adoption of additional cloud-based services.

Supplier readiness: Denotes the readiness of the service supplier to provide the expected service. In this context, vendor readiness is the readiness of the cloud service provider, including the readiness to deliver the solutions SMEs need, providing sufficient information about the service and vendor reputation (Trivedi, 2013). For example, an organization might require a service that is only available on the local or desktop version. It could hinder the adoption of cloud computing services.

4.2 Hypothesis of Adoption Factors

Hypothesis of Technological factors:

The technical context in the original TOE framework highlights factors such as the availability and characteristics of the technology, which may be related to the company's relevant internal or external context (Alshamaileh,2013). In the context of cloud-based solutions, the factors identified are comparative advantage, compatibility, complexity, security, and accessibility.

H1: Technological factors will positively relate to the public cloud adoption in UAE

Hypothesis of Organizational factors:

One of the influencing parts of cloud adoption is organizational factors (Trivedi 2013). In this context, three relevant factors have been identified, which are company size, top management support and technical readiness

H2: Organizational factors will positively relate to the public cloud adoption in UAE. The fig.1 shows the research modeling of the cloud computing adoption details.

Figure 1. Research modelling

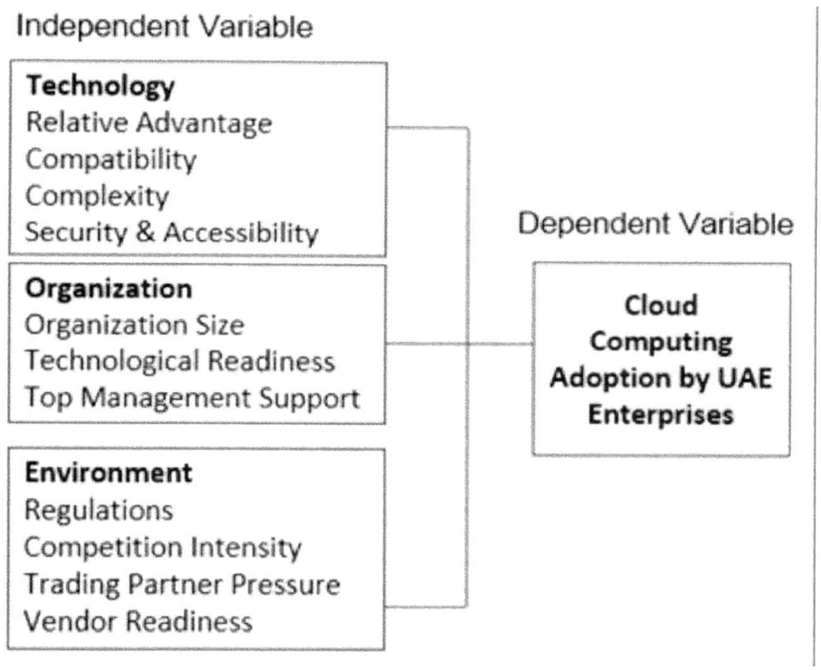

Hypothesis of Environmental factors:

The environmental construction of TOE is related to the external environment of the enterprise, including trade characteristics, market structure, technical support infrastructure, government guidelines and other factors. (DePietro, Wiarda, & Fleischer, 1990). The constructs identified by the researcher include regulations, competition Intensity, trading partner pressure and vendor readiness.

H3: Environmental factors will positively relate to the public cloud adoption in UAE

5. RESEARCH DESIGN AND METHODOLOGY

The below diagram depicts the overview of the research procedures performed for this study. This has been done with a clear plan to extend the research model into a logical sequence of research steps as depicted as Research Design and Methodology in Fig.2.

Figure 2. Research procedure

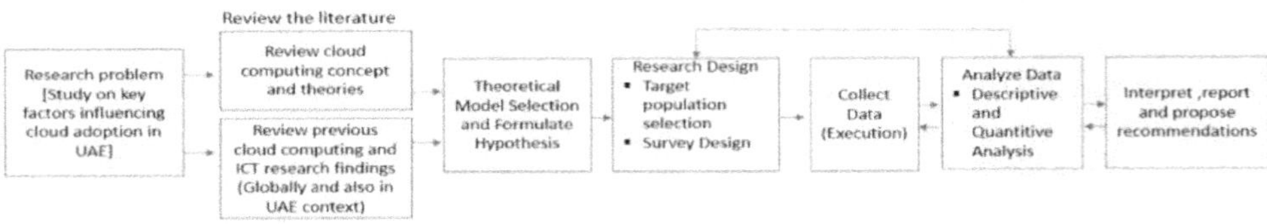

Literature review helped to draw conclusions about the desired model selection and survey conducted to obtain industry perceptions, hence the research is conclusive in nature from a taxonomic point of view. To generate insight and analyze the outcome quantitative data analysis and descriptive methods are used. The following sections are brief on the research activities and procedure used for developing the survey mechanism and data interpretations.

5.1 Research Design

The cross-section survey was done to get the representative of the UAE population. The research relies on sourcing information through surveys, expert feedback, and publicly available data sources. The scope of this research was only for UAE geography. Part of the analysis, an online survey (using Google form) was shared among potential decision-makers and influencers from various industry sectors in the UAE to determine cloud adoption factors. The findings of this survey are analyzed to draw conclusions. Secondary data confirmed the model selection and learning of similar previous research papers.

5.2 Data Collection

Based on our research problem and objective, the study uses both primary and secondary data collection methods. Online surveys and direct interviews performed to get the primary data. The online method uses surveying potential consumers to understand the cloud adoption strategies of businesses in UAE. And it factually aided to understand the existing cloud adoption market and assisted to correlate responded feedback. The study also made use of secondary data such as websites, journals, and reference books on the topic to capture the existing research findings.

5.3 Target Population

The target population for the research study comprises existing and potential cloud computing influencers and decision makers from the UAE based large enterprises. To ensure the validity, this study operationalised the variables based on previous relevant literature (Wambugu & Ndiege 2018).

5.4 Survey Design

The survey uses a five-point "Likert Scale" to measure the constructs on an interval ranging from "strongly disagree (1)" to "strongly agree (5)." Controls (screening questions) which included in the survey ensured that it captures the relevant work experience of the respondents and position in the company to understand the degree of the influence or decision-making power, and also the basic understanding of the cloud technology to exclude participants with no cloud knowledge. A pilot study was done to confirm the instrument accuracy in various aspects such as the content objectives, length, and the number of the questionnaire, usage of the wordings, and the format of the paper. Survey acknowledges the academic and practical nature of conducting research in the UAE. It also included questionnaires such as the number of employees in the organization, industry sector, whether the organization has dedicated IT personnel or not, does the organization have cloud strategy, existing cloud usage, yearly cost of the cloud solution, and satisfaction level of the cloud-based services. This design would ensure that the samples contribute meaningfully, both quantitatively and qualitatively. Succeeding are the criteria used for the sampling design. 1) Survey Target:Potential decision makers and influencers 2) Method: Convenient sampling 3) Survey duration: two weeks, 4) Sample size: between 50 and 60 5) Segmentation: Geography (UAE). The company size was measured using the number of employees. The purpose of the questionnaire design was to validate responses, to qualify and to distinguish factors influencing cloud adoption. This study recognized eleven independent variables and Survey resulted in more than fifty potential respondents. The Survey questionnaire and their sources is shown in Table.7.

Table 7. Survey questionnaire and their sources

A: General Information	**Personal information (4 questions)**	**Kumar (2017); Wambugu (2013) Tehrani (2013)**
	Basic organizational information (8 questions)	
B: Current ICT Setup	IT personnel and strategy (2 questions)	Kumar (2017); Wambugu (2013), Tehrani (2013)
	Software systems in place (2 questions)	
	Check on knowledge on cloud computing (1 question)	
C: Cloud-based services at the organization (For those who understand what is cloud computing)	Overview (4 questions)	Kumar (2017); Wambugu (2013)
	Technology factors (19 questions)	
	Organization factors (9 questions)	
	Environment factors (12 questions)	

Forty questions were used to assess and analyze factors influencing the perception of public cloud adoption in the UAE.

5.5 Data Analysis and Findings

This section captures the survey result and its analysis. Total of fifty-six responded completed the survey and two of them were excluded from the analysis considering they mentioned to not having any cloud knowledge. Most of the responses were from the Information technology sector and there was participation from different sectors as well.

Demographic characteristics of the survey analytics are given below.

- Received a total of fifty-six responses for our survey out of which 8.9% are female and 91.1% are male
- Majority of the population who took part in the survey (66.1%) come under the experience group of more than 15 years
- 96.4% of the respondents has some knowledge on cloud computing
- Majority of the survey responded were from information technology sector (73.2%)
- Majority of population who participated in the survey indicated their organization has dedicated IT personal (94.6%)
- Majority of individuals who participated in the survey indicated their organization has cloud strategy (85.7%)
- Majority of population who participated in the survey indicated they are satisfied with cloud-based services (46.4%) and second majority said they are

very satisfied (32.1%). Below are the key tables and graphs (from google form) showing some of the key survey questionnaires and responses. The survey participants organization details are displayed in Fig.3. The participants were chosen from the various leading organizations like AD Polic, Cisco Systems, FAB, Maersk, etc.

Figure 3. Survey participants' organization details

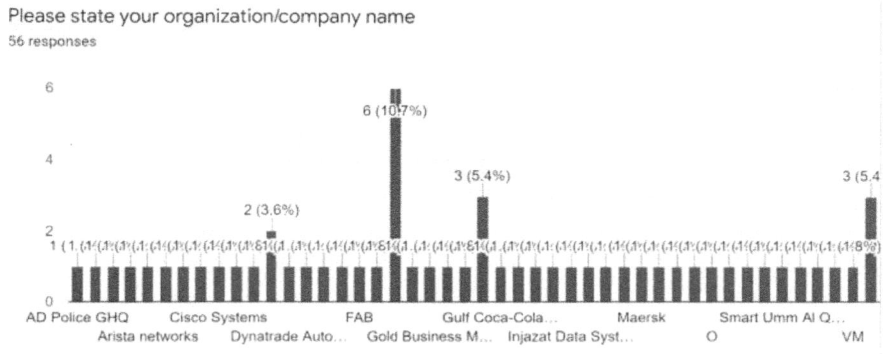

The Participant Job role varies with in the participants. 5.4% of the participants fall under the category of Owner or Investor. 10.7% people fall under the category of Executives and 30.4% of the people have participated from the manager category. The details of the participant's job role is depicted in Fig.4.

Figure 4. Survey participant job role details

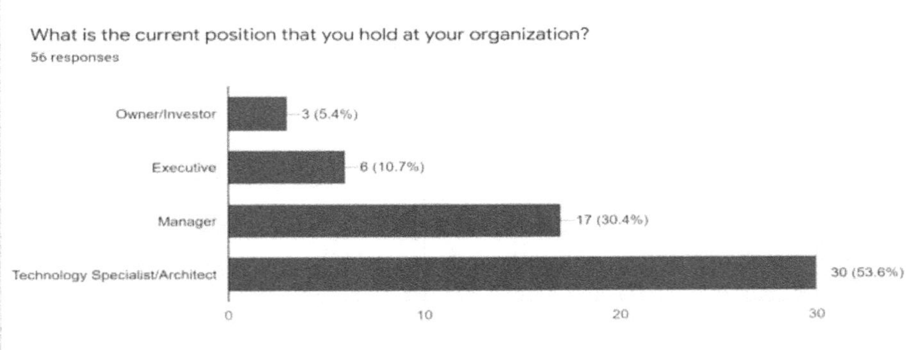

Fig. 5 explores the Survey participant gender ratio details. 91.1% of the participants are Male and 8.9% of the survey participants are females.

Figure 5. Survey participant gender ratio details

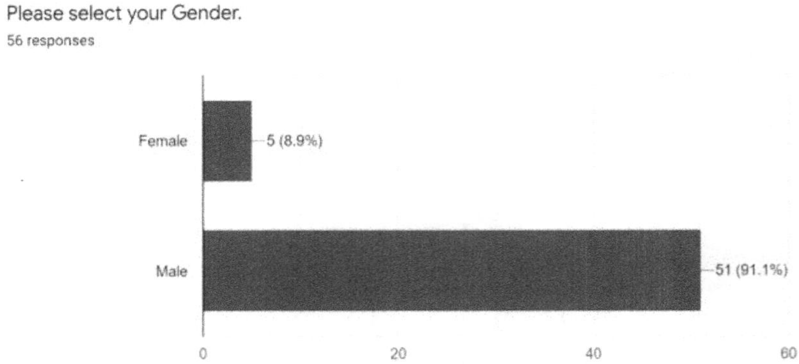

Fig.6 displays the cloud strategy survey result. Out of 56 responses, 85.7% answered with yes and 8.9% of the responses were no. 5.4% of the participants were unaware of the institution's cloud strategy result.

Figure 6. Cloud strategy survey result

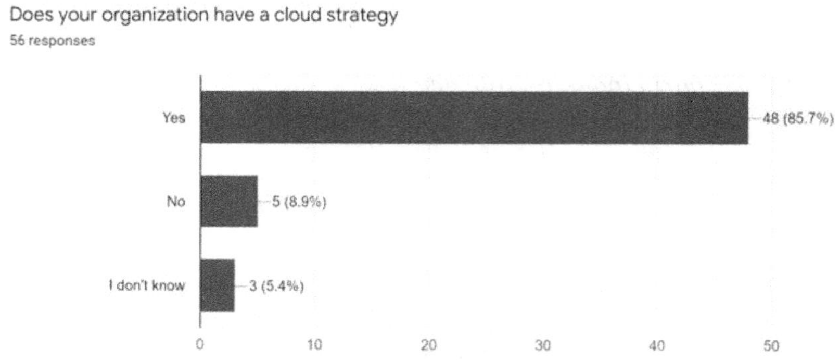

The cloud hosted applications, hosted in the public cloud is displayed in the Fig. 7.

Figure 7. Cloud-hosted application survey

a. Descriptive Analysis

Descriptive statistics gives a summary of the data, such as measuring the distribution of the data using the standard deviation, it describes the normal distribution, a measure of the mean (mean) and skewness to see how symmetrical the distribution is. It shown in Fig.8.

Figure 8. Descriptive analysis

Descriptive Statistics

	N	Minimum	Maximum	Mean	Std. Deviation	Skewness		Kurtosis	
	Statistic	Statistic	Statistic	Statistic	Statistic	Statistic	Std. Error	Statistic	Std. Error
TC	54	1.7292	5.0000	3.5502	.6387	.183	.325	1.333	.639
OG	54	1.5833	5.0000	3.7145	.6142	-.338	.325	1.527	.639
EN	54	2.1667	5.0000	3.7180	.5664	-.054	.325	.159	.639
CA	54	2	5	3.56	.634	.244	.325	-.273	.639
Valid N (listwise)	54								

TC – Technology, OG- Organization, EN – Environment and CA – Cloud adoption

The following observation is made from the above table

- The lowest values recorded for TC, OG and CA are close to "Disagree" and the highest value is "Strongly Agree."
- The mean value shows most of the respondents agree with the survey questions and opt for cloud adoption in UAE based on the given TOE-based factors.

b. Reliability Test

Cronbach's alpha is the measure of reliability and used to determine whether the scale is reliable. From the test, Cronbach's alpha value is "0.944," which shows high level of internal consistency for the scale used and considered highly reliable. Fig.9 shows the reliability statistics of Cronbach's alpha

Figure 9. Reliability statistics

Reliability Statistics

Cronbach's Alpha	N of Items
.944	40

c. Pearson Correlation

Correlation is the connection or relationship to each other. Pearson' r is the correlation coefficient, and the value range of "r" is between +1 and -1. If the "r" value is +1, then it is a perfect positive correlation and if it is "-1" then it is a perfect negative correlation. There is no correlation if the value is "0." The below table shows a strong positive correlation between the factors selected. And also, the 2-tail significance value which is 0.01 shows the correlation between the factors is highly significant.

Figure 10. Correlation analysis

Correlations

		TC	OG	EN	CA
TC	Pearson Correlation	1	.736**	.533**	.753**
	Sig. (2-tailed)		<.001	<.001	<.001
	N	54	54	54	54
OG	Pearson Correlation	.736**	1	.534**	.818**
	Sig. (2-tailed)	<.001		<.001	<.001
	N	54	54	54	54
EN	Pearson Correlation	.533**	.534**	1	.642**
	Sig. (2-tailed)	<.001	<.001		<.001
	N	54	54	54	54
CA	Pearson Correlation	.753**	.818**	.642**	1
	Sig. (2-tailed)	<.001	<.001	<.001	
	N	54	54	54	54

**. Correlation is significant at the 0.01 level (2-tailed).

d. Linear Regression

This section uses linear regression to analyze the relationship between the independent variables (TC-Technology, OG-Organization, and EN-Environment) and the dependent variable (CA-Cloud Adoption). It evaluates assumptions about how technical, organizational, and environmental factors determine cloud adoption The key important value in the following regression analysis is Sig. value. For a 95% confidence interval, the value should be lower than 0.05. Since Sig. value, < 0.05, indicating that technical, organizational, and environmental factors have a substantial impact on cloud acceptance in the UAE. And this result in hypothesis H1, H2, and H3 fail to reject. Also, from the data given below, it shows that out of the three key factors, the environmental considerations the (EN-.148), and that, especially regulation (RG-.283) are major factor determining the cloud adoption. The table. 8 shows the Linear regression analysis Coefficients of various models.

Table 8. Linear regression analysis Coefficients

Model		Unstandardized Coefficients		Standardized Coefficients	t	Sig.	
		B	Std. Error	Beta			
1	(Constant)	5.782	.192		4.850	.000	
	TC	.155	.388	.084	.400	.001	
	OR	.005	.404	.003	.013	.000	
	EN	.307	.351	**.148**	.874	.002	

Coefficients

Model		Unstandardized Coefficients		Standardized Coefficients	t	Sig.
		B	Std. Error	Beta		
1	(Constant)	5.556	1.365		4.070	.000
	RA	.300	.381	.197	.786	.006
	CO	.003	.402	.002	.007	.005
	CX	.011	.407	.007	.028	.000
	SA	.047	.435	.029	.108	.000
	TR	.182	.400	.097	.454	.005
	TM	.234	.325	.148	.721	.006
	RG	.422	.278	**.283**	.518	.007
	CI	.087	.370	.053	.235	.000
	TP	.043	.231	.035	.185	.000
	VR	.033	.430	.017	.077	.000

a. Dependent Variable: CA
RA – Relative Advantage, CO – Compatibility, CX- Complexity, SA – Security and access, TR – Technology Readiness, TM – Top Management support, RG – Regulations, CI – Competitive Intensity, TP – Technology Partner and VR is the vendor readiness.

6. CONCLUSION

This study investigates several specific factors guiding the adoption of public cloud in the UAE context and provides insight into the perceptions of public cloud adoption. According to the study, it clearly shows technical, organizational, and environmental factors significantly influence cloud adoption. Specifically, environmental factors are the main influencing factors in the UAE. The study also explores other areas such as organizations with cloud strategies, organization with dedicated IT personnel, satisfactory level of cloud services, various applications hosted on the cloud, annual spending on cloud-based services, different industry sectors adopting cloud, and more.

6.1 Recommendations

The study attempts to explore in detail the contributing factor of cloud adoption in the UAE with the help of a survey mechanism based on the TOE framework. The findings presented in this paper provide a guideline for cloud service providers, system integrators, and contractors on the adoption of public cloud for developing their products and services. The top management and policy decision-makers can use this to implement measures that can accelerate the awareness and adoption process between the enterprises. The findings also could help in evaluating the current government initiatives such as incentive programs and policies to speed up the adoption process.

6.2 Future Scope of Research

Due to the evolving nature of public cloud computing, in the future, factors may need to adjust as the technology progresses. Future research should focus on collecting more samples and gaining more representation from a broad range of organizations involving key stakeholders, including application owners, infrastructure owners, security owners, and finance and procurement leaders and other decision makers.

REFERENCES

Alsafi, T., & Fan, I. S. (2020, June). Cloud computing adoption barriers faced by Saudi manufacturing SMEs. In *2020 15th Iberian Conference on Information Systems and Technologies (CISTI)* (pp. 1-6). IEEE. 10.23919/CISTI49556.2020.9140940

Avram, M. G. (2014). Advantages and challenges of adopting cloud computing from an enterprise perspective. *Procedia Technology*, *12*, 529–534. doi:10.1016/j.protcy.2013.12.525

Davis, F. D. (1985). *A technology acceptance model for empirically testing new end-user information systems: Theory and results* [Doctoral dissertation]. Massachusetts Institute of Technology.

Depietro, R., Wiarda, E., & Fleischer, M. (1990). The context for change: Organization, technology and environment. *The Processes of Technological Innovation, 199*(0), 151-175.

Dewar, R. D., & Dutton, J. E. (1986). The adoption of radical and incremental innovations: An empirical analysis. *Management Science*, *32*(11), 1422–1433. doi:10.1287/mnsc.32.11.1422

El-Gazzar, R. F. (2014). A literature review on cloud computing adoption issues in enterprises. In *Creating Value for All Through IT: IFIP WG 8.6 International Conference on Transfer and Diffusion of IT, TDIT 2014, Aalborg, Denmark, June 2-4, 2014. Proceedings* (pp. 214-242). Springer Berlin Heidelberg. 10.1007/978-3-662-43459-8_14

Erl, T., Puttini, R., & Mahmood, Z. (2013). *Cloud computing: Concepts, technology & architecture*. Pearson Education.

Fisher, C. (2018). Cloud versus on-premise computing. *American Journal of Industrial and Business Management*, *8*(09), 1991–2006. doi:10.4236/ajibm.2018.89133

Frambach, R. T., & Barkema, H. G. (1998). Adoption of a service innovation in the business market: An empirical test of supply-side variables. *Journal of Business Research*. https://www.sciencedirect.com/science/article/abs/pii/S0148296397000052

Frambach, R. T., Barkema, H. G., Nooteboom, B., & Wedel, M. (1998). Adoption of a service innovation in the business market: An empirical test of supply-side variables. *Journal of Business Research*, *41*(2), 161–174. doi:10.1016/S0148-2963(97)00005-2

Fujitsu, S. (2011). *Cloud Adoption The definitive guide to a business technology revolution*. https://www.fujitsu.com/us/Images/WBOC-1-Adoption-US.pdf

Gutierrez, A., & Lumsden, J. R. (2014). *Key management determinants for cloud computing adoption*. Academic Press.

Kamra, V., Sonawane, K., & Alappanavar, P. (2012). Cloud computing and its pricing schemes. *International Journal on Computer Science and Engineering*, *4*(4), 577.

Kushwaha, A. (2020). Research Paper on AWS Cloud Infrastructure vs Traditional On-Premises. *International Research Journal of Engineering and Technology (IRJET), 7*(1).

Leavitt, N. (2009). Is cloud computing really ready for prime time. *Growth*, *27*(5), 15–20.

Mell, P., & Grance, T. (2011). *The NIST definition of cloud computing*. Academic Press.

Microsoft. (2019). *Microsoft Cloud datacenter regions now available in the UAE to help fuel the Middle East's future economic ambitions*. https://news.microsoft.com/en-xm/2019/06/19/microsoft-cloud-datacenter-regions-now-available-in-the-uae-to-help-fuel-the-middle-easts-future-economic-ambitions/

Oguntala, G. A., Abd-Alhameed, P., Raed, A., Odeyemi, D., & Janet, O. (2017). Systematic analysis of enterprise perception towards cloud adoption in the African states: The Nigerian perspective. *The African Journal of Information Systems*, *9*(4), 1.

Oliveira, T., & Martins, M. F. (2011). Literature review of information technology adoption models at firm level. *Electronic Journal of Information Systems Evaluation, 14*(1), 110-121.

Ross, P. K., & Blumenstein, M. (2015). Cloud computing as a facilitator of SME entrepreneurship. *Technology Analysis and Strategic Management*, *27*(1), 87–101. doi:10.1080/09537325.2014.951621

Sultan, N. (2010). Cloud computing for education: A new dawn? *International Journal of Information Management*, *30*(2), 109–116. doi:10.1016/j.ijinfomgt.2009.09.004

Trivedi, J. Y. (2013). *A study on marketing strategies of small and medium sized enterprises. Research Journal of Management Sciences.*

Vize, R., Coughlan, J., Kennedy, A., & Ellis-Chadwick, F. (2013). Technology readiness in a B2B online retail context: An examination of antecedents and outcomes. *Industrial Marketing Management*, *42*(6), 909–918. doi:10.1016/j.indmarman.2013.05.020

Wilson, B. M. R., Khazaei, B., & Hirsch, L. (2015, November). Enablers and barriers of cloud adoption among Small and Medium Enterprises in Tamil Nadu. In *2015 IEEE International Conference on Cloud Computing in Emerging Markets (CCEM)* (pp. 140-145). IEEE. 10.1109/CCEM.2015.21

Young, R., & Jordan, E. (2008). Top management support: Mantra or necessity? *International Journal of Project Management*, *26*(7), 713–725. doi:10.1016/j.ijproman.2008.06.001

ADDITIONAL READING

Escrich, P., Baig, R., Vilata, I., Neumann, A., Aymerich, M., Lopez, E., . . . Navarro, L. (2013, September). Community home gateways for p2p clouds. In IEEE P2P 2013 Proceedings (pp. 1-2). IEEE. doi:10.1109/P2P.2013.6688732

Fedushko, S., Ustyianovych, T., & Gregus, M. (2020). Real-time high-load infrastructure transaction status output prediction using operational intelligence and big data technologies. *Electronics (Basel)*, *9*(4), 668. doi:10.3390/electronics9040668

McGuirk, H., Lenihan, H., & Hart, M. (2015). Measuring the impact of innovative human capital on small firms' propensity to innovate. *Research Policy*, *44*(4), 965–976. doi:10.1016/j.respol.2014.11.008

Parthasarathy, V., & Kumar, V. (2016). Determinants of cloud computing adoption by SMEs. *International Journal of Business Information Systems*, *22*(3), 375–395.

Chapter 5
Fortifying Cloud Storage Using Hash Code

N. Ambika
https://orcid.org/0000-0003-4452-5514
St. Francis College, India

ABSTRACT

The data owner has complete control over it under the previous paradigm. Data owners set smart contracts. In smart contracts, the data owner stores data hash. On data, Ethereum performs encryption. It is also in charge of creating data hashes. The data owner receives a request from the user. The data owner updates information in smart contracts. After that, smart contracts provide access permissions and duration to the data user. After that, users of data can access data stored in the cloud. The recommendation suggests tracing the user and his doings.

INTRODUCTION

Cloud computing (Devare, 2019; Nagaraj, 2021) is a technology that allows individuals and organizations to access and use computing resources and services over the Internet, typically on a pay-as-you-go basis. Instead of owning and maintaining physical servers and data centers, cloud computing users can rent resources from cloud providers, which host and manage these resources in their data centers.

Cloud computing refers to the delivery of computing services, including servers, storage, databases, networking, software, analytics, and intelligence, over the Internet to offer faster innovation, flexible resources, and economies of scale. Instead of owning and managing physical hardware and software, individuals and organizations

DOI: 10.4018/979-8-3693-3249-8.ch005

can access and use these resources on a pay-as-you-go or subscription basis from cloud service providers.

In simpler terms, cloud computing allows users to rent computing resources and services from remote data centers (the "cloud") over the internet. These resources are typically scalable, meaning users can increase or decrease their usage as needed, and maintained by the cloud provider. Cloud computing has transformed businesses and individuals' access and use of computing power, enabling greater flexibility, cost-efficiency, and accessibility to range of applications and services.

Figure 1. Cloud deployment models and infrastructure
Source: Khalil et al. (2014)

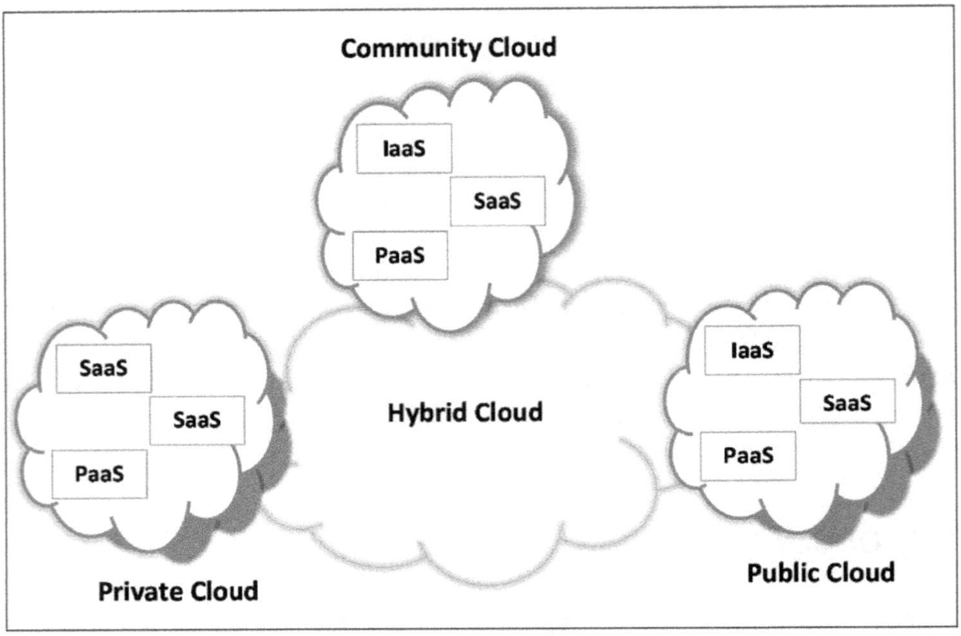

Cloud architecture refers to the design and structure of cloud computing systems, including the components, services, and organizations to deliver various cloud computing capabilities. Cloud architecture can vary depending on the specific needs of an organization. The architectural components and principles that are typically present in most cloud environments. Here are the key aspects of cloud architecture:

1. **Front-end and Back-end Components:**

   - **Front-end:** This is a client-side component of the cloud architecture. It includes applications, web browsers, and client devices used to interact with cloud services.
   - **Back-end:** The back-end component consists of cloud servers, data storage, databases, and the many services and resources provided by the cloud provider.
2. **Infrastructure as a Service (IaaS) Layer:**
   - This layer provides virtualized computing resources, including virtual machines, storage, and networking infrastructure.
   - Components include virtualization technologies, hypervisors, and hardware resources managed by the cloud provider.
3. **Platform as a Service (PaaS) Layer:**
   - PaaS offers a platform and runtime environment for developing, deploying, and managing applications.
   - Components may include application servers, databases, development frameworks, and middleware.
4. **Software as a Service (SaaS) Layer:**
   - SaaS applications are hosted in the cloud and accessible over the internet.
   - Components include the application, user data, and user interfaces accessed through web browsers or client applications.
5. **Storage and Data Management:**
   - Cloud storage services, both object storage and block storage, are essential for storing data in the cloud.
   - Data management components include databases, data warehouses, and data analytics services.
6. **Networking and Connectivity:**
   - Cloud architecture includes network infrastructure, load balancers, content delivery networks (CDNs), and Virtual Private Cloud (VPC) configurations.
   - Networking components enable secure and efficient data transfer within the cloud environment.
7. **Security and Identity Management:**
   - Security measures, such as firewalls, encryption, access control, and authentication, are crucial to protect data and resources in the cloud.
   - Identity and access management (IAM) components manage user access and permissions.
8. **Scalability and Elasticity:**
   - Cloud architecture is designed for scalability, allowing resources to be added or removed as needed to handle varying workloads.

- Autoscaling mechanisms automatically adjust resource allocation based on demand.

9. **Monitoring and Management:**
   - Cloud architecture includes tools and services for monitoring the health and performance of cloud resources.
   - Management components enable the provisioning, configuration, and maintenance of cloud resources.
10. **Fault Tolerance and High Availability:**
    - Cloud architectures are designed to minimize downtime and ensure high availability through redundancy, failover mechanisms, and data replication.
11. **Compliance and Governance:**
    - Cloud environments often include compliance and governance tools to adhere to regulatory requirements and organizational policies.
12. **Cost Management:**
    - Cloud cost management tools help organizations track and optimize their cloud spending by monitoring resource usage and managing budgets.

Cloud architecture can vary based on the specific cloud provider (e.g., AWS, Azure, Google Cloud) and the requirements of an organization. It's vital to design cloud architectures that align with business objectives, security needs, and performance requirements while taking advantage of the scalability and flexibility offered by cloud computing.

Some key aspects of cloud computing:

1. **Service Models:**
   - **Infrastructure as a Service (IaaS) (Janbi, Katib, Albeshri, & Mehmood, 2020):** This model provides virtualized computing resources over the Internet. Users can rent virtual machines, storage, and networking infrastructure. Examples of IaaS providers include Amazon Web Services (AWS), Microsoft Azure, and Google Cloud Platform (GCP).
   - **Platform as a Service (PaaS) (Pandit, et al., 2022):** PaaS offers a platform that includes the hardware and software required for application development and deployment. Developers can focus on coding and not worry about managing the underlying infrastructure. Examples of PaaS providers include Heroku and Google App Engine.
   - **Software as a Service (SaaS):** SaaS delivers software applications over the Internet on a subscription basis. Users can access these applications through a web browser, eliminating the need for local installation and

maintenance. Examples include Google Workspace (formerly G Suite), Microsoft 365, and Salesforce.

2. **Deployment Models:**
   - **Public Cloud:** In a public cloud, resources are owned and operated by third-party cloud providers and are made available to the general public. These resources are shared among multiple users and organizations.
   - **Private Cloud:** A private cloud is dedicated to a single organization. It can be hosted on-premises or by a third-party provider. Private clouds offer greater control and customization but may require more management.
   - **Hybrid Cloud:** Hybrid cloud combines public and private cloud resources, allowing data and applications to move between them. It provides flexibility and can help organizations balance cost, security, and performance requirements.
   - **Multi-Cloud:** Multi-cloud involves using services from multiple cloud providers to avoid vendor lock-in and enhance redundancy and resilience.
3. **Benefits of Cloud Computing:**
   - **Scalability:** Cloud resources can be easily scaled up or down to meet changing demands.
   - **Cost-Efficiency:** Pay-as-you-go pricing models can reduce capital expenditure and allow for cost optimization.
   - **Flexibility:** Users can access resources from anywhere with an internet connection.
   - **Reliability:** Cloud providers often offer high availability and redundancy.
   - **Security:** Cloud providers invest in robust security measures, but users are also responsible for securing their applications and data.

BACKGROUND

Cloud security is a critical aspect of cloud computing, focusing on protecting data, applications, and infrastructure hosted in cloud environments from security threats and risks. Cloud security is a shared responsibility between the cloud service provider and the customer, with each party having distinct responsibilities. Here are key considerations and best practices for cloud security:

1. Shared Responsibility Model:
   - Understand the shared responsibility model, which defines the security responsibilities of the cloud service provider and the customer.

Typically, the provider is responsible for the security of the cloud infrastructure, while the customer is responsible for securing their data and applications.

2. Identity and Access Management (IAM):
    - Implement strong identity and access controls to ensure authorized individuals and services can access cloud resources.
    - Use multi-factor authentication (MFA) for added security.
    - Regularly review and audit user permissions to avoid over-privileged accounts.
3. Data Encryption:
    - Encrypt data in transit and at rest to protect it from unauthorized access.
    - Use encryption protocols and encryption keys.
    - Consider using encryption services provided by the cloud provider.
4. Network Security:
    - Implement network security best practices such as firewalls, intrusion detection/prevention systems, and Virtual Private Cloud (VPC) configurations.
    - Use network segmentation to isolate sensitive data and applications.
5. Security Patch Management:
    - Keep all cloud resources, including virtual machines and software, up to date with security patches and updates.
    - Regularly monitor for vulnerabilities and apply patches promptly.
6. Logging and Monitoring:
    - Enable cloud logging and monitoring services to detect and respond to security incidents.
    - Set up alerts for suspicious activities or security breaches.
    - Consider using Security Information and Event Management (SIEM) solutions.
7. Incident Response Plan:
    - Develop an incident response plan that outlines how to respond to security breaches or incidents.
    - Conduct regular security drills and simulations to ensure preparedness.
8. Data Backup and Recovery:
    - Implement regular data backup and recovery procedures to protect against data loss.
    - Test backup and recovery processes to ensure they work as expected.
9. Compliance and Governance:
    - Understand the regulatory requirements that apply to your industry and ensure that your cloud environment complies with these standards.

  - Use cloud compliance and governance tools to enforce policies and track compliance.

10. Employee Training and Awareness:
  - Train employees on cloud security best practices and the importance of following security policies.

Blockchain

Blockchain (Vranken, 2017) is a decentralized and distributed digital ledger technology that records transactions across multiple computers for security, transparency, and immutability. It was created to support the cryptocurrency Bitcoin, but its applications have expanded far beyond digital currencies. Figure 2 represents architecture of the blockchain-enabled cloud computing system.

Figure 2. Architecture of blockchain-enabled cloud computing system
Source: Habib et al. (2022)

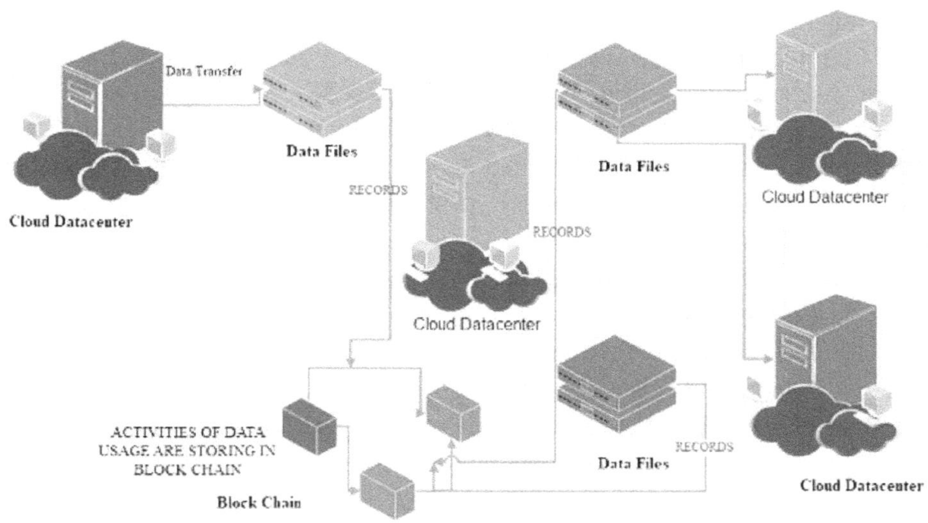

Here are key concepts and characteristics of blockchain:

1. **Decentralization:** Blockchain (Zarrin, Wen Phang, Babu, & Zarrin, 2021; Zheng, Xie, Dai, Chen, & Wang, 2018) operates on a decentralized network of computers (nodes) rather than a central authority. Each node in the network

has a copy of the entire blockchain, and transactions are validated collectively through a consensus mechanism.

2. **Distributed Ledger:** The blockchain ledger is distributed across all participating nodes. This distribution ensures no single point of failure, making it highly resistant to tampering and fraud.
3. **Transparency:** Transactions recorded on a blockchain are visible to all participants in the network. This transparency enhances trust and accountability.
4. **Immutability:** Once a transaction is added to the blockchain, it is nearly impossible to alter or delete. This immutability is achieved through cryptographic hashing and consensus mechanisms.
5. **Consensus Mechanisms:** Blockchain networks rely on consensus algorithms to agree on the validity of transactions and the order in which they are added to the blockchain. Common consensus mechanisms include Proof of Work (PoW) and Proof of Stake (PoS).
6. **Cryptography:** Cryptographic techniques are used to secure transactions and control access to the blockchain. Private and public keys are used to sign and verify transactions.
7. **Smart Contracts:** Smart contracts are self-executing contracts with the terms of the agreement directly written into code. They automatically execute when predefined conditions are met, without the need for intermediaries.
8. **Use Cases:** Blockchain has applications across various industries, including finance (for cryptocurrencies and digital assets), supply chain management (for tracking and tracing goods), healthcare (for securely managing patient data), and more.
9. **Public vs. Private Blockchains:**
    - **Public Blockchain:** Open to anyone and permissionless, where anyone can participate, read, and write to the blockchain. Examples include the Bitcoin and Ethereum networks.
    - **Private Blockchain:** Restricted and permission, often used by organizations for internal purposes. Participants are controlled, and access is limited.
        1. **Tokens and Cryptocurrencies:** Many blockchains have their native cryptocurrencies or tokens, used for various purposes within the network, such as paying transaction fees or accessing specific features.
        2. **Scalability and Performance:** Blockchain networks face challenges related to scalability and transaction throughput. Various solutions, such as layer-2 scaling solutions and alternative consensus mechanisms, aim to address these issues.

3. **Challenges:** Blockchain technology faces challenges like scalability, energy consumption (for PoW-based networks), regulatory concerns, and interoperability between different blockchain platforms.
4. **Blockchain Platforms:** There are various blockchain platforms, each with its own features and use cases. Ethereum, Binance Smart Chain, and Hyperledger are examples of blockchain platforms.

Blockchain technology continues to evolve and find applications in diverse fields beyond finance. Its potential to provide trust, security, and transparency makes it a promising tool for transforming industries and processes.

LITERATURE SURVEY

The system (Esposito, De Santis, Tortora, Chang, & Choo, 2018) aims to provide a comprehensive and secure view of a patient's healthcare records by leveraging blockchain technology. It offers transparency, data integrity, and trust among healthcare providers while maintaining patient privacy through robust data protection measures. Blockchain is used as the underlying technology to create a distributed ledger where healthcare data is stored in a secure and immutable manner. Each patient has a blockchain network, and data is organized in blocks. Whenever new healthcare data for a patient is generated, a new block is instantiated. This block includes relevant patient information, such as medical records, test results, and treatment history. The newly created block is distributed to all peers (healthcare providers) in the patient's network. Peers in this context could include hospitals, clinics, laboratories, and any other entities involved in the patient's care. Before a block is added to the blockchain, it must undergo an approval process. Most of the peers in the network must approve the new block. This ensures that data added to the blockchain is accurate and trusted by multiple providers. Once the majority of peers approve the new block, it is inserted into the blockchain. This action creates a permanent and verifiable record of the patient's medical history. If an agreement is not reached among peers (i.e., they don't approve the new block), a fork in the blockchain is created. The block that was not approved is defined as an orphan and does not belong to the main chain. This mechanism maintains data integrity by only adding trusted information to the main chain. Once a block is inserted into the blockchain, its contents cannot be modified without modifying all subsequent blocks. This ensures that any attempt to alter historical healthcare data can be easily detected, providing data integrity and security. As block content is publicly accessible, healthcare data needs to be protected before being added to the blockchain. This can be achieved through encryption and access control mechanisms, ensuring that sensitive patient information remains confidential.

The owner of the data has complete control over it under this paradigm (Kollu, 2021). Smart contracts are set by data owners. In smart contracts, the data owner stores data hash. On data, Ethereum performs encryption. It is also in charge of creating data hashes. The data owner receives a request from the user. The data owner updates information in smart contracts. After that, smart contracts provide access permissions and duration to the data user. After then, users of data can access data stored in the cloud.

This system (Wei, Wang, Zhao, Tyagi, & Kumar, 2020) combines mobile agent technology, blockchain, and cryptographic techniques to create a secure and trustworthy environment for data storage and verification in the cloud. It aims to provide data integrity, reliability, and transparency while enabling multi-tenancy and cooperation among users or organizations. It consists of virtual machine agents deployed in the cloud. These agents are software entities that can execute tasks independently or collaboratively. In this context, they are responsible for ensuring data verification and maintaining data integrity. The virtual machine agents enable multiple tenants (users or organizations) to cooperate. This cooperation likely involves sharing and accessing data while maintaining data security and trust. The virtual machine agents are responsible for verifying the trustworthiness of data. It involves various checks and validations to ensure that data is accurate and has not been tampered with. The virtual machine agent mechanism includes mechanisms for storing data reliably. It involves redundancy, backups, or other techniques to ensure data availability in case of hardware failures or other issues. The system utilizes monitoring mechanisms to monitor the data stored in the cloud. It includes regular checks to detect unauthorized changes or tampering with data. The blockchain stores records of data changes in a tamper-proof ledger. Each change to data is recorded as a transaction on the blockchain. A Merkle hash tree is used to create a unique hash value corresponding to a file or a set of data. This hash value acts as a digital fingerprint for the data. Any change to the data will result in a different hash value. Smart contracts on the blockchain are used to monitor data changes. These contracts can be programmed to trigger actions when data tampering is detected. For example, if the hash value of a file changes, a smart contract can issue a warning message to notify the user or organization that owns the data. When data tampering is detected through changes in the hash values, the system promptly issues warning messages to inform the relevant users or organizations about the potential security breach.

Federation-as-a-Service (FaaS) (Gaetani, et al., 2017) facilitates the secure creation and management of cloud data and services within a cloud federation. It emphasizes advanced data security services. It implies that the service provides robust security measures to protect data stored and processed within the cloud federation.

Data security may include encryption, access controls, authentication, and other security mechanisms. It is built on innovative design principles. These principles likely incorporate modern cloud computing and distributed computing paradigms, making the service efficient, scalable, and adaptable to various use cases. It promotes a distributed and democratic governance model for cloud federations. It means that decisions regarding the management and operation of the cloud federation are made collectively and involve input from various stakeholders. It ensures control by a single entity but operates collaboratively and fairly. The primary objective of cloud federations is to enable secure and regulated inter-cloud interactions. Members of the federation can share cloud services and resources while adhering to specific rules and regulations. These interactions allow for efficient resource utilization and collaboration among different cloud providers. The contracts specify the rules and terms of cloud services and resources that can be accessed and shared among members. It provides the legal and operational framework for the federation.

PREVIOUS STUDY

It (Kollu, 2021) outlines a decentralized and automated system for managing data access and permissions using blockchain technology (Ethereum) and cloud computing. Such systems can provide enhanced security, transparency, and trust in data sharing and access control by leveraging the immutability of the blockchain and the flexibility of cloud resources.

1. **Data Ownership and Control**: The data owner has complete control over their data in this paradigm. This control likely includes determining who can access the data, for how long, and under what conditions.
2. **Smart Contracts**: Smart contracts are self-executing contracts with the terms of the agreement directly written into code. Smart contracts manage and enforce data access permissions and conditions. These smart contracts are created and configured by the data owner.
3. **Data Hashing**: The data owner stores a hash of the data on the Ethereum blockchain. Hashing is a cryptographic process that generates a fixed-size string of characters from data of any size. Storing the hash on the blockchain provides a tamper-evident way to verify the integrity of the data.
4. **Encryption**: Ethereum performs encryption on the data. Encryption is the process of converting data into a secure format be decrypted with the appropriate key. Encrypting data before storing it in the cloud enhances security and privacy.

5. **Access Requests**: Users of the data send access requests to the data owner. This step likely involves communication between the data owner and the data user, facilitated by the smart contract.
6. **Smart Contract Updates**: Upon receiving an access request, the data owner updates the information in the smart contracts. This update could include granting or denying access, specifying the duration of access, and possibly other conditions or terms.
7. **Access Permissions**: The smart contracts provide access permissions and duration to the data user based on the updates made by the data owner. This step automates the process of granting or revoking access rights.
8. **Data Access**: Once the smart contract's conditions are met, users can access the data stored in the cloud. This access is likely controlled and monitored through the smart contract, ensuring that data access aligns with the agreed-upon terms.

Drawbacks

- The cloud owner owns the infrastructure.
- The client can either read the data stored or can also write on it.
- The client can also erase the files stores. If multiple users are using the dataset, it is necessary to know who has done what modification and its details.

PROPOSED WORK

Assumptions

- The cloud assigns internal code to the username.
- The user has to use the same username for all kinds of services he avails.
- The user is provided with a provision of changing the password.

Table 1. Notations used in the work

Notations	*Description*
S	Cloud server
U_i	Username
H	Hash algorithm
L_i	Location details of the user (from where he is accessing the cloud)
A_i	User activity
IC_i	Internal code

The suggestion keeps track of the doings of the users. The user will login using his credentials (username and password). The cloud server assigns an internal code to the username. In the equation (1), user U_i assigns internal code IC_i.

$$S: U_i \rightarrow IC_i \tag{1}$$

The cloud server S generates a hash code using the internal code IC_i, activities in the session A_i and L_i. the same is represented in equation (2).

$$S \rightarrow H(IC_i || A_i || L_i) \tag{2}$$

ANALYSIS OF WORK

The suggestion generates a hash code to enable tracking of user activities.

1. **Activities**: These could refer to a wide range of actions and behaviors that a user engages in online. Examples might include browsing habits, application usage, and actions that can be tracked or recorded.
2. **Internal Code**: Internal code likely refers to a unique identifier or code associated with the user. It could be a user ID, a device identifier, or any other means of distinguishing one user from another.
3. **Location Details**: Location information can provide valuable context for user activities. It could involve tracking a user's geographical location through GPS or IP address to understand where they are when engaging in various activities.
4. **Analysis**: The core purpose of this methodology is to analyze the user's activities. This analysis can yield insights into user behavior, preferences, patterns, and trends. It can be valuable for various purposes, such as user profiling and security monitoring.

Simulation Details

The work is simulated in NS2. Table 2 represents the simulation details.

Table 2. Simulation details

Parameters Used in the Study	*Description*
Dimension of the network	200m*200m
Number of cloud servers	01
Number of users	05
Length of username	Up to 32 characters
Length of generated internal code	20 bits
Length of location details	32 bits
Length of activities	256 bits
Length of hash code	84 bits

Stage 1 – input internal code (20 bits), location details (32 bits) and activities (256 bits)
For number of bits <= 32 bits
Do

Step 2.1 – Replace activities bits by its complement ('1' is replaced by '0' and '0' by '1')
Step 2.2- Divide the activities bits into two halves (128 bits each;64 bits;32 bits)
Step 2.3 – Xor first set of bits from second set of bits (resultant – 128 bits; 64 bits;32 bits)
Step 3 – Combine internal code with location details bits and activities bits (20+32+32 bits)
Step 4 – Apply right shift by 2 on the bits
Step 5 – Complement all the bits
Step 5- Apply left circular shift by 2 on bits (resultant – 84 bits)

Visibility

The suggestion creates more visibility compared to previous work by 95.08%. Figure 3 portrays the same.

Figure 3. Visibility in the system

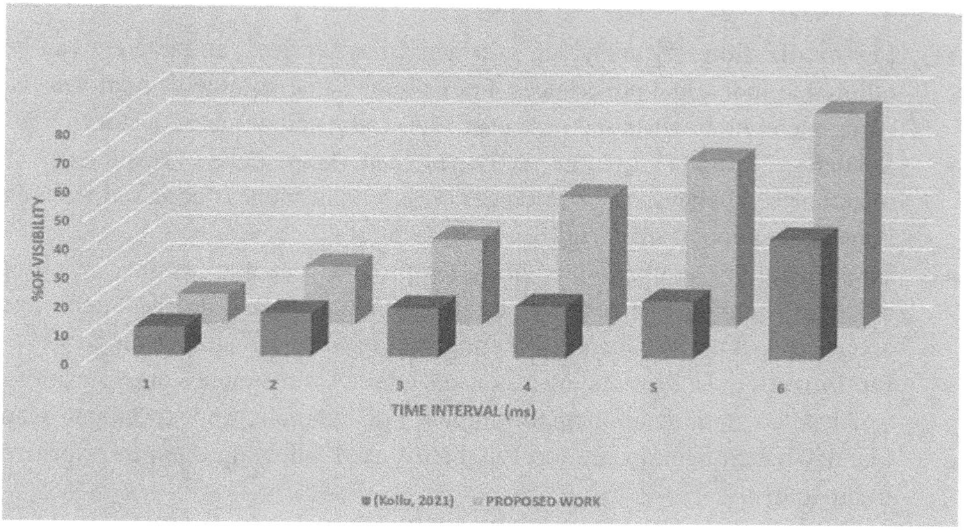

Security

The suggestion improves security in the system by 32.4% compared to previous work. Figure 4 portrays the same.

Figure 4. Security in the system

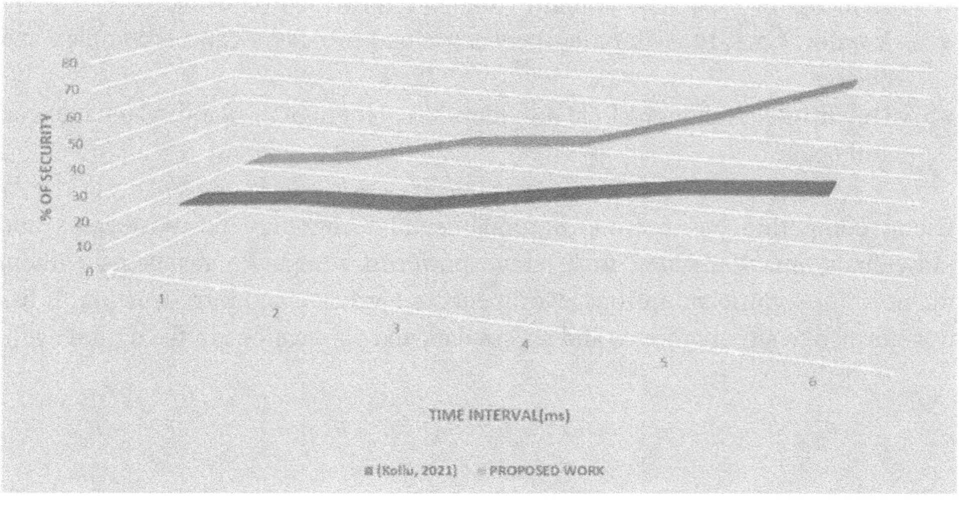

Benefits of this methodology may include:

- **Personalization**: By analyzing user activities, services, and content can be tailored to individual preferences. For example, an e-commerce platform can recommend products based on a user's browsing and purchase history.
- **Security**: Monitoring user activities can help detect suspicious or unauthorized behavior. For instance, if a user's account is accessed from an unusual location, it may trigger a security alert.
- **User Insights**: Analyzing activities can provide valuable insights into user behavior, helping businesses and organizations make informed decisions about product development, marketing strategies, and customer support.
- **Optimization**: Understanding how users interact with systems or applications can lead to optimization opportunities. For example, app developers can identify which features are most and least used, allowing them to prioritize improvements.

CHALLENGES

- **Security Concerns:** While cloud providers implement security measures, users must also take steps to secure their data and applications.
- **Data Privacy:** Compliance with data protection regulations can be challenging, especially in multi-cloud or hybrid environments.
- **Vendor Lock-In:** Migrating between cloud providers can be complex and costly.
- **Downtime:** Although cloud providers strive for high availability, outages can still occur.

Cloud computing has become a fundamental technology for businesses and individuals, enabling them to leverage powerful computing resources without the need for significant upfront investments in hardware and infrastructure. It has transformed to store, process, and access data and applications in the digital age.

FUTURE SCOPE

The future of cloud computing is expected to be marked by significant advancements and innovations, driven by evolving technology trends and changing business needs. Here are some key aspects of the future of cloud computing:

1. **Edge Computing Integration:** As the Internet of Things (IoT) and edge computing continue to grow, cloud providers will work on integrating edge computing capabilities into their services. It will enable faster processing of data at or near the source, reducing latency and improving real-time decision-making for applications like autonomous vehicles, smart cities, and industrial automation.
2. **AI and Machine Learning Integration:** Cloud providers will increasingly offer AI and machine learning services to make it easier for businesses to develop and deploy AI-driven applications. These services range from pre-trained models to specialized hardware like GPUs and TPUs for accelerated AI workloads.
3. **Quantum Computing:** While quantum computing is still in its infancy, cloud providers are already exploring ways to offer quantum computing as a service. As this technology matures, it has the potential to revolutionize fields like cryptography, optimization, and materials science.
4. **Serverless and Event-Driven Architectures:** The adoption of serverless computing and event-driven architectures will continue to rise. This approach allows developers to focus on writing code without worrying about server management, and it can lead to more efficient and cost-effective application development.
5. **Multi-Cloud and Hybrid Cloud Strategies:** Organizations will increasingly adopt multi-cloud and hybrid cloud strategies to avoid vendor lock-in, improve redundancy, and meet specific regulatory and compliance requirements. Cloud providers will offer more tools and services to facilitate seamless multi-cloud management.
6. **Security and Compliance:** Cloud providers will continue to invest in security and compliance measures to address evolving cybersecurity threats and regulatory requirements. It includes enhanced identity and access management, encryption, and monitoring capabilities.
7. **Sustainability and Green Computing:** As concerns about environmental sustainability grow, cloud providers will focus on improving the energy efficiency of their data centers and reducing their carbon footprint. It may lead to more renewable energy usage and carbon offset programs.

8. **Containerization and Kubernetes:** The use of containers and container orchestration platforms like Kubernetes will remain a fundamental part of cloud-native application development. Cloud providers will continue to offer container services and tools to simplify container management.
9. **Blockchain Integration:** Blockchain technology will find applications in cloud computing, particularly in areas like supply chain management, identity verification, and secure data sharing. Cloud providers may offer blockchain-as-a-service solutions.
10. **Advanced Data Analytics:** Cloud providers will offer increasingly sophisticated data analytics and business intelligence services, enabling organizations to extract valuable insights from their data using advanced analytics, machine learning, and data warehousing.
11. **Robotic Process Automation (RPA):** Cloud providers may integrate RPA capabilities into their services, allowing businesses to automate routine tasks and workflows.
12. **Augmented and Virtual Reality (AR/VR):** Cloud computing will play a role in delivering AR and VR experiences, particularly for gaming, training, and collaborative work environments.

Overall, the future of cloud computing is characterized by innovation, flexibility, and accessibility. Cloud services will continue to evolve to meet the ever-expanding demands of businesses and individuals, enabling them to harness the power of advanced technologies without the need for extensive infrastructure investments. However, it's important to note that with these advancements come new challenges, including increased focus on security, data privacy, and ethical considerations related to emerging technologies like AI and quantum computing.

CONCLUSION

Cloud blockchain is the integration of blockchain technology into cloud computing platforms or services. It allows organizations to securely store, manage, and verify data and transactions in the cloud using blockchain's decentralized and tamper-resistant features. This combination can provide additional layers of trust and security for various applications, including supply chain tracking, financial transactions, healthcare records, and more. In a cloud blockchain environment, users can leverage the scalability and convenience of cloud computing while benefiting from the enhanced data integrity and transparency offered by blockchain technology. This combination is valuable for scenarios where data security and trust are critical factors.

The core purpose of this methodology is to analyze the user's activities. This analysis can yield insights into user behavior, preferences, patterns, and trends. The system improves visibility by 95.08% and security by 32.4% compared to previous work.

REFERENCES

Ambika, N. (2019). Energy-Perceptive Authentication in Virtual Private Networks Using GPS Data. In Security, privacy and trust in the IoT environment (pp. 25-38). Cham: Springer. doi:10.1007/978-3-030-18075-1_2

Devare, M. H. (2019). Cloud Computing and Innovations. In G. Kecskemeti (Ed.), *Applying Integration Techniques and Methods in Distributed Systems and Technologies* (pp. 1–33). IGI Global. doi:10.4018/978-1-5225-8295-3.ch001

Esposito, C., De Santis, A., Tortora, G., Chang, H., & Choo, K. K. (2018). Blockchain: A panacea for healthcare cloud-based data security and privacy? *IEEE Cloud Computing, 5*(1), 31-37.

Gaetani, E., Aniello, L., Baldoni, R., Lombardi, F., Margheri, A., & Sassone, V. (2017). Blockchain-based database to ensure data integrity in cloud computing environments. In *Italian Conference on Cybersecurity* (p. 10). University of Southampton.

Habib, G., Sharma, S., Ibrahim, S., Ahmad, I., Qureshi, S., & Ishfaq, M. (2022). Blockchain Technology: Benefits, Challenges, Applications, and Integration of Blockchain Technology with Cloud Computing. *Future Internet, 14*(11), 341. doi:10.3390/fi14110341

Janbi, N., Katib, I., Albeshri, A., & Mehmood, R. (2020). Distributed Artificial Intelligence-as-a-Service (DAIaaS) for Smarter IoE and 6G Environments. *Sensors (Basel), 20*(20), 5796. doi:10.339020205796 PMID:33066295

Khalil, I., Khreishah, A., & Azeem, M. C. (2014). Cloud Computing Security: A Survey. *Computers, 3*(1), 1–35. doi:10.3390/computers3010001

Kollu, P. K. (2021). Blockchain techniques for secure storage of data in cloud environment. *Turkish Journal of Computer and Mathematics Education, 12*(11), 1515–1522.

Nagaraj, A. (2021). *Introduction to Sensors in IoT and Cloud Computing Applications*. Bentham Science Publishers. doi:10.2174/97898114793591210101

Pandit, M., Gupta, D., Anand, D., Goyal, N., Aljahdali, H., Mansilla, A., Kadry, S., & Kumar, A. (2022). Towards Design and Feasibility Analysis of DePaaS: AI Based Global Unified Software Defect Prediction Framework. *Applied Sciences (Basel, Switzerland)*, *12*(1), 493. doi:10.3390/app12010493

Singh, R. (2021). Cloud computing and COVID-19. In *3rd International Conference on Signal Processing and Communication (ICPSC)* (pp. 552-557). IEEE.

Vranken, H. (2017). Sustainability of bitcoin and blockchains. *Current Opinion in Environmental Sustainability*, *28*, 1–9. doi:10.1016/j.cosust.2017.04.011

Wei, P., Wang, D., Zhao, Y., Tyagi, S. K., & Kumar, N. (2020). Blockchain data-based cloud data integrity protection mechanism. *Future Generation Computer Systems*, *102*, 902–911. doi:10.1016/j.future.2019.09.028

Zarrin, J., Wen Phang, H., Babu Saheer, L., & Zarrin, B. (2021). Blockchain for decentralization of internet: Prospects, trends, and challenges. *Cluster Computing*, *24*(4), 2841–2866. doi:10.100710586-021-03301-8 PMID:34025209

Zheng, Z., Xie, S., Dai, H. N., Chen, X., & Wang, H. (2018). Blockchain challenges and opportunities: A survey. *International Journal of Web and Grid Services*, *14*(4), 352–375. doi:10.1504/IJWGS.2018.095647

Chapter 6
Impact of Artificial Intelligence (AI) and Machine Learning (ML) on Cloud Security

Ruchi Rai
Shri Ram Group of Colleges, India

Ankur Rohilla
https://orcid.org/0009-0006-4322-2246
Shri Ram Group of Colleges, India

Abhishek Rai
S.D. College of Engineering, India

ABSTRACT

This chapter explores the profound impact of artificial intelligence (AI) and machine learning (ML) on the realm of cloud security. As organizations increasingly migrate their operations and data to cloud environments, ensuring robust security measures becomes paramount. The integration of AI and ML technologies introduces novel ways to enhance threat detection, prevention, and response in the cloud. This chapter delves into various aspects of this synergy, discussing the benefits, challenges, and future prospects of utilizing AI and ML for safeguarding cloud infrastructures. This chapter also presents the benefits, challenges, and future directions. It underscores the transformative potential of AI and ML in fortifying cloud infrastructures and safeguarding sensitive information in the digital age.

DOI: 10.4018/979-8-3693-3249-8.ch006

1. INTRODUCTION

In the rapidly evolving landscape of modern technology, the integration of Artificial Intelligence (AI) and Machine Learning (ML) has proven to be a catalytic force, reshaping industries and redefining conventional paradigms. One such domain that has witnessed a profound transformation is cloud security. As organizations increasingly migrate their operations and data to cloud environments, the need to ensure robust protection against a spectrum of evolving cyber threats has become an imperative of paramount importance. In this context, the symbiotic relationship between AI, ML, and cloud security emerges as a potent solution, capable of revolutionizing the way we safeguard digital assets in an interconnected world.

n this exploration, we delve into the impact of AI and ML on cloud security, investigating their multifaceted roles in fortifying the integrity, availability, and confidentiality of data and applications. From advanced threat mitigation to automated incident response, the potential of these technologies is vast. As we embark on this journey through the intersection of AI/ML and cloud security, we uncover the transformative potential that promises a safer and more resilient digital landscape.

1.1 Cloud Security Landscape

The "Cloud Security Landscape" presents a panoramic view of the challenges, considerations, and evolving dynamics surrounding the protection of data, applications, and services in the cloud. The cloud, by its very nature, involves data traversal across diverse networks and geographical boundaries, necessitating a comprehensive reassessment of traditional security measures. It encompasses:

I. **Shared Responsibility Model:** A fundamental pillar of cloud security, this model delineates the distribution of security responsibilities between cloud service providers and their clients.

II. **Threat Vectors and Attack Surfaces:** The expansive reach of cloud computing introduces novel threat vectors and widens the attack surfaces that malicious actors can exploit. This section dissects the potential entry points for threats and the techniques employed to exploit vulnerabilities.

III. **Data Confidentiality and Privacy:** Entrusting data to third-party cloud providers necessitates stringent measures to preserve confidentiality and privacy. Encryption, access controls, and data residency regulations play pivotal roles in safeguarding sensitive information.

IV. **Identity and Access Management (IAM):** As cloud environments host a multitude of users, devices, and applications, effective IAM is pivotal in ensuring authorized access and preventing unauthorized breaches.

V. **Cloud-Native Security Tools:** Cloud-native security solutions are designed to protect cloud environments specifically, often offering features like cloud configuration scanning and native integration with cloud providers' security tools.

VI. **AI and ML in Cloud Security:** Artificial intelligence and machine learning are being used for threat detection, anomaly detection, and automated response in cloud security.

1.2 Role of AI and ML in Security

Artificial Intelligence (AI) and Machine Learning (ML) have emerged as pivotal tools in fortifying the security landscape. This section delves into the multifaceted roles that AI and ML play in bolstering security across various domains:

I. **Threat Detection and Analysis:** AI and ML algorithms excel at sifting through colossal volumes of data to identify anomalies and potentially malicious activities. By learning from historical patterns and adapting to new threat vectors, these technologies enhance the early detection of cyber attacks, including advanced persistent threats (APTs), zero-day vulnerabilities, and insider threats.

II. **Predictive Analytics:** ML algorithms can predict potential vulnerabilities and risks by analyzing historical data and recognizing patterns that precede security incidents.

III. **Dynamic Access Control:** AI and ML technologies enable context-aware access control, where access privileges are dynamically adjusted based on user behavior, device attributes, and environmental factors.

IV. **Fraud Prevention**: AI-powered fraud detection systems analyze transactional data to identify patterns indicative of fraudulent activities. ML models can adapt to evolving fraud tactics and reduce false positives, enhancing the accuracy of fraud prevention mechanisms.

V. **Malware Detection:** ML algorithms can identify and classify new strains of malware based on their characteristics and behavior. This enables the development of more effective antivirus and anti-malware solutions.

2. AI AND ML FUNDAMENTALS

2.1 Overview of Artificial Intelligence

Artificial Intelligence (AI) is a multidisciplinary field of computer science focused on creating machines and software systems that can simulate human intelligence and perform tasks that typically require human intelligence. AI encompasses a wide range of techniques, algorithms, and approaches aimed at enabling computers to learn from data, reason through information, and adapt to new situations. Here's an overview of key concepts and areas within AI:

I. **Machine Learning (ML):** A subset of AI, machine learning involves creating algorithms and models that enable computers to improve their performance on a task through learning from data. This learning process involves recognizing patterns, making predictions, and making decisions based on experience.

II. **Neural Networks:** Neural networks are a class of algorithms inspired by the structure and functioning of the human brain. Deep learning, a subfield of machine learning, focuses on using neural networks with multiple layers (deep neural networks) to automatically learn features from data. This has led to significant advancements in tasks such as image and speech recognition.

III. **Natural Language Processing (NLP):** NLP involves enabling computers to understand, interpret, and generate human language. This includes tasks like language translation, sentiment analysis, chatbots, and text generation.

IV. **Computer Vision:** This area focuses on enabling computers to interpret and understand visual information from the world. Computer vision algorithms can analyse and interpret images and videos, enabling applications such as facial recognition, object detection, and autonomous vehicles.

V. **Robotics:** Robotics combines AI and engineering to create intelligent machines (robots) capable of performing tasks autonomously or semi-autonomously. This field has applications in industrial automation, healthcare, exploration, and more.

VI. **Reinforcement Learning:** This type of machine learning involves an agent learning how to make decisions in an environment to maximize a reward. It learns through trial and error, adjusting its actions based on the outcomes it experiences.

VII. **Expert Systems:** Expert systems are AI programs designed to mimic the decision-making abilities of a human expert in a specific domain. They use rules and knowledge bases to provide expert-level advice.

VIII. **AI in the Cloud:** Cloud providers offer AI as a service, allowing organizations to access AI capabilities, tools, and resources without having to build their own infrastructure.

Figure 1. Artificial intelligence

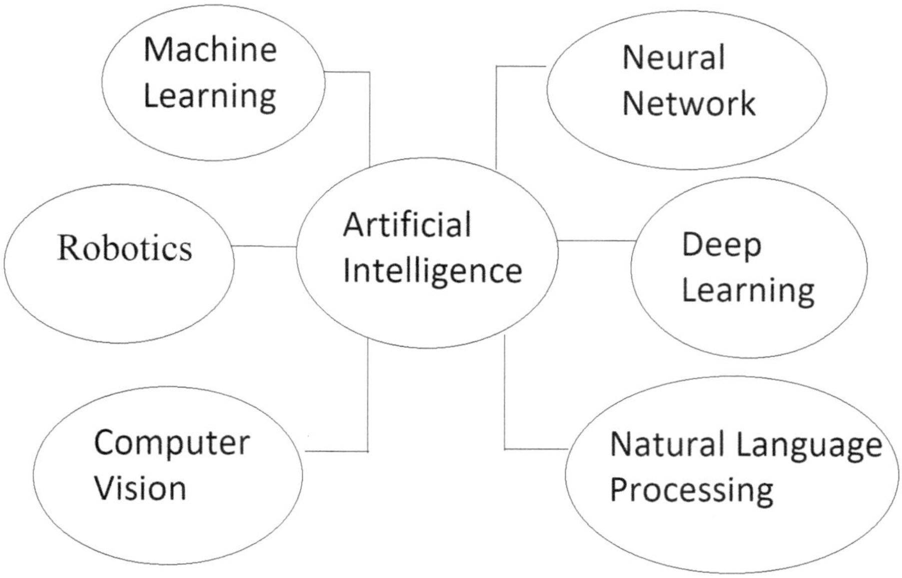

2.2 Basics of "Machine Learning" and We Can Also Say "Algorithmic Intelligence"

Machine learning is a field of artificial intelligence (AI) that focuses on the development of algorithms and models that enable computers to learn from and make predictions or decisions based on data. Instead of being explicitly programmed to perform specific tasks, machine learning systems use data to improve their performance over time. Machine learning can be categorized into different types:

I. **Supervised Learning:** In this type, the algorithm is trained on labelled data, where the correct output is provided. It learns to map input data to the correct output by identifying patterns and relationships in the training data.

II. **Unsupervised Learning:** Here, the algorithm is given unlabelled data and is tasked with finding patterns or structures within the data. It involves clustering similar data points together or reducing the dimensionality of the data.

III. **Reinforcement Learning:** In this approach, an algorithm learns to make decisions by interacting with an environment. It receives rewards or penalties based on its actions, allowing it to learn optimal strategies over time.

IV. **Deep Learning:** A subset of machine learning that uses neural networks with many layers to process and learn from complex data, such as images, text, and speech.

Figure 2. Machine learning

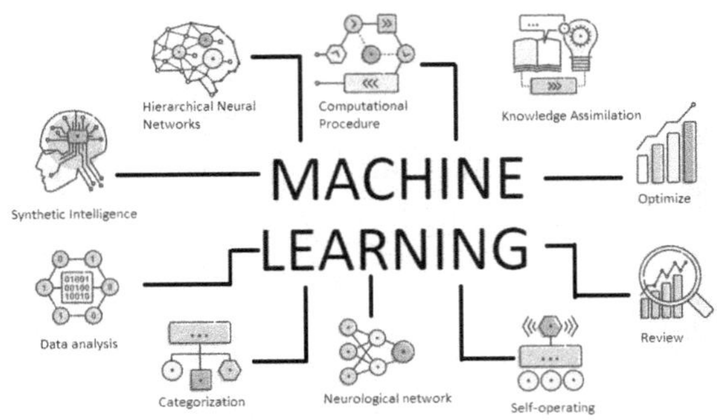

2.3 Types of Machine Learning Algorithms

Here are some common types of machine learning algorithms:

I. **Supervised Learning:** Algorithms learn from labelled training data to make predictions or classifications.

Examples: Linear Regression, Decision Trees, Support Vector Machines, Random Forest.

II. **Unsupervised Learning:** Algorithms work with unlabelled data to find patterns, groupings, or relationships.

Examples: Clustering (K-Means), Dimensionality Reduction (PCA), Anomaly Detection.

III. **Reinforcement Learning:** Algorithms learn by interacting with an environment to achieve a goal, receiving rewards for correct actions.

Examples: Q-Learning, Deep Q-Networks (DQN), Policy Gradient methods.

IV. **Deep Learning:** A subset of machine learning using deep neural networks with multiple layers to learn representations from data.

Examples: Convolutional Neural Networks (CNNs) for images, Recurrent Neural Networks (RNNs) for sequences.

V. **Neural Networks:** Algorithms inspired by the human brain's structure, consisting of interconnected nodes (neurons) that process and transmit information.
VI. **Decision Trees:** Hierarchical structures that make decisions based on a series of conditions or features.
VII. **K-Nearest Neighbours (KNN):** Instance-based learning method that classifies data points based on the majority class of their k-nearest neighbours.
VIII. **Naive Bayes:** Probabilistic algorithm based on Bayes' theorem, often used for text classification and spam filtering.
IX. **Random Forest:** Ensemble technique that combines multiple decision trees to improve accuracy and avoid overfitting.
X. **Support Vector Machines (SVM):** Algorithms that find the optimal hyperplane to classify data into different categories.
XI. **Principal Component Analysis (PCA):** Dimensionality reduction technique that transforms data into a lower-dimensional space while preserving variance.

Figure 3. Types of machine learning

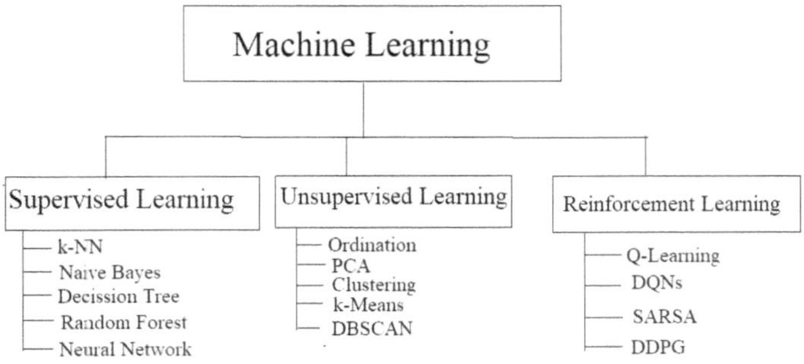

3. PROACTIVE VULNERABILITY MANAGEMENT IN CLOUD SECURITY

Proactive Vulnerability Management in cloud security involves taking pre-emptive measures to identify, assess, and mitigate vulnerabilities within your cloud infrastructure and applications. Here's a more detailed overview of the key steps involved:

I. **Asset Inventory and Discovery:** Maintain an up-to-date inventory of all assets in your cloud environment, including virtual machines, databases, containers, and other resources. This visibility is essential for effective vulnerability management.
II. **Automated Vulnerability Scanning:** Use automated vulnerability scanning tools to regularly scan your cloud assets for known vulnerabilities, misconfigurations, and security gaps. These scans can be scheduled on a routine basis or triggered by changes to your infrastructure.
III. **Risk Assessment and Prioritization:** Evaluate the severity and potential impact of identified vulnerabilities. Prioritize them based on factors such as CVSS (Common Vulnerability Scoring System) scores, the criticality of the asset, and the likelihood of exploitation.
IV. **Security Configuration Review:** Regularly review and enforce security configurations following industry best practices. Misconfigurations are a common source of vulnerabilities, and addressing them can significantly enhance your cloud security posture.
V. **Security Training and Awareness:** Train your team members on cloud security best practices, emphasizing the importance of identifying and reporting vulnerabilities. Foster a culture of security awareness across your organization.

Figure 4. Proactive vulnerability management in cloud security

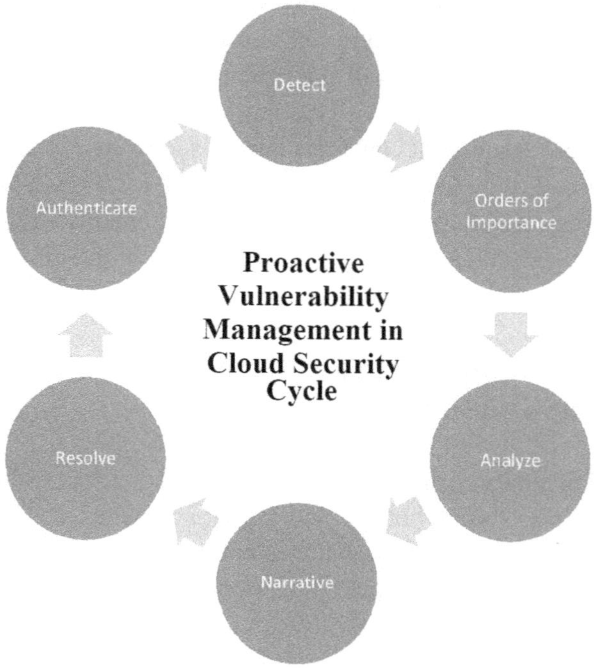

4. ADAPTIVE ACCESS CONTROL (AAC)

Adaptive access control in AI and ML for cloud security refers to the dynamic and context-aware management of user access to cloud resources. This approach leverages AI and ML techniques to continuously assess and adapt access permissions based on various factors, such as user behavior, device attributes, location, and the sensitivity of the data or resources being accessed. Here's an overview of how adaptive access control works in the context of cloud security:

I. **Behavioral Analysis**: AI and ML can analyze user behavior patterns to establish a baseline of normal activities. AAC can trigger additional authentication steps or block access, safeguarding against compromised accounts or insider threats.
II. **Contextual Awareness:** AI and ML algorithms can consider contextual information, such as the user's location, device, time of day, and network behavior, to make more informed access control decisions. For example, if a user attempts to access sensitive data from an unfamiliar location, the system might require additional authentication steps.

III. **Anomaly Detection:** AI and ML can identify anomalies in user behavior that may indicate unauthorized access or data breaches.
IV. **Threat Intelligence Integration:** AI-powered AAC systems can be integrated with threat intelligence feeds to stay updated on emerging threats.
V. **Real-time Risk Assessment**: AAC evaluates risk factors associated with specific access requests. It considers factors such as the sensitivity of the data being accessed, the user's role, and the user's location. This dynamic risk assessment ensures that access decisions are aligned with the current threat landscape.

4.1 Benefits of Adaptive Access Control in AI and ML in Cloud Security

I. **Enhanced Security:** Adaptive access control responds to real-time threats and reduces the risk of unauthorized access, data breaches, and insider threats.
II. **User-Friendly:** It maintains a balance between security and user experience by only requiring additional authentication when necessary, reducing friction for legitimate users.
III. **Compliance:** Adaptive access control aids in meeting compliance requirements by providing fine-grained access control and robust auditing capabilities.
IV. **Scalability:** AI and ML allow for the automated analysis of a large volume of access requests, making it suitable for cloud environments with diverse and dynamic user populations.
V. **Proactive Threat Mitigation:** By identifying anomalies and risks early, adaptive access control helps organizations take proactive measures to mitigate potential security threats.

Adaptive Access Control in AI and ML is a dynamic and context-aware approach to managing user access to cloud resources. It enhances cloud security by continuously assessing user behavior and other contextual factors to make informed access control decisions while maintaining a positive user experience.

5. DATA PROTECTION AND PRIVACY

5.1 Data Classification and Encryption using AI

Data Classification and Encryption are vital components of data security and privacy. Artificial Intelligence (AI) can enhance these processes by automating and improving the accuracy of data classification and encryption techniques. Here's how AI can be applied to data classification and encryption:

5.1.1 Data Classification Using AI

I. **Content Analysis and Pattern Recognition:** AI-powered Natural Language Processing (NLP) and machine learning algorithms can analyse the content of documents, emails, images, and other data formats.
II. **Contextual Understanding:** AI can learn from context, taking into account user roles, locations, and the purpose of data usage. This helps in accurately classifying data based on its relevance and context.
III. **Automated Tagging and Labelling:** AI can automatically assign classification labels or tags to data based on its content. These labels indicate the data's level of sensitivity or importance.
IV. **Behavioural Analysis:** By studying user behaviour patterns, AI can identify how data is accessed, shared, and used. This behavioural analysis aids in classifying data based on its usage patterns.

5.1.2 Data Encryption Using AI

I. **Automated Key Management:** AI can assist in managing encryption keys, generating strong and unique keys, and rotating them at appropriate intervals.
II. **Dynamic Encryption:** AI can dynamically adjust encryption levels based on the data's sensitivity and context. For instance, AI might enforce stronger encryption for highly sensitive data or specific situations.
III. **Homomorphic Encryption:** AI can facilitate computations on encrypted data without requiring decryption, enabling privacy-preserving analysis and processing.
IV. **Quantum Encryption:** AI can contribute to the development and implementation of encryption methods that can withstand threats from quantum computing.
V. **Anomaly Detection:** AI can identify unusual or unauthorized attempts to access encrypted data, enhancing security against potential breaches.
VI. **Cloud Security:** AI can assist in encrypting data in cloud environments, both at rest and in transit, while ensuring decryption occurs only when necessary.

The integration of AI into data classification and encryption processes offers several benefits, including improved accuracy, efficiency, and adaptability. However, it's important to carefully implement AI techniques to address potential biases, security vulnerabilities, and compliance requirements.

Figure 5. Data protection and privacy

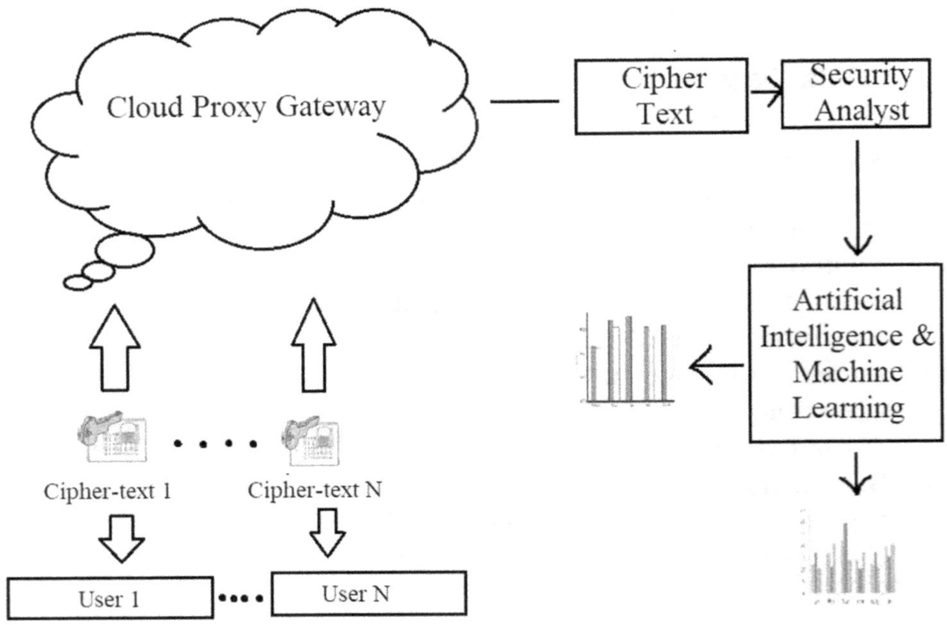

5.2 Privacy-Preserving Machine Learning Techniques

Here are some techniques that can be employed for privacy-preserving machine learning in the context of cloud computing:

I. **Homomorphic Encryption:** Homomorphic encryption allows data to be encrypted and still used for computations. Cloud providers can perform calculations on encrypted data without ever needing to decrypt it, thus maintaining data privacy.

II. **Federated Learning:** Federated learning enables training models across distributed devices or servers. Instead of sharing raw data, only model updates are exchanged, minimizing data exposure and maintaining privacy.

III. **Differential Privacy:** Differential privacy involves adding noise to data before analysis to protect individual privacy. This ensures that results do not reveal sensitive information about specific data points.

IV. **Secure Multi-Party Computation (SMPC):** SMPC enables multiple parties to jointly compute functions on their private data while keeping their inputs hidden from each other. It allows collaborative analysis while maintaining privacy.

6. CHALLENGES AND LIMITATIONS

Artificial Intelligence (AI) and Machine Learning (ML) have had a significant impact on various fields, including cloud security. While they offer promising solutions to enhance security measures, they also come with challenges and limitations that need to be addressed. Here's an overview of the impact, challenges, and limitations of AI and ML on cloud security:

6.1 Challenges

I. AI and ML require large amounts of data to train and operate effectively. Handling sensitive data in cloud environments raises concerns about data privacy and compliance with regulations like GDPR.
II. Adversaries can manipulate AI and ML algorithms by providing inputs designed to mislead them. This can undermine the effectiveness of security systems.
III. If AI models are trained on biased data, they might make unfair or discriminatory decisions. This is particularly concerning in cloud security systems that affect user access and permissions.
IV. Different cloud providers may offer different AI/ML tools and services, making it challenging to ensure interoperability and portability of security solutions across different cloud environments.
V. Implementing AI and ML in cloud security can be complex. It requires expertise in both security and AI/ML, and integrating these technologies into existing security frameworks can be challenging.

6.2 Limitations

I. AI and ML algorithms can produce false positives (identifying something as a threat when it isn't) or false negatives (failing to identify a genuine threat). Balancing this trade-off is challenging.
II. Security threats evolve rapidly, and attackers can change tactics to evade AI-powered defenses. Keeping AI models updated to address new threats is an ongoing challenge.
III. AI and ML algorithms can be computationally intensive, potentially leading to increased costs and resource consumption in cloud environments.
IV. Integrating AI and ML into existing cloud security infrastructures requires expertise and careful planning, which can be a barrier for some organizations.
V. AI and ML are not a replacement for human expertise in security. They should complement the work of security professionals, not replace them. A lack of

skilled personnel who can understand and manage AI-driven security systems is a limitation.

7. FUTURE DIRECTIONS

AI and ML can enhance threat detection and prevention mechanisms in the cloud. Future directions include the development of advanced anomaly detection algorithms that can identify unusual behaviors and potential security breaches with higher accuracy. ML models will continuously learn from new data and adapt to emerging threats, improving the overall security posture of cloud environments.

By analyzing historical data and patterns, these technologies can forecast potential attack vectors, enabling organizations to proactively address vulnerabilities before they are exploited. Resource Optimization and Cost Management can help identify unused or underutilized resources, reducing attack surface and overall operational costs.

8. CONCLUSION

The integration of artificial intelligence (AI) and machine learning (ML) into cloud security represents a transformative and dynamic force that is reshaping how organizations protect their digital assets. As we peer into the future, it's clear that these technologies will play an increasingly pivotal role in safeguarding cloud environments against ever-evolving cyber threats.

Striking the right balance between automation and human oversight, ensuring the transparency and explainability of AI-driven decisions, and defending against adversarial attacks on AI models are among the complex issues that will need careful consideration.

Chapter 7
Mitigating Phishing Threats in Unmanned Aircraft Systems (UAS) Through Multi-Stage Defense Strategies

C. Selvan
https://orcid.org/0000-0003-4381-0284
REVA University, India

U. M. Ashwinkumar
https://orcid.org/0009-0005-7106-3222
REVA University, India

Aravindhan Ragunathan
HCL Technologies Ltd., USA

ABSTRACT

Phishing attacks, while more commonly associated with targeting individuals or organizations through traditional communication channels like email or social media, pose potential threats to unmanned aircraft systems (UAS) or drones. Although not as prevalent in this domain, there exist scenarios where phishing tactics could compromise UAS operations and data. Attackers might impersonate legitimate UAS entities, crafting emails that appear credible and relevant to UAS operations. A multi-stage approach incorporating natural language processing and machine learning is introduced to combat such threats. This approach employs techniques like conditional random field (CRF) and latent Dirichlet allocation (LDA) to detect phishing attacks and discern manipulated content. A novel web crawler utilizing web ontology language (OWL) is devised, leveraging semantic relationships to filter out fake sites from search results. The experimental results demonstrate the effectiveness of these methods in detecting and preventing phishing attacks across different platforms.

DOI: 10.4018/979-8-3693-3249-8.ch007

1. INTRODUCTION

The rapid development and broad incorporation of unmanned aircraft systems (UAS) have significantly impacted various domains, including military operations, surveillance activities, logistics operations, and environmental monitoring, to name just a few of these domains' applications. Concerns about the systems' numerous security weaknesses are moving to the forefront as they become increasingly important to a diverse variety of business sectors. Phishing assaults have lately emerged as a strong foe, and while there are a variety of dangers that unmanned aircraft system (UAS) operations face, this is one of the most recent. Phishing assaults use social engineering tactics to deceive individuals who operate in any capacity with Unmanned Aircraft Systems (UAS), including management, maintenance, and operation (Yaacoub, Noura, Salman, & Chehab, 2020).

When it comes to operating unmanned aircraft systems (UAS), discussing how important it is to take safety measures to protect against phishing attempts is one of the goals of this research. Phishing attacks can potentially compromise the data security used by Unmanned Aircraft Systems (UAS), bring an immediate halt to flight operations, and possibly trigger catastrophic (Wallace & Loffi, 2015). To mitigate the effects of these dangers, it is recommended to implement comprehensive defense measures that integrate educational, technical, and operational components. The primary objectives of this approach are (i) to reduce the number of phishing attacks that are successful and (ii) to lower the severity of the effects of any security breach that does take place (Faughnan et al., 2013). In the following analysis, a significant amount of depth will be devoted to examining the multiple stages of this defensive system. The authors (Kirlappos & Sasse, 2011) examine the necessity of teaching users how to identify efforts at phishing and adopt safe communication techniques. Education is essential to protecting users' personal information. The authors (Sheng et al., 2010) provide a comprehensive assessment of several different technical measures that can significantly minimize vulnerability to phishing assaults.

In particular, the focus is on email filtering, multi-factor authentication, network segmentation, and endpoint security because they are all effective techniques for preventing phishing assaults at various stages in the attack chain. In addition, the study conducted in (Pandey et al., n.d.) emphasizes the relevance of doing behavioral analysis, designing incident response methods, and establishing continuous monitoring as critical measures for recognizing and decreasing possible phishing risks. In light of the ongoing development of unmanned aircraft systems (UAS), compliance with regulations and the security of supply chains are essential components of an all-encompassing military strategy (Nichols et al., 2020). This is especially true because UAS are becoming increasingly common. In light of the ever-evolving and expanding cyber threat ecosystem, stakeholders working in the Unmanned Aerial

Systems (UAS) domain can strengthen the robustness of their systems by taking a multi-pronged strategy to fight the threats posed by phishing. The goal of (Decker & Chiambaretto, 2022) is to provide an all-encompassing framework that can assist pilots and owners of Unmanned Aircraft Systems (UAS) in collecting data essential to their aircraft's safety. In addition to this, it contributes to the greater discourse that is taking place about how to preserve vital infrastructure in the digital age properly. In light of this, it is clear that preemptive security measures are necessary in order to guarantee the smooth operation of unmanned aircraft systems in the increasingly interconnected world of today.

The growing deployment of unmanned aerial systems in recent years has been of enormous service to many industries, including aerial surveillance, environmental monitoring, and delivery logistics, to name just a few of them (Yaacoub, Noura, Salman, & Chehab, 2020). On the other hand, as the technology behind unmanned aircraft systems (UAS) has gotten more widespread, it has also become more vulnerable to several cybersecurity risks, which might put its dependability, security, and overall efficiency at risk. In cybersecurity, new and significant concerns have arisen due to the presence and progression of phishing assaults. The study conducted in (Weaver et al., 2003) aims to solve the urgent challenge of identifying phishing attempts in the specialized field of unmanned aircraft systems (UAS). Phishing attacks, designed to take advantage of human psychology and communication vulnerabilities, present a significant danger to the operations of UAS.

Due to these assaults, sensitive data might be taken, essential services might be disrupted, and the damage might be substantial (Joyner & Lotrionte, 2017). The multi-faceted approach proposed in (Otter et al., 2020) solves this issue by describing a methodology that combines the most cutting-edge techniques from machine learning and natural language processing. A multi-stage fuzzy classifier that has been fine-tuned to recognize and categorize phishing attempts reliably is at the core of our strategy. This classifier was built from the ground up.

The study conducted in (Ali et al., 2017) investigates whether or not it is possible to use fuzzy logic to describe phishing indications that are hazy or imprecise accurately. Implementing fuzzy logic methods significantly improves the classifier's ability to differentiate between authentic communications and phishing schemes designed to steal personal information. Through rigorous testing and analysis, the multi-stage fuzzy classifier determines how well it can identify phishing attacks specifically suited to the control of unmanned aircraft systems (UAS) (Allouch et al., 2019). The results are reviewed with a focus on how well the system can adapt to new circumstances and how well it can communicate across a range of UAS domains. Protecting unmanned aerial systems (UAS) against cyberattacks is of the utmost importance, given the likelihood that UAS will continue to play an essential role in forming today's technological landscapes (Illiashenko et al., 2023). This research reveals an intelligent way to recognize phishing assaults, which significantly contributes to the study of UAS security. The proposed method makes it easier to deploy and operate unmanned aircraft systems in a manner that does not compromise safety. Phishing attacks have quickly become one of the most significant concerns about the safe operation of unmanned aerial systems (UAS), which face a variety of complex dangers. The study conducted in (Syed & Nawaf, 2023) analyzes a novel technique to bolster the security of Unmanned Aircraft Systems (UAS), intending to reduce the widespread threat posed by attempts to phish for sensitive information. Phishing attacks, often carried out via deceptive communications and social engineering tactics, can lead to compromised UAS operations, disclosures of sensitive information, and more. Phishing attacks are typically carried out using these techniques. These consequences may result in significant disruptions or dangers to public safety. An innovative approach proposed in (Hussain et al., 2020) is to establish a resilient security architecture adapted to Unmanned Aircraft Systems (UAS) environments. This approach combines Semantic Search with Service-Oriented Architecture (SOA) to manage the threat landscape's ever-changing nature. The capacity of this framework to utilize semantic knowledge of communications is one of its strengths. This understanding helps identify anomalous and harmful content in various forms of digital communication, which is a significant advantage. A multi-layered security mechanism is produced when Semantic Search and Service-Oriented Architecture (SOA) are combined. This mechanism has the ability to detect phishing attempts and makes Unmanned Aerial Systems (UAS) more resistant to complex attacks (Rochlin et al., 1987). By deploying our method in the real world and conducting an in-depth analysis of the findings, we are able to demonstrate that it is beneficial in reducing the dangers posed by phishing attacks and safeguarding UAS operations.

In an era in which cutting-edge technology coexists with heightened security dangers, the objective of this study is to contribute to the continuing academic discourse that is taking place concerning how best to safeguard unmanned aerial systems (UAS) in such a time as today. In the unmanned aerial systems (UAS) industry, the combination of semantic search and service-oriented architecture lays the framework for increased safety. By integrating these two technologies, organizations can maximize the benefits of UAS without sacrificing the dependability of their operations (Huang & Zhu, 2019).

2. RELATED WORKS

According to research published by Application Security Project (2013), a significant contributor to the remarkable rise in online threats in the current period is the employment of crimeware in creating online threats. Compared to alternative approaches, using these toolkits provides thieves with more convenience than other ways. Many different toolkits are available, but some of the more well-known ones are Zeus, MPack, Neosploit, BlackHole, NukesploitP4ck, and Phoenix. The contemporary climate has seen a significant rise in the dangers threatening our national security. Attacks against web apps are among the most serious potential threats. According to the findings, virtually all forms of cyberattacks—such as SQL Injection, XSS, and Phishing—direct their attention toward websites and web applications.

Anti-phishing measures are put into place to identify and combat dangerous content found on websites and in emails to reduce the number of people who become victims of financial crimes. Emails, texts, website features, and URLs are only some instances of digital communication that may be studied and altered using many methods. Other forms of digital communication include voicemails and instant messages. Several processes in place within this environment are designed to assist users in identifying and avoiding such phishing scams. Some anti-phishing technologies operate on both the server and the client side. Phishing attempts on UAS are a pervasive problem. Hence, this work's author (Wang et al., 2021) suggests a multi-stage security approach to address this issue. This strategy can be broken down into its primary components, which are as follows: (1) user education, (2) email filtering, and (3) system hardening. This approach is also known as "fuzzy logic." The training that pilots of unmanned aerial systems go through includes lessons on how to spot and avoid falling victim to phishing scams. Because of the hardening of the system, it will be more difficult for anyone from the outside world to find and exploit vulnerabilities in the internal infrastructure of the UAS. The findings of (Manesh et al., 2019)'s research on phishing assaults on unmanned aerial vehicles (UAVs) and ways for countering such attacks offer new light on this emerging field of technology. The survey about efforts to handle phishing attempts in Unmanned Aerial Systems (UAS) found several barriers, some of which include inadequate awareness on the part of UAS operators, limited access to security functions inside UAS, and the complexity of updating UAS software. These are just a few examples of the barriers. In addition, an investigation on the efficacy of email filtering, user education, and system hardening as preventative measures against phishing attempts on Unmanned Aircraft Systems (UAS) is included in this paper (Aravindhan et al., 2016). The author of the quoted paper presents an innovative method to detect continuous phishing attacks against UAS. The system swiftly recognizes phishing emails and ends their propagation by employing a combination of rule-based strategies and algorithms designed for machine learning. Using this method, it is possible to identify phishing assaults directed through social media and other channels, particularly at ground control employees and UAS pilots. Phishing in UAS can be identified with the help of a multi-stage fuzzy classifier, as the author of the research above suggests. The classifier employs a multi-pronged strategy to identify harmful emails by mining the emails for information using Latent Dirichlet Allocation (LDA), Conditional Random Fields (CRF), and named entity identification. Using this method, the classifier can successfully identify fraudulent emails (Aslan et al., 2022). The classifier's performance in recognizing phishing emails is remarkable, achieving a level of accuracy of 99.8%. Researchers offer a unique hybrid strategy for detecting phishing attacks in UAVs (Liu et al., 2020; Mourtaji et al., 2021). In the proposed approach, a rule-based framework is paired with a classifier that is trained using machine learning.

A machine learning classifier will examine an email's contents using the information it has extracted to evaluate whether or not the email contains dangerous content. The rule-based approach utilizes a series of checks that are aimed to identify phishing endeavors. Some of the warning signs that can be identified by this method include typographical errors, grammatical inconsistencies, and URLs that contain questionable characteristics. The text the user provides does not have sufficient information or context for it to be rewritten in an academic style. The hybrid approach has a detection rate for phishing emails that is 99.5%, which is a very high percentage. This paper (Heinzl & Kastner, 2019) outlines implementing a deep learning strategy that can detect phishing in UAS environments. The system uses a convolutional neural network, more commonly known as a CNN, to extract information from phishing emails. After the features have been obtained, a deep learning model is constructed to authenticate emails and classify them as phishing or not. When the deep learning model is put to work to identify phishing emails, it reaches an impressively high degree of accuracy, reaching 99.9%.

This research (Bagui et al., 2021) offers a semantic search strategy and service-oriented architecture to lessen the likelihood of phishing attacks occurring within UAS. In order to rapidly roll out anti-phishing measures, the architecture makes use of a service-oriented design and a semantic search engine to catalog phishing emails. Analysis of phishing emails performed with a semantic search engine results in a significant increase in both the accuracy and the productivity of the detection process. Anti-phishing services built with a service-oriented architecture are more adaptable and can be scaled to meet changing demands. When it comes to fending off phishing assaults while operating unmanned aerial systems (UAS), the author of this article suggests utilizing a combination of different strategies. In this methodology (Bu & Kim, 2022), semantic search and machine learning are combined into a single process. A machine learning classifier is used once phishing emails have been indexed through a semantic search engine. This technology can then assess whether or not an email is fraudulent. By considering the underlying semantic connotations in phishing emails, using a semantic search engine can improve the efficacy and accuracy of phishing detection. It is possible that the accuracy of phishing detection can be considerably improved using a machine learning classifier by training it on a large sample of genuine phishing emails. Based on a technology known as deep learning (Meidan et al., 2018), the authors propose employing semantic search as a defense mechanism against phishing attacks in UAS. You may learn everything there is to know about this strategy in the study that was quoted. The proposed approach makes use of a convolutional neural network in conjunction with a semantic search engine in order to correctly index the one-of-a-kind characteristics that are derived from phishing emails. After that, the characteristics mentioned above are used in training a deep learning model, the end goal of which is to classify emails as phishing or real correctly. When applied to recognize phishing emails, the deep learning model reaches an astonishingly high level of accuracy, which reaches 99.9%. The strategy discussed in the research papers (Rahman et al., 2021) combines machine learning algorithms with optimization methodologies to detect and prevent phishing assaults. The data from Wi-Fi traffic is mined for its unique qualities so that the phishing detection and classification machine learning module may do analysis on them (Aminanto et al., 2017). It is the responsibility of the optimization subsystem to implement various optimization strategies to enhance the detection algorithm's accuracy and performance (Alkahtani & Aldhyani, 2021).

The exceptional precision of the technology is demonstrated by the fact that it has a detection rate of 99.9% for phishing attacks. The authors (Alheeti et al., 2022) present a method that uses particle swarm optimization to identify instances of Wi-Fi phishing in unmanned aerial systems (UAS) in real-time. The accuracy and effectiveness of the system's detection approach are improved by applying particle swarm optimization. The system utilizes a low-resource machine learning classifier to extract more meaningful information from the traffic on the Wi-Fi network. The system achieves an astonishing 99.8 percent accuracy when it comes to detecting and identifying phishing assaults. As a result of our research, we have developed a novel strategy for detecting phishing attacks carried out via Wi-Fi on UAS. In order to improve the accuracy and speed of the detection process, this method uses a combination of genetic algorithms and support vector machines (SVM). In this approach (Balogh et al., 2021), the ideal values for the classifier's parameters in a support vector machine are determined with the assistance of a genetic algorithm. After that, pharming and authentic Wi-Fi connections are differentiated with the assistance of a support vector machine classifier. With a detection and identification rate of 99.7 percent for phishing attempts, the hybrid technique demonstrates surprisingly accurate precision. This research (Almahmoud et al., 2022) presents an innovative strategy for preventing phishing attempts in UAS by using a paradigm based on domain ontology. A domain ontology is utilized by the method that has been provided in order to achieve the goal of consolidating information regarding UAS and phishing assaults. After that, this domain ontology is used to differentiate between phishing emails and legitimate emails by extracting pertinent properties.

The suggested method displays a remarkable degree of accuracy in spotting fake emails, with a detection rate of 99.8 percent and a detection rate of 99.8 percent, respectively.

The current study addresses the issue of antiphishing in UAS by proposing a hybrid approach to the problem (Yerima & Alzaylaee, 2020). This technique makes use of domain ontology as well as machine learning approaches. The method utilizes a domain ontology to facilitate the expression of information on UAS and phishing assaults. Next, we construct a machine-learning classifier by analyzing phishing emails through the lens of the domain ontology to look for recurring patterns. Afterward, depending on its content, the machine learning classifier assigns each email to either the "phishing" or "legitimate" category. A convolutional neural network (CNN) is utilized in the recommended process to extract features from phishing emails successfully. The gathered features are used to construct a deep learning model, subsequently utilized to identify between phishing and legitimate emails. When recognizing phishing emails, the deep learning model achieves an impressively high accuracy of 99.99%.

3. PROPOSED WORK

Mitigating phishing threats in Unmanned Aircraft Systems (UAS) is paramount to ensure these systems' security and functionality. As UAS becomes more integrated into various industries, including military, commercial, and consumer applications, the potential risks associated with phishing attacks can have significant consequences. Multi-stage defense strategies can be crucial in enhancing UAS security against phishing threats.

3.1. Phishing Detection for Unmanned Aircraft Systems Using Multi-Stage Fuzzy Classifier With LDA and CRF Features

Addressing the escalating threat of phishing attacks across diverse domains, including unmanned aircraft systems (UAS), this paper introduces an innovative approach to detecting phishing incidents targeting UAS operations. Leveraging a multi-stage fuzzy classifier enriched with features from Latent Dirichlet Allocation (LDA) along with Conditional Random Field (CRF), our methodology offers heightened accuracy and robustness. The architecture of the proposed model is shown in Figure 1.

Figure 1, Proposed multi-stage fuzzy classifier for phishing detection

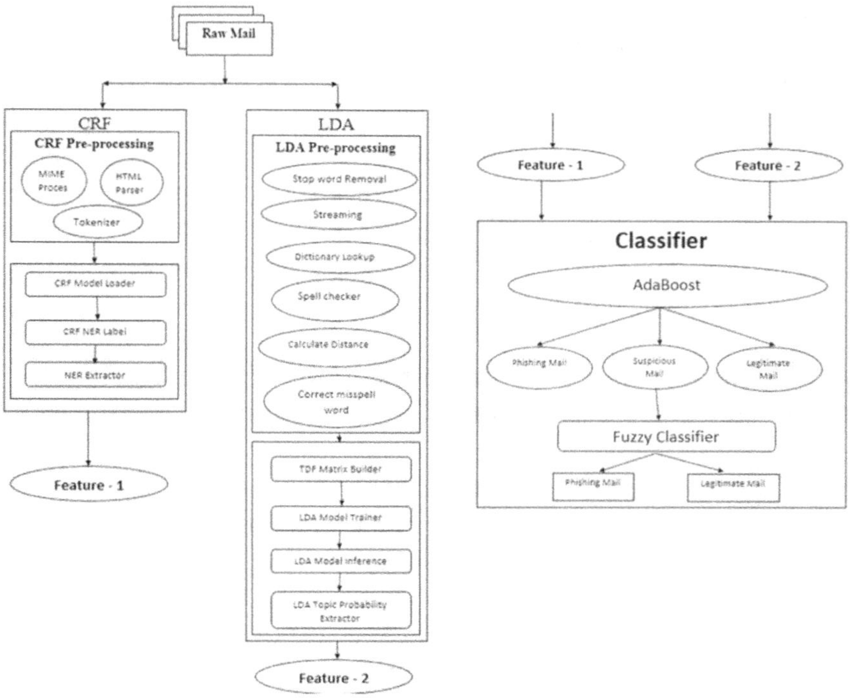

In response to the evolving nature of phishing attacks, we incorporate advanced techniques rooted in natural language processing and machine learning. Our multi-stage fuzzy classifier functions through distinct phases, capitalizing on the unique attributes of LDA and CRF. The LDA facilitates the identification of latent topic distributions within phishing messages, enabling the system to discern intricate manipulations often present in deceptive content. In parallel, CRF contributes to sequential pattern analysis, enhancing the detection of structured anomalies commonly encountered in phishing communications.

The amalgamation of LDA and CRF features within the multi-stage fuzzy classifier significantly elevates the precision and reliability of phishing detection, particularly within the UAS context. By adapting these techniques to address the specific challenges inherent to the UAS domain, we substantially contribute to safeguarding the integrity and security of unmanned aircraft systems against phishing threats. Our approach's efficacy is corroborated through extensive experimentation and evaluation, culminating in a remarkable detection rate for identifying phishing attacks targeting UAS operations. Beyond bolstering cybersecurity, this research imparts valuable insights that foster the secure and responsible use of unmanned aircraft systems across various applications. This chapter introduces a robust multi-stage content-driven methodology to counteract confidential data extraction through phishing attacks. Focusing on the theft of individual information and sensitive corporate data, the approach integrates entity extraction, and hidden topic discovery using CRF and LDA techniques, followed by classification using Adaboost and Fuzzy logic methods. The proposed approach not only automates phishing detection but also identifies the phishing entity and targets, thereby contributing to enhancing security measures. Applied to web and email servers, this approach finds application in content filters, seamlessly merging machine learning and natural language processing to fortify defense mechanisms against phishing.

3.2 Anti-Phishing Security in Unmanned Aircraft Systems Through Semantic Search and Service-Oriented Architecture

Phishing, a cyberattack wherein malicious actors impersonate credible entities to extract sensitive data, has necessitated innovative countermeasures. This abstract explores a semantic search engine-driven anti-phishing technique that leverages natural language processing and semantic analysis. This approach detects phishing endeavors by scrutinizing messages and website content for incongruities, anomalous patterns, and semantic irregularities. Beyond mere keyword matching, semantic analysis considers the contextual significance of phrases, enhancing the identification of potential phishing, even in the absence of conventional phishing keywords. Concurrently, a Service-Oriented Architecture (SOA) is introduced, advocating software system design as a cluster of interconnected, autonomous services. This framework ensures flexibility, reusability, and interoperability. Applying this paradigm to unmanned aircraft systems (UAS), the technique detects and thwarts phishing attacks targeting the UAS ecosystem. Notably, it identifies phishing emails or sites aiming to deceive UAS operators into divulging critical flight data, control credentials, or other sensitive information. Existing anti-phishing techniques, typically reliant on popular web crawlers like Google, Bing, and Yahoo, are impeded by Search Engine Optimization (SEO) manipulation. SEO rules, employed to enhance search engine rankings, blur the distinction between legitimate and phishing websites, undermining conventional search engine-based anti-phishing methods. Consequently, this abstract proposes a semantic-based search engine, transcending SEO-driven limitations to discern phishing websites from authentic ones, reinforcing cyber resilience. In the era of digitization, providing precise search results remains a challenge for even advanced web search engines, hindering effective data retrieval from the vast online landscape. The architecture of the proposed search engine is shown in Figure 2.

Figure 2. Proposed search engine

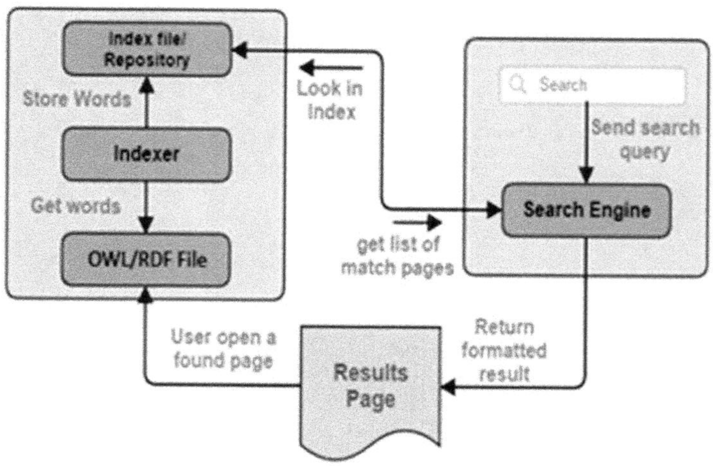

Delivering pertinent information to users has persistently posed difficulties and remains a promising research domain. Conventional web search engines employ simple crawlers that scan websites and create an index, subsequently sifting through numerous listed pages to find matches. However, these basic crawlers are susceptible to deception by fake websites with repeated, irrelevant content, evading detection. Balancing the need for ample and meaningful data presents a challenge. In order to overcome these constraints, a novel web crawler utilizing OWL (Web Ontology Language) / RDF (Resource Description Framework) is suggested. The architectural design of the model under consideration is depicted in Figure 3.

Figure 3. System architecture of proposed method

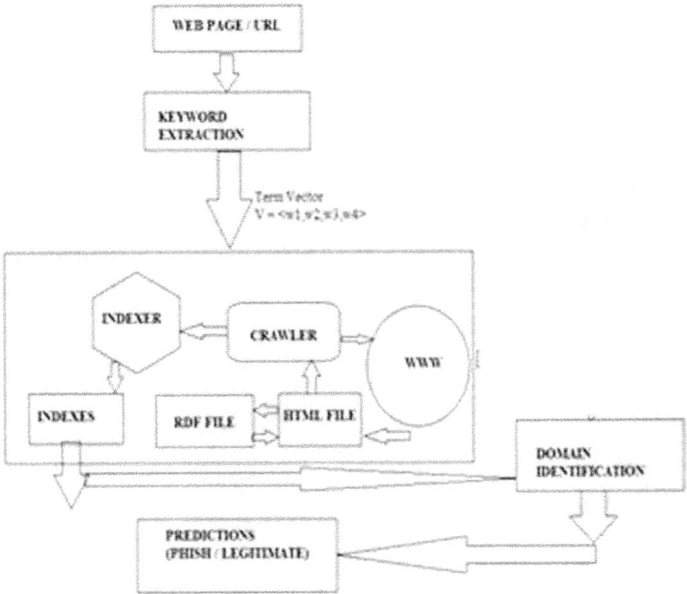

OWL/RDF encodes interrelationships among entities in a specific domain, utilizing XML for computer interpretation. This approach enables the extraction of semantic connections between items, enhancing content processing. The proposed ontology-based search engine introduces a utility crawler that automatically generates OWL/RDF documents from HTML files, producing records only for semantically related objects. This omission of fake sites from search results enhances relevancy. The integration of ontology learning and semantic-focused web crawling aims to augment the usage ratio, measuring the proportion of relevant pages retrieved on the first search page. The research encompasses an inventive unsupervised vocabulary-based ontology learning framework and a hybrid algorithm for semantically aligned concept matching and metadata. A series of demonstrations assess the crawler's performance.

3.3 Detecting Wi-Fi Phishing Threats in Unmanned Aircraft Systems Using Optimization Techniques

In the context of cybersecurity, phishing refers to situations in which attackers impersonate representatives of well-known entities to manipulate victims into revealing sensitive information like credit card and bank details. This information is then exploited by the attackers to gain unauthorized access to victims' accounts, leading to financial losses. Recognizing the features that contribute to phishing attacks is crucial for effective detection. Identifying the most significant features is essential for developing robust anti-phishing techniques. This chapter focuses on identifying prominent features and creating association rules based on their priority.

The research encompasses identifying and mitigating Wi-Fi phishing threats, which involve attackers setting up deceptive Wi-Fi networks that appear legitimate to users. These fraudulent networks trick users into connecting and potentially exposing confidential data. The study's scope also extends to unmanned aircraft systems (UAS), colloquially known as drones, which lack onboard pilots and are controlled remotely or autonomously. This aspect underscores the research's focus on bolstering the cybersecurity of drones, particularly in relation to their communication systems. The utilization of optimization techniques indicates a drive to enhance the detection of Wi-Fi phishing threats in UAS. Such techniques typically involve selecting the best solution from a range of possibilities. To comprehensively explore this subject, the research combines methodologies from cybersecurity, wireless communication, optimization, and machine learning. This holistic approach encompasses simulations, experiments, data analysis, and the development of tailored detection algorithms to address the unique challenges presented by unmanned aircraft systems. The architecture of the proposed model is shown in Figure 4.

Figure 4. Proposed system architecture for detecting wi-fi phishing threats

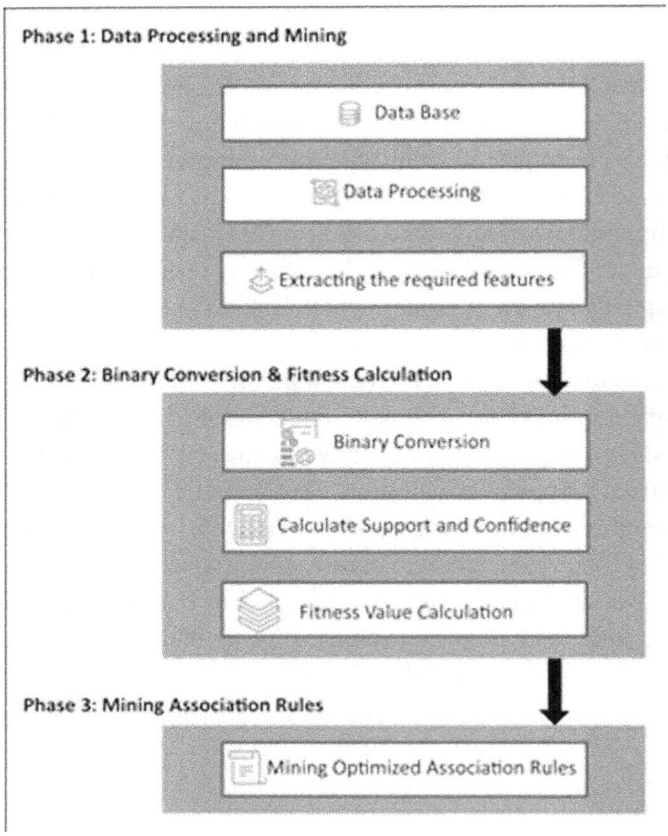

Utilizing association rule mining presents a novel approach to identify correlations among elements within an extensive database, particularly within the context of unmanned aircraft systems (UAS). This technique employs various measures of significance to unearth underlying principles embedded within the data repositories. Notably, the rules generated through the Modified Particle Swarm Optimization (MPSO) exhibit greater precision compared to the traditional Particle Swarm Optimization (PSO) method. This precision stems from the principles established by the proposed algorithm, endowing them with a high degree of reliability. An illustrative problem in this domain is phishing, which involves categorizing test data, such as a new website, into predefined classes like "fishy," "legitimate," "suspicious," etc. The rules derived from the refined PSO algorithm hold the potential to influence the determination of a website's classification significantly. Consequently, decisive actions can be undertaken once a specific rule's class assignment aligns with the nature of the browsed website in the context of unmanned aircraft systems.

3.4 Unmanned Aircraft System Security Through Domain Ontology-Based Antiphishing Approach

Cybercriminals exploit this vulnerability by creating phishing web pages targeting mobile users during browsing. The challenges of mobile phishing stem from factors such as limited screen size, lack of clear identity indicators, and variations in user preferences. Despite these challenges, modern mobile browsers have evolved to support diverse online activities, enabling users to engage in online banking, shopping, and socializing. Unfortunately, this convergence of capabilities also presents opportunities for sensitive data to be shared with malicious phishing websites. The realm of mobile platforms introduces users to a distinct set of experiences, with hardware limitations being a crucial aspect. As major companies develop mobile applications to enhance user experiences, the spotlight on mobile phishing intensifies. Phishing applications exploit unsuspecting users to obtain their credentials, which are then stored on phishing servers. Detecting mobile phishing has proven challenging due to the lack of means to verify user credentials. This challenge is compounded by factors such as limited resources on mobile devices, the small screen size making it hard to distinguish phishing sites, and the lightweight nature of mobile browsers with limited security capabilities.

To address these complexities, specialized anti-phishing methods are necessary for both web pages and applications. This chapter introduces an effective strategy called Ontology-based Mobile Phishing Defense (OMPD) to counter phishing attacks on mobile platforms. OMPD leverages domain ontology to address identity theft issues. Optical Character Recognition (OCR) is employed to extract content from login interface screenshots. The extracted characters and URL-derived identity are then compared, and the user is alerted if discrepancies arise. OMPD targets account registry phishing variations by assessing account label consistency, application names, and authorized communication goals. The domain ontology provides insights into the safety of web page usage, identifying attack types and indicating whether a web page is secure.

In a parallel domain, the security of Unmanned Aircraft Systems (UAS), colloquially known as drones, is a paramount concern. UAS operates autonomously or under remote control and must be safeguarded against unauthorized access, breaches, and physical attacks. A promising approach involves integrating domain ontology to create a foundation for an antiphishing strategy. By defining legitimate entities, communication protocols, and behaviors in the UAS domain, such an approach could enhance the identification and prevention of phishing attacks, ultimately fortifying UAS security. A system based on a domain ontology is planned to be incorporated into the system's architecture. The architecture of the proposed Ontology-based Webpage Phish Defense (OWPD) is shown in Figure 5.

Figure 5. Architecture of the proposed ontology-based webpage phish defense

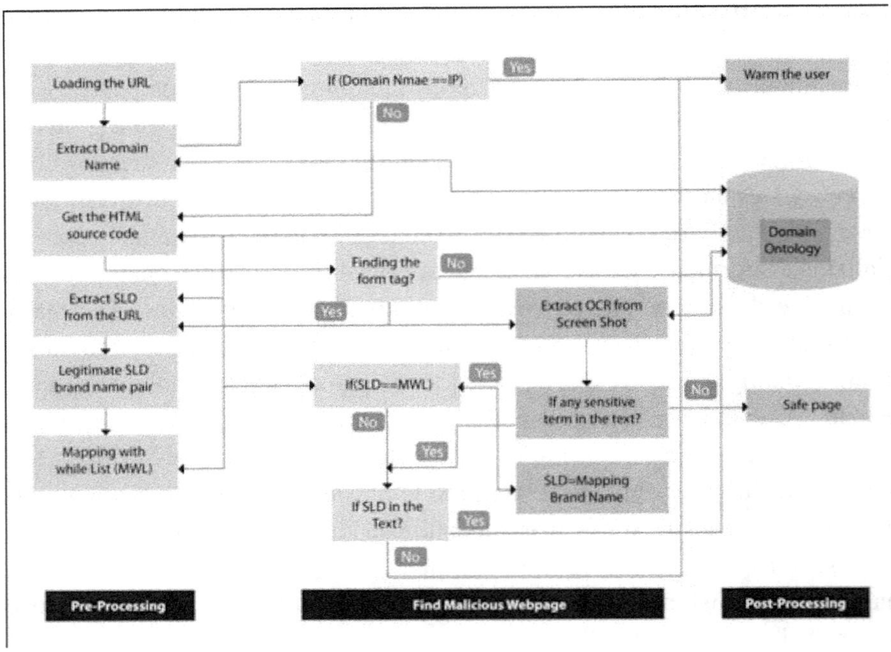

As an automated method of countering mobile phishing attacks, the OMPD system is recommended. Ontology-based Webpage Phish Defense (OWPD) and Ontology-based Account Phish Defense (OAPD) are the two main parts of the OMPD system. These features are meant to safeguard both persistent accounts and mobile web pages. The OWPD scheme starts with the loading of the URL. The OWPD scans the URL when the browser loads the webpage, and then it is sent to the ODB (Ontology Database) to investigate if the URL is valid or trusted. The contrast between an original site and a phishing site is that domain names are utilized as confirmations in the event of the trusted web pages, whereas the phishing site uses IP addresses. The user is intimated about a fake web page in case an IP address is used. The OWPD gets the loading page's HTML source code to find the page's form. The architecture of the proposed Ontology-based Account Phish Defense (OAPD)is shown in Figure 6.

Figure 6. Architecture of the proposed ontology-based account phish defense

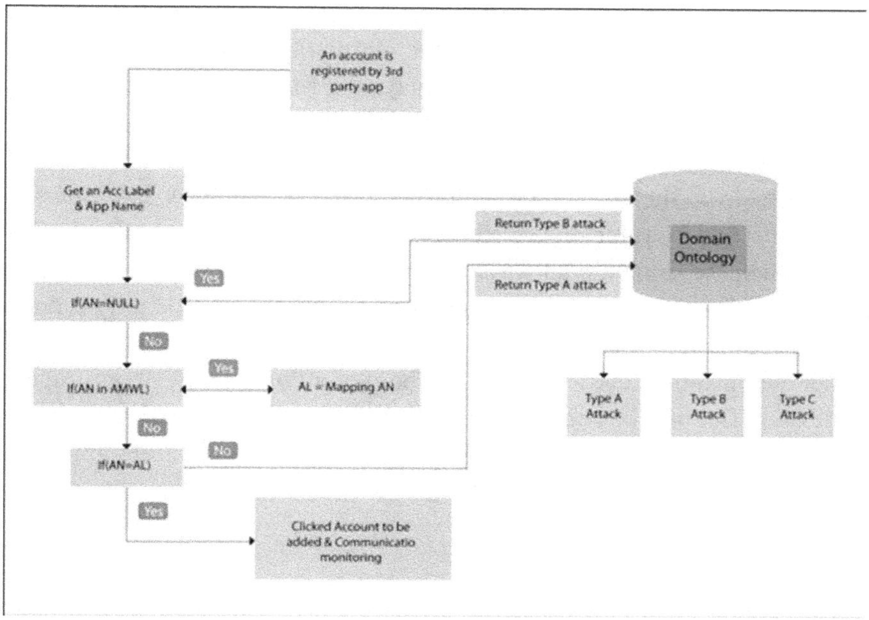

Here OCR and Mapping white list (MWL) is used for extracting the text from webpage screenshots and indexing SLD (second-level domain name). All the applications in the mobile are powerless against account registry phishing attacks as the clients may not recollect all the applications introduced in the gadget. The domain ontology is grouped in light of the three sorts of phishing attacks, specifically sort A, B, and C. In the sort A attack, the objective account gets an unexpected application compared to the original application (e.g., an amusement application enrolls a Facebook account). When an attack of type B is carried out, the malicious software is not presented in any capacity within the primary menu. In a type C attack, the harmful software is made to look like the lawful one, and the most common way this is accomplished is by adapting the same name. Because of this, the phony application will show up in the main menu with a name that is deceptively similar to the name of a valid account that can be discovered in the directory of accounts. It is feasible to detect phishing efforts directed at Account Type A and Account Type B by using a strategy that considers both the program name displayed in the main menu and the account name included in the account menu.

4. RESULTS AND DISCUSSION

The findings of the trials that evaluate the multi-stage structure are presented in Tables 1 and 2, respectively. Table 1 displays the findings obtained from putting the Latent Dirichlet Allocation (LDA) themes model through its paces. In order to evaluate how well the Latent Dirichlet Allocation (LDA) model holds up over time, datasets from the years 2006 and 2012 were compared. A 200 topics model produced a perplexity value of 230.15 when it was applied to the dataset from 2006; however, when the same model was applied to the dataset from 2012, it produced a perplexity value of 199.62. The enigma could not be significantly reduced by increasing the number of topics; hence, a model with 500 topics was utilized to construct the phishing classifier. With the help of all of these attributes together, a phishing classifier may be constructed. Probabilities of topic distributions using the Latent Dirichlet Allocation (LDA) algorithm and the formation of named entities using Conditional Random Fields (CRF).

Table 1. Time taken for computation

Total Number of Topic	Perplexity	Computation Time (Min)
100	245.85	6
200	230.15	15
300	214.65	25
400	199.62	33
500	186.15	48
Data Set : 6700- Phishing Email from Enron Email Dataset, 2014. 5687-Non Phishing Email from CSMINING Group, 2012.		

AdaBoost with a Random Forest weak learned are used to build the classifier. The 8-fold cross-validation results are shown in Table 2.

Table 2. Validation of phishing emails

Ratio of Phishing Emails	TPR	FPR	Precision	Recall	F-measure
50%	0.961	0.039	0.961	0.961	0.961
40%	0.987	0.013	0.987	0.987	0.987
30%	0.988	0.012	0.988	0.988	0.988
20%	1.0	0.0	1.0	1.0	1.0
10%	1.0	0.0	1.0	1.0	1.0
2.5%	1.0	0.002	1.0	1.0	1.0
Strategy: 8 fold Data Source : Enron Email Dataset(2006), CSMINING Group(2015), PhishTank (2010) Data Range: 10000 to 20000 (Number of emails)					

The comparison of multi-stage architecture in Table 1 is presented to show the effectiveness of architecture. The word orders are considered in CRF, and LDA does not consider them. Both Conditional Random Fields (CRF) and Latent Dirichlet Allocation (LDA) are mutually beneficial, as they produce reliable outcomes (see Figure 7). The comparative analysis of the suggested method's uniqueness and advantages is presented in Figure 7 in relation to other anti-phishing technologies such as Fuzzy DM, Phishguard, PhishWish, PHONEY, and FRALEC. Each algorithm has its own drawbacks. PILFER lacks in classifying the emails. PhishWish fails in the case of updating the patterns of phishing. FRALEC consumes more time because of layered design. But multi-stage fuzzy classifier overcomes all these drawbacks with better accuracy of 96.76%.(figure 8). The conventional single-stage fuzzy inference may not be well-suited for human activities due to the requirement of a substantial number of rules for developing the proposed approach. But multi-stage fuzzy needs a small set of rules to implement the proposed model. This is the major benefit brought by the proposed method.

Figure 7. Comparison of the multi-stage fuzzy classifier with other algorithms

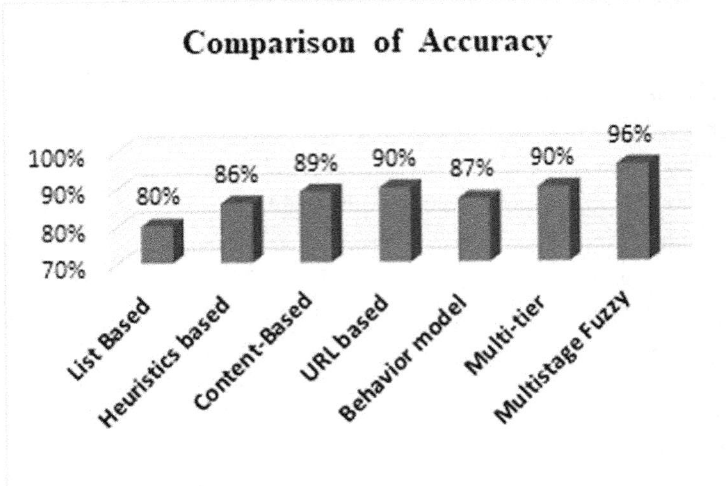

We compare the results of our suggested model to those of other Anti-Phishing Methods. Table 3 shows the comparison of anti-phishing techniques with a dataset.

Table 3. Comparison of anti-phishing techniques with a dataset

Phishing detectors/ parameters	Number of Legitimate Pages	Number of Phishing Pages	Total Pages in Dataset	TPR	FPR	ACC	Running Time (Min)
List-Based Anti-Phishing Approaches	100	200	300	88%	10%	80%	4
Heuristics based anti-phishing approaches	100	500	600	90%	13%	86%	5
Content-Based Phishing Analysis	500	1500	2000	89%	5%	89%	4
Detection of social profile cloning	300	800	1100	79%	12%	83%	7
URL based Phishing detectors	400	100	500	92%	10%	90%	4
Behavior model approach for testing phishing sites	1000	700	1700	88%	13%	87%	3
Hybrid neuro-fuzzy phishing detectors	5000	4000	9000	90%	8%	91%	4
Anti-phishing through Phishing Target Discovery	4000	2000	6000	85%	7%	92%	2
Multi-tier phishing detectors	3000	900	3900	90%	20%	90%	4
Our Model (Multi-Stage Classifier)	400	400	800	94%	2%	96%	6

Proposed method comes with many advantages compared to other methods in phishing webpage detection; it shows a low false positive rate and high accuracy. The running time is the main issue of this approach. The multi-stage classifier will take more time.

Figure 8. Accuracy comparison of different anti-phishing methods with multi-stage fuzzy classifier

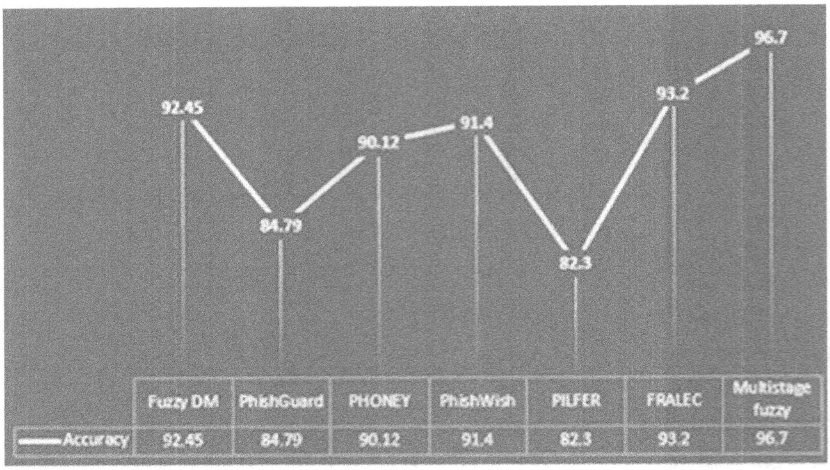

Additionally, the advocated methodology is successful in detecting forgeries. Our entity discovery technique is effective based on evidence gleaned from various data sources, including phishing emails, phishing URLs, and phishing websites. Any industry would benefit from utilizing our methodology. The prevention of phishing attempts and the detection of counterfeit goods are also possible applications for this method. When designing our methodology, we considered the many types of messages that MIME and HTML parsers can simply process. Our strategy took into account the availability of text as well as hyperlinks within the communication itself. Because of the visual character of some phishing communications, these attempts to deceive users cannot be uncovered using conventional parsing approaches. The primary focus of our subsequent research will be the development of improved techniques for recognizing phishing communications in all of its guises. The scalability problem must be the primary focus of future analyses. Our findings indicate that a more controlled experimental environment may produce more conclusive findings. The email server processes a significant amount of email daily, estimated to number in the billions of messages. Utilizing a framework like Hadoop MapReduce, explicitly designed with managing huge volumes of data in mind, is a common method for determining scalability. This is because this kind of framework was established specifically for Big Data.

In order to achieve the objectives of the Anti-Phishing Security for Unmanned Aircraft Systems initiative, a combination of semantic search and service-oriented architecture is being deployed. To determine how effective our system is, we measure it based on three different metrics: the True Positive Rate (TPR), the False Positive

Rate (FPR), and the Accuracy (ACC). For the purpose of this study, a dataset of 1200 authentic pages and 3374 phishing pages was utilized. The genuine web pages used to compile our dataset were acquired from the three different sources outlined in Table 4.

Table 4. Experimental results

	Phishing Pages	Legitimate Pages	Total
Total number of pages	10000	9800	19800
Number of correctly classified pages	9850	9600	19450

The pages included in our collection primarily focus on well-established and highly regarded websites that are widely recognized and referenced in reputable sources. Table 5 compares our test results and those obtained from different anti-phishing technologies.

Table 5. Comparison of our test results with those of other anti-phishing methods

Phishing detectors/ parameters	Number of Legitimate Pages	Number of Phishing Pages	Total Pages in Dataset	TPR	FPR	ACC	Running Time (Min)
List-Based Anti-Phishing Approaches	100	200	300	88%	10%	80%	4
Heuristics-based anti-phishing approaches	100	500	600	90%	13%	86%	5
Content-Based Phishing Analysis	500	1500	2000	89%	5%	89%	4
Detection of social profile cloning	300	800	1100	79%	12%	83%	7
URL based Phishing detectors	400	100	500	92%	10%	90%	4
Behavior model approach for testing phishing sites	1000	700	1700	88%	13%	87%	3
Hybrid neuro-fuzzy phishing detectors	5000	4000	9000	90%	8%	91%	4
Anti-phishing through Phishing Target Discovery	4000	2000	6000	85%	7%	92%	2
Multi-tier phishing detectors	3000	900	3900	90%	20%	90%	4
Multi-Stage Classifier	400	400	800	94%	2%	96%	6
Proposed Model	400	478	478	98%	1%	97%	9

This approach utilizes search engine results to distinguish fishiness from Webpages. Our semantic web crawler changes over HTML documents into OWL/RDF record format. Consequently, the temporal estimation of our framework is contingent upon the efficiency of the web crawler. The temporal duration would be increased as a result of any delays imposed by external factors. However, the current widespread access to high-speed internet and the abundance of other sources have effectively resolved this issue of bottleneck. According to Figure 9, the semantic search engine has a notably higher level of accuracy in comparison to both the fuzzy classifier and other anti-phishing strategies.

Figure 9. Comparison of semantic search engine with other algorithms

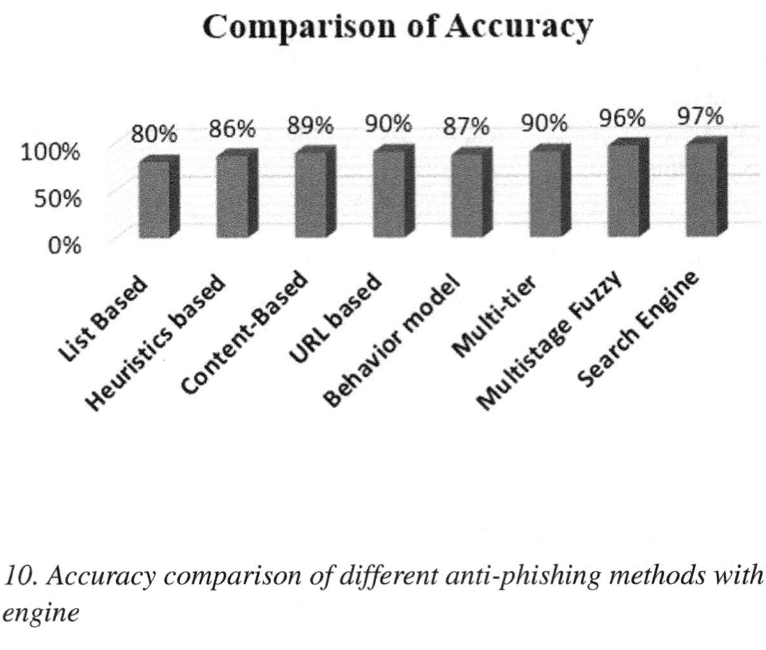

Figure 10. Accuracy comparison of different anti-phishing methods with semantic search engine

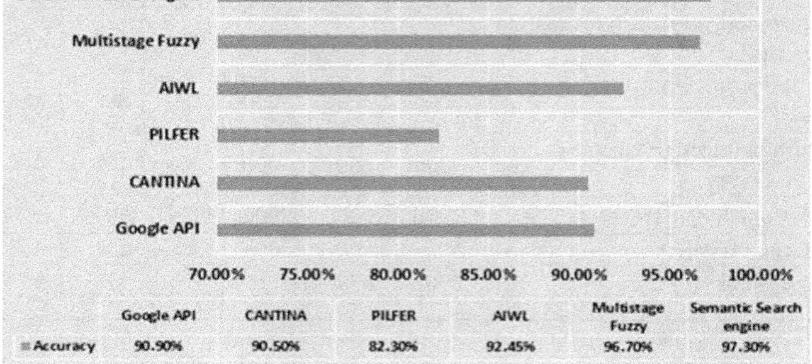

The novelty and advantages of the proposed approach are compared with other existing approaches, such as Google API, CANTINA, PILFER, and AIWL, as shown in Figure 10. AIWL is depending on how the user trains the dataset and browser. Google API needs high bandwidth in some cases and the CANTINA delays in queuing the search engine. The semantic search engine has overcome this drawback with a better accuracy of 97.3%. The top features of phishing is identified to improve the quality of the anti-phishing techniques.

4.1. In Sort of Detecting Wi-Fi Phishing Threats in Unmanned Aircraft Systems

Using Optimization Techniques, A query request is a strategy for identifying the type of a site. Different features have been used to learn about the particular information from those requests. We are in a position to hazard some educated predictions about the kind of website the user is attempting to access based on this data. This collection of roughly 1640 websites derived from various sources spans a broad spectrum of subjects and areas of interest. In a recent article, the distinctions between legitimate websites and phishing websites were examined. In Table 6, we have a list of 15 different phishing instances, along with the characteristics that are connected with them. Several different categories encompass a broad variety of characteristics, such as "Legitimate," "Suspicious," and "Phishy." The characteristics are partitioned into subsets according to the individual values of one, zero, and negative ones that they each have. Two classifications can be applied to a website: legitimate or phishing. The under-consideration algorithm generates a new category for websites, which it calls "Suspicious," and it bases this category on its own rules. If you have reason to doubt the authenticity of a website, you can divide it into one of two categories: either it exhibits characteristics common in phishing scams, or it is genuine and trustworthy. The customer is able to make a final decision after considering the relative weight that the criterion attaches to the test results. During the course of the experiment, a variety of rule acceptance and decision tree analysis techniques were put to the test. These techniques included CBA, MCAR, MMAC, C4.5, PART, and RIPPER. Most selection algorithms are rule-based and employ a wide range of learning approaches to compare and evaluate various scenarios.

Table 6. Sample phishing data for ten features

Request URL	Age	Sub domain	IP address	DNS record	URL length	Web traffic	URL with @	Prefix suffix	URL anchor
0	1	1	1	1	-1	0	1	1	1
1	1	1	-1	1	1	1	1	1	1
1	1	-1	1	1	1	1	1	1	1
0	0	1	1	1	0	-1	-1	1	0
1	-1	0	-1	1	0	1	1	1	1
-1	1	0	1	-1	1	1	1	1	1
1	0	1	1	1	-1	-1	1	1	1
1	1	1	1	1	1	1	0	1	-1
1	1	1	1	-1	0	0	1	-1	0
-1	1	-1	1	1	1	1	1	1	0
1	-1	1	1	-1	1	1	-1	1	1
1	1	0	-1	1	0	-1	1	1	1
0	0	1	1	1	1	1	-1	1	1
-1	1	-1	1	-1	1	-1	0	0	-1
1	1	0	1	1	-1	1	1	1	1

Accurately categorizing a phishing website is the goal of phishing categorization techniques. Table 7 shows the distinction between a legitimate website and a phishing page.

Table 7. Classification of phishing page

Actual Classes	**Predicted Classes**		
		Phishing	Legitimate
	Phishing	True Positive (TN)	False Negative (FN)
	Legitimate	False Positive (FP)	True Negative (TN)

To calculate the True Positive Rate (TPR), we divide the actual number of phishing sites found by the expected number of phishing sites. Using the following equation, we can determine the TPR.

$$TPR = \frac{TP}{P} = \frac{TP}{(TP + FN)}$$

In this context, TP represents the measure of phishing pages that have been correctly classified and grouped together. The variable P represents the total number of phishing pages, which is calculated by adding the number of correctly classified phishes (TP) to the number of missed phishes (FN). The False Positive Rate (FPR) quantifies the percentage of legitimate websites that are erroneously identified as phishing sites. The false positive rate (FPR) is calculated using the subsequent mathematical expression.

$$FPR = \frac{FP}{L} = \frac{FP}{(FP + FN)}$$

Let FP represent the number of authentic website pages that have been inaccurately classified as phishing, and let L denote the total number of legitimate pages.

Table 8. Evaluation of phishing and legitimate pages

Actual Classes	Predicted Classes		
		Phishing	Legitimate
	Phishing	100%	0%
	Legitimate	3.1%	96.9%

The findings of a study performed on both phishing and genuine online banking websites included in our dataset are displayed in Table 8. The findings demonstrate that the recommended rule-based extension is successful one hundred percent of the time in spotting phishing URLs when applied in online banking. Despite this, it is only accurate 3.1% of the time when attempting to recognize authentic websites. Rearranging the features does not change the sensitivity of the proposed model. Based on the accuracy rate and fitness value, features are rearranged in Table 9. The rearrangement is mainly based on the highly influenced feature in phishing that comes first in order. The optimally performing rearrangement features for phishing detection are depicted in Figures 8 and 9, which show the true positive rate and false positive rate patterns, respectively.

Table 9. Rearranged features

Extracted Website Feature	TPR %	FPR%
Request URL	99.31%	0.69%
Age of domain	99.12%	0.88%
Website Traffic	99.02%	0.98%
Misuse of HTTP protocol	98.97%	1.03%
Long URL	98.81%	1.19%
Subdomain	98.63%	1.37%
Prefix and suffix	98.47%	1.53%
URL of anchor	98.32%	1.68%
Hiding the links	98.28%	1.72%
IP address	98.20%	1.8%
Abnormal URL	98.14%	1.86%
Pop up window	98.08%	1.92%
Redirect page	97.65%	2.35%
DNS record	97.42%	2.58%
URL with @ symbol	97.31%	2.69%
Server form handler	96.85%	3.15%

The following is a list of the most typical indicators that are used to assess the effectiveness of the algorithm: The level of accuracy achieved by the classifiers. The size of the classifier has been brought up as a potential source of disagreement. As a result of decreasing the number of available features, the accuracy has suffered.

Figure 11. Flow of TPR percentage of the arranged features

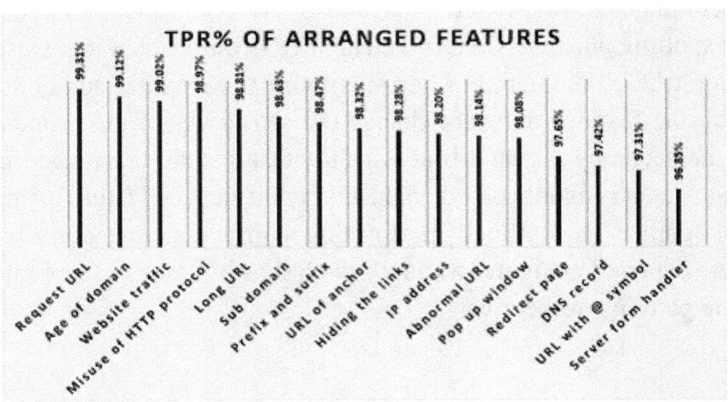

Figure 12. Flow of FPR percentage of the arranged features

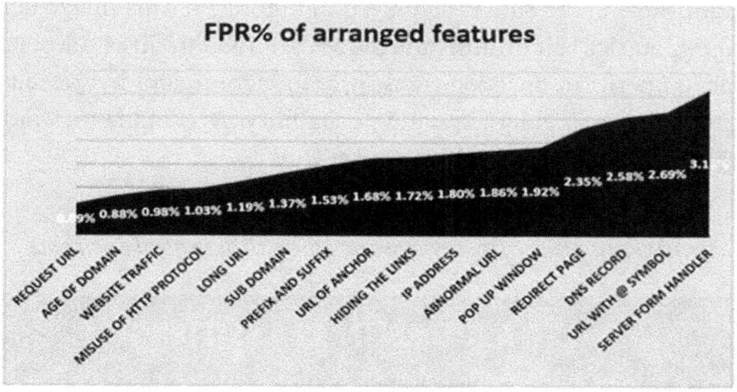

Figure 13. Accuracy percentage of different algorithms

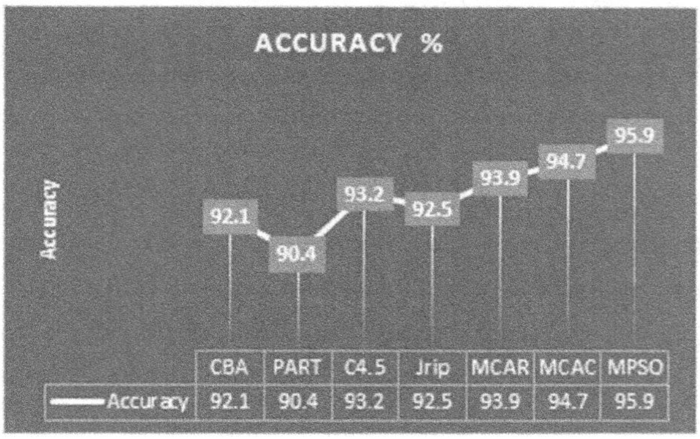

Figure 13 summarizes the prediction accuracy (expressed as a percentage) reached by the algorithms applied to the dataset used for the larger-featured phishing challenge. The visual depiction demonstrates that the PSAO algorithm fared significantly better than any of the other algorithms when it came to accurately predicting the sorts of websites based on the provided rules. In conclusion, it can be observed that the accuracy of the algorithms' predictions was significantly higher than the average. Because it can extract numerous classes from a single rule and generate all potential classes in a manner that is unique to each one, the MPSO technique demonstrates impressively accurate prediction.

It is uncommon for existing algorithms to consider additional variables, even though doing so could improve their capacity for prediction and make them more appropriate for end users. The total number of rules that were generated by applying all of the algorithms to the data is displayed in Figure 14. This image demonstrates how AC (Aho-Corasick) algorithms and the MCAR (Multi-Class Association Rule), in particular, outperform decision trees, rule induction, and hybrid classification approach regarding their rule-generating capability. AC stands for Aho-Corasick, while MCAR is for Multi-Class Association Rule.

Figure 14. Average number of rules generated by different algorithms

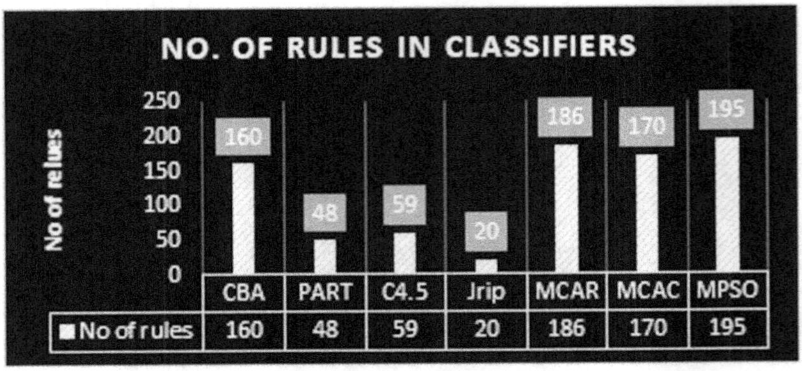

Exhaustive classifiers are utilized by every Aho-Corasick (AC) algorithm throughout the training phase to accurately compute the associations between the values of the attributes and the values of the classes. This function, which originates from the field of association rule mining, enables the training instance to be utilized multiple times in the rule learning process. This function was brought over from that field. On the other hand, conventional classification methods are only capable of applying a single rule to every training example. When contrasted with the MCAR methodology, the MPSO algorithm generates a greater number of rules. Using the MPSO method, we determined the fitness value and established a select few of the elements that make up the experimental setup. Because of this, it is possible to make an educated guess as to the category the website falls under based on its features. In addition, during the process of selecting the features to be used, having fewer characteristics to choose from makes it easier to eliminate attributes that are not relevant. This transpires due to the training dataset containing qualities that are not pertinent to the task at hand. The primary purpose of this investigation is to identify the minimum number of features that can adequately describe the phenomenon under investigation. Nine of a website's fifteen components have been found to have a substantial correlation, leading researchers to hypothesize that these components could play a role in the phishing detection technique. Various characteristics are taken into consideration and examined, including IP Address Use, Request URL, Domain Age, HTTPS, Website Traffic, Long URL, SFH, Pop-Up window, Anchor URL, and Redirect URL.

Table 10. Comparison of different algorithms

Algorithms	CBA	PART	C4.5	Grip	MCAR	MCAC	MPSO
No rules generated	160	48	59	20	186	170	195
Accuracy rate after reducing features	92.1	90.4	92.2	91.5	92.4	94.7	95.1
Execution time	4.128	4.937	4.273	4.682	4.015	3.997	3.619

In order to highlight how distinctive and advantageous the proposed method is, it is contrasted with established methodologies such as CBA, PART, C4.5, MCAR, and MPSO. The results of the experiment's methodology, when applied to a more limited number of attributes, are outlined in Table 10. These results illustrate how accurate the classification was. The following table provides a summary of the required amount of time and the total number of rules generated by the various approaches. According to the findings, there was no significant deviation from the original accuracy of the classification. When all of the feature sets are considered, the results show that there is only an average loss in classification accuracy of 0.8%. Therefore, it can be deduced that feature sets with fewer options help classify the different kinds of websites. Everyone who connects their device to a public Wi-Fi network should take additional precautions to ensure the privacy of their data while it is being transmitted over the network. However, it is essential to remember that connecting to the internet over a public Wi-Fi hotspot does not necessarily ensure a secure connection. In this chapter, the problem mentioned above was analyzed, and a workable solution was suggested in the following manner:

Participants in a phishing scam showed no concern or suspicion in controlled studies within real-world networks. The association-mining rule is a new approach used in this chapter to determine the solution. The algorithm, Modified Particle Swarm Optimization (MPSO), has been developed that helps the user to find out if the website is genuine or fake. Implementing Unmanned Aircraft System Security through Domain Ontology-Based Antiphishing Approaches there involves the Disregarding of how the PC programs have blocked the phishing sites; they can be identified using versatile programs. The "repackaged" Twitter application has been produced to outline the sort C attack, and again, it likewise gets distinguished by the OAPD amid the account enlistment, as shown in Figure 15.

Figure 15. Performance of OWPD and OAPD

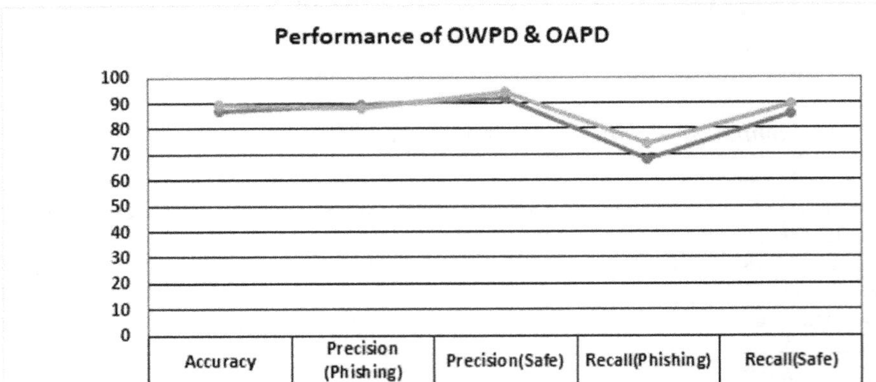

	Accuracy	Precision (Phishing)	Precision(Safe)	Recall(Phishing)	Recall(Safe)
OWPD	87.02	89.21	92.12	68.32	85.67
OAPD	89.28	88.05	94.15	74.15	89.2

The execution of the OWPD is evaluated by the estimation of the execution time of this plan. The OWPD uses three primary approaches, namely, the building of a domain ontology, the extraction of SLD from the isolated content of a snapshot, and the brief blocking of SMS and socket connections. Reading issues that take up a lot of a person's time can be alleviated with the help of optical character recognition (OCR) technology for people with specific learning disabilities (SLD). The processing time for a document can then be compared with OCR-based approaches and others that do not depend on optical character recognition in this manner. The findings are presented in Table 11. The OCR-based solutions consist of three discrete phases: capturing a screenshot, isolating the textual data within that screenshot, and determining whether or not a particular structured layout design (SLD) is present. These steps are performed in order.

Table 11. Average execution time of OMPD scheme

Techniques	Phases	Execution time	
OCR Based techniques	Taking screenshot	0.017	3.328
	OCR extraction	3.212	
	SLD searching	0.099	
Non-OCR technique	Timestamp comparison	0.027	

It takes around 0.017 seconds to complete the first step, 3.212 seconds to complete the second, and 0.099 seconds to complete the third. It has been determined that the OCR extraction phase accounts for 3.212 seconds out of the total 3.328-second delay. In an experiment developed for non-OCR systems, the amount of time it takes for a text message and its attachment to a link was measured. The latency overhead is extremely low, clocking in at only 0.027 seconds, as only a single correlation of two timestamps is required to determine if the blocking time frame has ended. Figure 16 illustrates the various ways in which OMPD stands apart from other anti-phishing strategies.

Figure 16. Comparison of different anti-phishing methods with OMPD

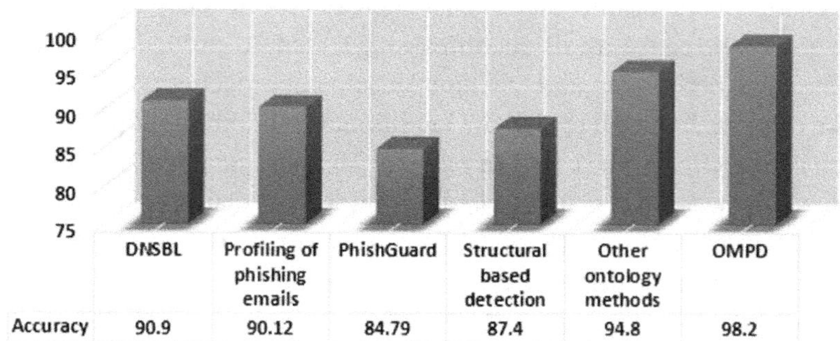

The novelty and advantages of the OMPD approach are compared with other phishing detection methods like DNSBL, profiling of phishing emails, phishing guard, structural feature-based detection, and other ontology methods, as shown in Figure 14. In DNSBL, if packages associated with the web server and system are not reliable, addresses from which the system could get mail may get blocked. PhishGuard needs an updation of rules for every detection. Structural feature-based detection and other ontology methods only apply to small data sizes. However, OMPD provides better accuracy of 98.2 than other approaches. The benefit brought by the proposed method is that OMPD can be used for large data sets and there is no need for a rule upgrade.

5. CONCLUSION

In conclusion, while phishing attacks have traditionally targeted individuals and organizations through conventional communication channels, their potential impact on unmanned aircraft systems (UAS) or drones cannot be ignored. Although less frequent in this domain, UAS operations and data can be compromised through phishing tactics. This chapter highlighted the vulnerabilities and potential risks of phishing attacks on UAS and proposed strategies to counter them. The chapter shed light on the deceptive techniques attackers could employ to impersonate legitimate UAS entities, exploiting the operators' trust. These tactics involve crafting convincing emails containing attachments or links that lead to malware infiltration. The malware jeopardizes the operators' systems and can infect the drones themselves when connected for operational purposes.

Furthermore, the chapter outlined how phishing attacks could be used to extract login credentials, providing unauthorized access to operational systems and data. Additionally, attackers might use fraudulent payment requests to deceive recipients into disclosing financial information. To decrease the severity of the damage that these dangers could cause, an all-encompassing and multi-pronged strategy that uses natural language processing and machine learning approaches was developed. This study takes a more in-depth look into Conditional Random Field (CRF) along with Latent Dirichlet Allocation (LDA) in recognizing manipulated data and identifying phishing attempts. A novel web crawler leveraging Web Ontology Language (OWL) was introduced to filter out fake sites from search results by exploiting semantic relationships. Moreover, the work extended its focus to Wi-Fi and mobile phishing, proposing countermeasures using Association Rule mining and an anti-phishing ontology scheme (OMPDef). These countermeasures aim to prevent attacks across various platforms. The experimental results showcased the efficacy of the proposed methods in detecting and preventing phishing attacks within the UAS domain and across different platforms. Considering the multi-faceted nature of phishing threats and employing advanced technological approaches, the research work offers a promising foundation for safeguarding unmanned aircraft systems against potential phishing risks.

REFERENCES

Alheeti, K. M. A., Al-Ani, M. S., Al-Aloosy, A. K. N., Alzahrani, A., & Rukan, D. A. S. (2022). Intelligent mobile detection of cracks in concrete utilising an unmanned aerial vehicle. *Bulletin of Electrical Engineering and Informatics*, *11*(1), 176–184. doi:10.11591/eei.v11i1.2987

Ali, Khan, Riaz, Kwak, & Abuhmed. (2017). A Fuzzy Ontology and SVM–Based Web Content Classification System. *IEEE Access*. doi:10.1109/ACCESS.2017.2768564

Alkahtani, H., & Aldhyani, T. H. (2021). Intrusion detection system to advance internet of things infrastructure-based deep learning algorithms. *Complexity*, *2021*, 1–18. doi:10.1155/2021/5579851

Allouch, A., Cheikhrouhou, O., Koubâa, A., Khalgui, M., & Abbes, T. (2019, June). MAVSec: Securing the MAVLink protocol for ardupilot/PX4 unmanned aerial systems. In 2019 15th International Wireless Communications & Mobile Computing Conference (IWCMC) (pp. 621-628). IEEE.

Almahmoud, S., Hammo, B., Al-Shboul, B., & Obeid, N. (2022). A hybrid approach for identifying non-human traffic in online digital advertising. *Multimedia Tools and Applications*, *81*(2), 1–34. doi:10.100711042-021-11533-4

Aminanto, M. E., Choi, R., Tanuwidjaja, H. C., Yoo, P. D., & Kim, K. (2017). Deep abstraction and weighted feature selection for Wi-Fi impersonation detection. *IEEE Transactions on Information Forensics and Security*, *13*(3), 621–636. doi:10.1109/TIFS.2017.2762828

Aravindhan, R., Shanmugalakshmi, R., Ramya, K., & Selvan, C. (2016). Certain investigation on web application security: Phishing detection and phishing target discovery. *3rd International Conference on Advanced Computing and Communication Systems (ICACCS).*

Aslan, M. F., Durdu, A., Yusefi, A., & Yilmaz, A. (2022). HVIOnet: A deep learning based hybrid visual–inertial odometry approach for unmanned aerial system position estimation. *Neural Networks*, *155*, 461–474. doi:10.1016/j.neunet.2022.09.001 PMID:36152378

Bagui, S., Nandi, D., Bagui, S., & White, R. J. (2021). Machine learning and deep learning for phishing email classification using one-hot encoding. *Journal of Computational Science*, *17*(7), 610–623. doi:10.3844/jcssp.2021.610.623

Balogh, S., Gallo, O., Ploszek, R., Špaček, P., & Zajac, P. (2021). IoT security challenges: Cloud and blockchain, postquantum cryptography, and evolutionary techniques. *Electronics (Basel)*, *10*(21), 2647. doi:10.3390/electronics10212647

Bu, S. J., & Kim, H. J. (2022). Optimized URL feature selection based on genetic-algorithm-embedded deep learning for phishing website detection. *Electronics (Basel)*, *11*(7), 1090. doi:10.3390/electronics11071090

Decker, C., & Chiambaretto, P. (2022). Economic policy choices and trade-offs for Unmanned aircraft systems Traffic Management (UTM): Insights from Europe and the United States. *Transportation Research Part A, Policy and Practice*, *157*, 40–58. doi:10.1016/j.tra.2022.01.006

Faughnan, M. S., Hourican, B. J., MacDonald, G. C., Srivastava, M., Wright, J. P. A., Haimes, Y. Y., Andrijcic, E., Guo, Z., & White, J. C. (2013, April). *Risk analysis of unmanned aerial vehicle hijacking and methods of its detection. In 2013 IEEE systems and information engineering design symposium*. IEEE.

Heinzl, B., & Kastner, W. (2019). Platform-independent Modeling for Simulation-based Energy Optimization in Industrial Production. *International Journal of Simulation: Systems, Science and Technology*, *20*(6), 10–11.

Hildmann, H., & Kovacs, E. (2019). Using unmanned aerial vehicles (UAVs) as mobile sensing platforms (MSPs) for disaster response, civil security and public safety. *Drones (Basel)*, *3*(3), 59. doi:10.3390/drones3030059

Huang, L., & Zhu, Q. (2019). Adaptive strategic cyber defense for advanced persistent threats in critical infrastructure networks. *Performance Evaluation Review*, *46*(2), 52–56. doi:10.1145/3305218.3305239

Hussain, F., Hussain, R., Hassan, S. A., & Hossain, E. (2020). Machine learning in IoT security: Current solutions and future challenges. *IEEE Communications Surveys and Tutorials*, *22*(3), 1686–1721. doi:10.1109/COMST.2020.2986444

Illiashenko, O., Kharchenko, V., Babeshko, I., Fesenko, H., & Di Giandomenico, F. (2023). Security-Informed Safety Analysis of Autonomous Transport Systems Considering AI-Powered Cyberattacks and Protection. *Entropy (Basel, Switzerland)*, *25*(8), 1123. doi:10.3390/e25081123 PMID:37628153

Joyner, C. C., & Lotrionte, C. (2017). Information warfare as international coercion: Elements of a legal framework. In *The Use of Force in International Law* (pp. 433–473). Routledge. doi:10.4324/9781315084992-18

Kirlappos, I., & Sasse, M. A. (2011). Security education against phishing: A modest proposal for a major rethink. *IEEE Security and Privacy*, *10*(2), 24–32. doi:10.1109/MSP.2011.179

Liu, Y., Wang, J., Niu, S., & Song, H. (2020). Deep learning enabled reliable identity verification and spoofing detection. *Wireless Algorithms, Systems, and Applications: 15th International Conference, WASA 2020, Qingdao, China, September 13–15, 2020 Proceedings*, *15*(Part I), 333–345.

Manesh, M. R., Kenney, J., Hu, W. C., Devabhaktuni, V. K., & Kaabouch, N. 2019, January. Detection of GPS spoofing attacks on unmanned aerial systems. In 2019 16th IEEE Annual Consumer Communications & Networking Conference (CCNC) (pp. 1-6). IEEE. doi:10.1109/CCNC.2019.8651804

Meidan, Y., Bohadana, M., Mathov, Y., Mirsky, Y., Shabtai, A., Breitenbacher, D., & Elovici, Y. (2018). N-baiot—Network-based detection of iot botnet attacks using deep autoencoders. *IEEE Pervasive Computing*, *17*(3), 12–22. doi:10.1109/MPRV.2018.03367731

Mourtaji, Y., Bouhorma, M., Alghazzawi, D., Aldabbagh, G., & Alghamdi, A. (2021). Hybrid Rule-Based Solution for Phishing URL Detection Using Convolutional Neural Network. Hindawi Wireless Communications and Mobile Computing. doi:10.1155/2021/8241104

Nichols, R. K., Mumm, H. C., Lonstein, W. D., Ryan, J. J., Carter, C., & Hood, J. P. (2020). *Counter unmanned aircraft systems technologies and operations*. New Prairie Press.

Otter, D. W., Medina, J. R., & Kalita, J. K. (2020). A survey of the usages of deep learning for natural language processing. *IEEE Transactions on Neural Networks and Learning Systems*, *32*(2), 604–624. doi:10.1109/TNNLS.2020.2979670 PMID:32324570

Pandey, Gurjar, Nguyen, & Yadav. (n.d.). Security Threats and Mitigation Techniques in UAV Communications: A Comprehensive Survey. *IEEE Access*. doi:10.1109/ACCESS.2022.3215975

Rahman, M. A., Asyhari, A. T., Wen, O. W., Ajra, H., Ahmed, Y., & Anwar, F. (2021). Effective combining of feature selection techniques for machine learning-enabled IoT intrusion detection. *Multimedia Tools and Applications*, *80*(20), 1–19. doi:10.100711042-021-10567-y

Rochlin, G. I., La Porte, T. R., & Roberts, K. H. (1987). The self-designing high-reliability organization: Aircraft carrier flight operations at sea. *Naval War College Review*, *40*(4), 76–92.

Sheng, S., Holbrook, M., Kumaraguru, P., Cranor, L. F., & Downs, J. (2010, April). Who falls for phish? A demographic analysis of phishing susceptibility and effectiveness of interventions. In *Proceedings of the SIGCHI conference on human factors in computing systems* (pp. 373-382). 10.1145/1753326.1753383

Syed, A. H. M., & Nawaf, Q. H. O. (2023). Yanlong Li1, Mohammed H. Alsharif, Muhammad Asghar Khan, Unmanned aerial vehicles (UAVs): Practical aspects, applications, open challenges, security issues, and future trends. *Intelligent Service Robotics*, *16*, 109–137. doi:10.100711370-022-00452-4 PMID:36687780

Wallace, R. J., & Loffi, J. M. (2015). Examining unmanned aerial system threats & defenses: A conceptual analysis. *International Journal of Aviation, Aeronautics, and Aerospace*, *2*(4), 1. doi:10.15394/ijaaa.2015.1084

Wang, J., Liu, Y., & Song, H. (2021). Counter-unmanned aircraft system (s)(C-UAS): State of the art, challenges, and future trends. *IEEE Aerospace and Electronic Systems Magazine*, *36*(3), 4–29. doi:10.1109/MAES.2020.3015537

Weaver, N., Paxson, V., Staniford, S., & Cunningham, R. (2003, October). A taxonomy of computer worms. In *Proceedings of the 2003 ACM workshop on Rapid Malcode* (pp. 11-18). 10.1145/948187.948190

Yaacoub, J.-P., Noura, H., Salman, O., & Chehab, A. (2020, September). Security analysis of drones systems: Attacks, limitations, and recommendations. *Internet of Things : Engineering Cyber Physical Human Systems*, *11*, 100218. Advance online publication. doi:10.1016/j.iot.2020.100218

Yerima, S. Y., & Alzaylaee, M. K. (2020, March). High accuracy phishing detection based on convolutional neural networks. In *2020 3rd International Conference on Computer Applications & Information Security (ICCAIS)* (pp. 1-6). IEEE. 10.1109/ICCAIS48893.2020.9096869

Chapter 8
Threat Modeling and Risk Analysis for Cloud Deployments

Prathibha Muraleedhara
https://orcid.org/0009-0004-5870-5633
Stanley Black & Decker, USA

ABSTRACT

Today, most of the solutions and applications are migrated to cloud platforms. All the cloud service providers (CSP) employ a shared responsibility model. This means the cloud providers are responsible for the security "of the cloud" and the customers are responsible for the security "in the cloud." Based on research it is stated that 95% of cloud security breaches are because of user misconfigurations. Cloud security almost entirely depends on the consumers configuring and using the cloud platform. Thus, it is important to understand the threat landscape of cloud implementations, the risks involved, and ways to remediate them. One of the earliest and most important processes is threat modeling. This process helps in analyzing the cloud architecture, identifying security threats, evaluating risks, and prioritizing remediation efforts. This chapter describes how to apply some of the popular threat modeling frameworks to access cloud architectures.

Today all small and large-scale enterprises are migrating their solutions from on-premises to cloud. Cloud deployments provide several benefits for organizations with limited processing capabilities, storage, resources, and workforce. It provides flexibility and scalability, where teams can easily spin up virtual machines and other resources based on demand. It does not require the maintenance of physical

DOI: 10.4018/979-8-3693-3249-8.ch008

servers and is cost-effective. Cloud deployments increase performance with hardly any downtime as it automatically launches load-balancing servers based on demand. It is easy to serve a global audience as it provides capabilities to split data across multiple regional data centers. Cloud platforms have simplified resource management by providing a central interface to configure and manage all services including backup and recovery tools that increase their reliability.

Cloud Service Providers (CSP) offer cloud services based on one of the three cloud service models. In the Software as a Service (SaaS) model, the CSPs manage all the underlying infrastructure including the storage drives, virtual machines, operating systems, network components, and application capabilities and services. The customers have no control over the underlying infrastructure, nor the applications hosted. In the Platform as a Service (PaaS) cloud service model, the CSPs manage all the underlying infrastructure, but the customers have control over the applications and services hosted. As part of the Infrastructure as a Service (IaaS) model, the CSP still manages all the underlying infrastructure, but the customers have more control over certain services like storage, operating systems, network components like host firewalls, and complete access to manage and configure the hosted applications.

With respect to security, cloud security providers follow the shared responsibility model (Shea Tally, 2023). This is a security and compliance framework that describes the responsibilities of the CSPs and the customers in securing the cloud environment including the network components, infrastructure, hardware, virtual machines, operating systems, storage, endpoints, and access controls. It states that the service providers are responsible for the security of the cloud environment itself and the underlying infrastructure like the data centers, hardware, storage drives, virtual machines, network components, and gateways. There is a misconception that the security of the cloud is completely the responsibility of the cloud service provider and that is not true. The customers are responsible for securely configuring the cloud services, the security of the applications hosted, and the data stored and processed in the cloud. Today, most of the security breaches in the cloud are due to insecure configurations and human errors made by the customers. Thus, customers play a significant role in securing the cloud environment. It is important to educate cloud customers regarding the cloud threat landscape and the security risks involved.

CLOUD COMPUTING SECURITY THREATS

The Cloud Security Alliance (CSA) (2022) recently published its annual report on cloud security top threats. The CSA working group surveyed over seven hundred experts and professionals in the cloud security domain to prepare this report. Below is the list of top cloud security threats in the order of significance:

Insufficient Identity, Credentials, Access, and Key Management

Access to cloud resources and services is provided by authenticating and validating the identity of the users. Identities are not only assigned to users but also to services like virtual machines, storage systems, databases, serverless functions, containers, and other resources. It is important to always follow the least privilege and zero trust policies. Frequent gap analysis should be performed to compare what permissions the users/roles are assigned versus what is really required so that unnecessary permissions can be removed. The service/client credentials, secrets, keys, and tokens should never be hardcoded in config files and client-side code. They must be securely stored and managed using cloud-native services like AWS Secrets Manager, Azure Key Vault, and CyberArk. These credentials and secrets should be frequently rotated as per the organization's IT policies.

Insecure Interfaces and APIs

Application Programming Interfaces (APIs) facilitate communication between applications and services. APIs are prone to several security exploits due to misconfigurations, broken authentication, improper access control, insecure coding practices, and lack of encryption. Application developers need to implement security controls like input validation, rate limiting, integrity validation, security headers, access controls, and sufficient logging and monitoring. Strong authentication methods like OAuth2 or mutual TLS should be implemented. APIs should use HTTPs with TLS version 1.2 or above. Internal APIs should not be exposed to the internet and must be restricted using appropriate security groups.

Misconfiguration and Inadequate Change Control

It's very easy to spin up new cloud services and resources like virtual machines, databases, and container nodes based on demand. However, this flexibility may lead to misconfigurations and security vulnerabilities. Services can be launched, replicated, and distributed in minutes and if there are any vulnerabilities or misconfigurations in the base image, it will be repeated throughout. Teams may spin up new servers or databases and continue to reconfigure them based on specific requirements. However, it is very difficult to keep track of all the changes in the whole infrastructure. It is the responsibility of the customers to keep track of what resources are used, how they are configured, and the history of all configuration changes made. Frequent configuration scans should be performed to detect any errors as the cloud environment and the threat landscape are ever-changing.

Lack of Cloud Security Architecture and Strategy

Every organization should publish cloud security guardrails that can be followed by all the application teams. The guardrails and policies should clearly define the responsibilities of the developers in securing the cloud deployments. The guardrails should highlight policies around principles of least privilege, encryption of data at rest and in transit, principles of separation of duties, sufficient logging and monitoring, server hardening requirements, network security, and establishing of segmented VLANs using firewalls to limit damage during an exploit.

Insecure Software Development

There are several options available for developers to build an application. They can use SDKs, and browser extensions, download code from public Git repositories, use containerized packages to deliver applications, and access cloud-based SaaS CI/CD tools to build, test, and deploy applications. All organizations should define and mandate Secure Development Lifecycle (SDLC) standards. If the development tools and processes are not properly defined and securely configured, it may lead to several security vulnerabilities.

Unsecured Third-Party Resources

Applications are built using several third-party components, libraries, packages, and open-source codes. If a vulnerability is identified in one such component, all the industry applications using that component will be affected. Thus, is it important to always patch and update the images, software, and libraries to the latest versions. Only use components from trusted suppliers who practice open reporting of vulnerabilities and commit to release fixes and patches regularly.

System Vulnerabilities

New security vulnerabilities are continuously discovered. Hence, it is important to run frequent scans to detect system security flaws. There are many third-party tools and cloud services available to scan the cloud resources used and to detect security vulnerabilities. Application teams must make sure that all the system images are patched and updated to the latest versions.

Accidental Cloud Data Disclosure

All cloud resources should have proper access control policies defined. The principle of least privilege should be followed when defining the identity and access policies. Otherwise, this may lead to unauthorized access to application data. Another scenario of data disclosure is developers hardcoding client credentials in config files and uploading the code to shared public repositories like GitHub. These credentials can be stolen and misused by malicious users. Proper precautions should be taken while handling credentials on the client side.

Misconfiguration and Exploitation of Serverless and Container Workloads

Today, most of the applications are containerized to make them platform agnostic. The container images should be scanned early in the development process to detect and prevent security vulnerabilities. Never download images from unknown sources. Also, continuous runtime security scanning should be performed to detect vulnerabilities, malware, and other security threats in the container images. The solution must capture and monitor OS logs, container logs, and application logs from the containers and host operating systems.

Organized Crime, Hackers, and APTs

There is always an attempt from advanced persistent threat groups to compromise exposed applications. Thus, organizations should proactively implement behavior-based detection capabilities to detect cloud security threats based on suspicious behaviors such as discovery, lateral movement, and vertical escalations.

Cloud Storage Data Exfiltration

Data exfiltration is the final goal of most of the hackers. Thus, extra measures should be taken to protect company data. The first step is to classify the organization's data into restricted, confidential, personally identifiable information (PII) and public data. Then apply security policies on the classified data, such as encrypt at rest and in transit, access restrictions, authentication, MFA, network segmentations, and data lifecycle policies.

CLOUD THREAT MODELING

It is important for organizations to evaluate the cloud architectures and designs early in the process, so that if any security threats are identified the architecture can be updated with additional security controls. Threat modeling can be performed to achieve this goal. It is a proactive analysis of the system/solution attack surface, point of entry, security threats, and ways to mitigate the identified risk. Threat modeling adopts the attacker's perspective to identify and analyze the security threats. Several threat modeling frameworks can be followed to identify the threats, such as OWASP Top 10, MITRE ATT&CK Framework, STRIDE, DREAD, PASTA, OCTAVE, and NIST.

The Process for Attack Simulation and Threat Analysis (PASTA) framework explains seven steps that should be followed to identify, count, and prioritize security threats (Tony & Marco, 2015). The framework elaborates the process of defining objectives, scope, decomposing the application, analyzing the security threats, vulnerabilities, modeling the attacks, and finally analyzing the risk and impact. It helps in archiving business objectives while complying with security policies.

STRIDE is a Microsoft threat modeling framework that describes ways to identify security attack vectors, analyze the threat risk/impact, and prioritize mitigation efforts (Hewko Alex, 2021). It is used to analyze the architecture diagram and enumerate different threats and vulnerabilities that a malicious user may exploit to compromise the system. This may include:

Spoofing – Violation of authenticity and pretending to possess the identity of someone or something other than yourself.

Tampering – Violation of integrity. Modifying information/data within the memory, disk, network, or any data in transit or at rest.

Repudiation – Performing an action and falsely claiming that you did not perform that action.

Information Disclosure – Violation of confidentiality. Providing unauthorized access to data/information.

Denial of Service – Violation of availability. Consuming all resources so that legitimate users are denied service.

Elevation of Privilege – Violation of authorization. Allowing unauthorized low-privilege users to access higher-privilege or admin features.

THREAT MODELING METHODOLOGY

The steps involved in cloud threat modeling are similar to on-prem systems. However, the architecture components, services, and mitigation requirements will differ. The cloud thread modeling includes the following steps:

Architecture Diagram

The first step in cloud threat modeling is to visually depict the solution architecture. Several tools can be used to create this visual depiction. The architecture diagram will include all network boundaries including VPCs, availability zones, private/public subnets, internal and external networks. Also, it includes cloud services used such as virtual machines, databases, middleware layers, serverless functions, container clusters, storage services, connection details including protocols/ports, authentication, authorization, and network services like load balances, NAT gateways, firewalls, and entry points. This gives a complete visual depiction of the implemented solution.

Asset Classification

Organization assets include data, software, hardware, technology, products, services, and other valuable resources owned. It is important to protect these assets from unauthorized malicious users and security breaches. Thus, an inventory of all the company assets should be created and maintained. Once all the assets are identified, they must be classified based on their criticality measured by accessing confidentiality, availability, and integrity impacts. The assets are mainly classified into private information, financial assets, application assets, computing, and network assets. Industrial asset management tools can be used to identify company assets, the security risk associated, and ways to mitigate the risk.

Threat and Vulnerability Identification

Most exploitable weaknesses in a solution are inherent to the technology stack used by the services incorporated, application frameworks, programming languages, open source, and third-party components. The vulnerabilities will arise due to insecure configurations, unpatched software, insecure secrets management, insecure coding, and a lack of security controls. In this step of threat modeling all the existing threats and vulnerabilities are identified.

Threat and Vulnerability Classification

Threat is defined as the technique used by the attackers to exploit the vulnerabilities present in the target solutions. Threats can be classified based on agents, localization, and motivation (Amini, Jamil, Ahmad & Z'aba, 2015). Agents are the attackers who perform the exploit to compromise the system and can be categorized as humans, technologies, and force majeure. Localization describes the origin of the threat and can be grouped into external or internal. Motivation answers the question of 'why' the exploit was performed. It can be classified as accidental or deliberate.

Remediation Recommendations

This step describes the security controls that should be implemented to address the identified threats and vulnerabilities. This may include using Security-as-a-Service solutions like Intrusion detection, Security information and event management (SIEM), WAF, network security, Identity, and access management, data loss prevention, logging and monitoring, web and email security, encryption of data at rest and in transit, business continuity and disaster recovery. The remediation efforts can be prioritized based on the risk rating assigned to each of the detected threats.

Risk Assessment

After identifying and classifying threats, vulnerabilities, and other potential weaknesses, the risk rating is assigned based on likelihood/ease of exploitation and impact such as reputational damage, loss of data, damage of asset/property/equipment, technical and financial consequences. Refer Appendix for the security risk matrix. As per OWASP, the formula used is - Risk = Likelihood×Impact. The overall risk status is aligned with the organization's risk and compliance policies. This will enable the teams to define a strategic plan to remediate the identified security threats.

CLOUD THREAT MODELING EXAMPLE

This section will walk through the detailed methodology of performing threat modeling for a web application hosted in AWS. Figure 1 shows the basic web application architecture diagram (AWS Cloud Whitepaper, 2021).

The key components of the web application architecture are:

Amazon Route 53 – This AWS component provides DNS services.

Amazon CloudFront – This AWS service provides high-volume data edge caching to increase performance by reducing latency.

AWS WAF – A web application firewall is used to detect security exploits like SQL injection, cross-site scripting, redirection attacks, XML external entity attacks, remote code executions, and other web-based attacks.

Elastic Load Balancer (ELB) – This service is used to distribute traffic across EC2 auto-scaling groups and multiple Availability Zones.

EC2 instances – They are virtual machine instances on which applications can be developed and deployed.

Amazon RDS – This is a relational database service that can be used to store application data.

AWS S3 – Amazon simple storage service provides HTTP-based object storage and backup.

AWS Shield – Protects applications from Distributed Denial of Service (DDoS) attacks.

NAT gateway - This is hosted in the VPC public subnet to route internet traffic from EC2 instances in the private subnet.

Figure 1. Web application architecture diagram

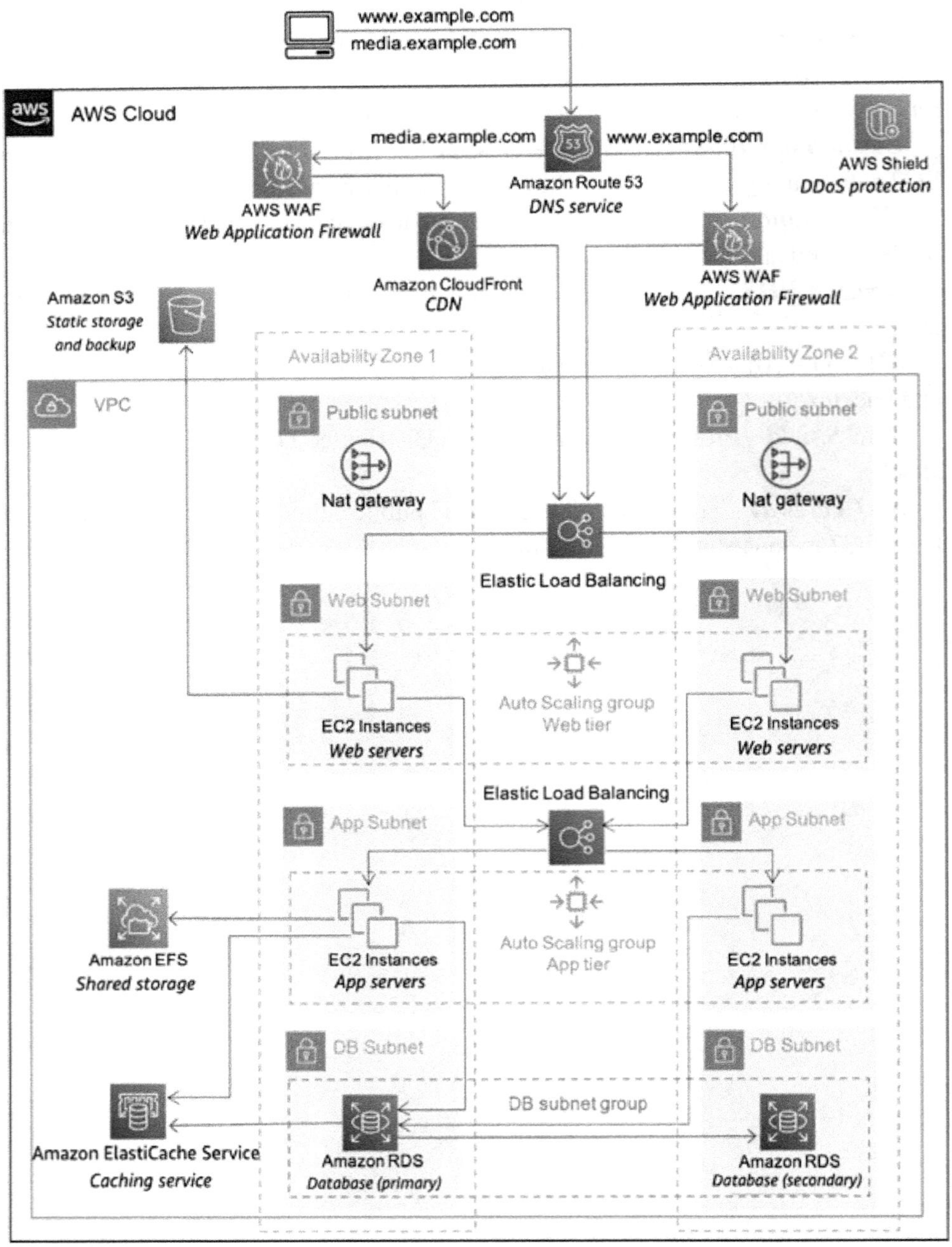

Asset Classification

Assets refer to key attributes, organization data, or functionalities that an attacker intends to acquire. In this solution, the key assets are the application data, authentication credentials, authorization tokens or session IDs, application logs, and administrative functionalities.

Threat Actors

Threat actors are malicious users or hackers who intend to steal application data or compromise the application's normal behavior. In this scenario, the threat actors can be external hackers over the internet, compromised external services, internal malicious users, and internal compromised systems/services.

Threat Motivation

The attacker's goal and motive in this example can be to gain access to application data, compromise the integrity of the stored data, bypass security controls, redirect to malicious websites, steal user credentials, host malicious contents, consume all resources to cause a denial of service attacks, gain admin privileges, gain shell access to the backend server, or reach internal servers through server-side request forgery attacks.

Potential Security Threats and Remediation Recommendations

Many industrial tools like Microsoft Threat Modeling tool, OWASP Threat Dragon, IriusRisk, SDElements by Security Compass, and Threagile can be used for threat modeling. For this example, the Microsoft Threat Modeling Tool is used to identify the security threats. After analyzing all the components, connections, and configurations defined in the architecture diagram, below is the list of potential security threats (Vincent, Brian, William & Han, 2018):

T01 – An advisory can steal user credentials and session tokens

Description – An attacker can steal user credentials through brute force and dictionary attacks. Session tokens can be stolen through cross-site scripting and other session-hijacking exploits

STRIDE Category – Spoofing, Elevation of privilege

Risk Rating - High

Remediation – Implement a strong password policy and multi-factor authentication. Have input validation on the server side and incorporate strong session management controls.

T02 – An advisory can steal AWS platform credentials.

Description – An attacker can steal AWS platform credentials through brute force attacks. Some developers create IAM user credentials and insecurely store them. These IAM keys can be compromised if not securely managed.

STRIDE Category – Spoofing, Information Disclosure

Risk Rating - High

Remediation – Avoid using root accounts. Integrate with organization SSO and MFA for user authentication. Each AWS account should have only one or two admin users. For service authentication use IAM roles. All secrets must be stored in AWS Secrets Manager.

T03 – An advisory can access application features and data without authentication

Description – An attacker can bypass authentication through SQL injection or attempt to access application features without authentication.

STRIDE Category – Spoofing, Elevated privilege

Risk Rating - High

Remediation – Use parameterized queries to remediate SQL injection. Make sure all the application features and data are rendered only after successful authentication and authorization validation on the server side.

T04 – An advisory can delete or modify application data

Description – An attacker can gain unauthorized access, delete, and modify application data through SQL injection or privilege escalation through parameter/URL manipulation.

STRIDE Category – Tampering, Escalated privilege

Risk Rating - High

Remediation – Use parameterized queries to remediate SQL injection. User authorization must be properly mapped and validated on the server side. Client-side validations can be bypassed. Encrypt data at rest and in transit.

T05 – The web application may become unavailable

Description – An attacker can send a large number of requests, consume all the resources, and may cause denial of service attacks.

STRIDE Category – Denial of Service

Risk Rating - High

Remediation – Use load balancers and distribute traffic across multiple regions for high availability. Implement SIEMs, logging, and monitoring capabilities. Web applications should have rate-limiting features.

T06 – Logging may not capture sufficient data

Description – Logs may not have captured sufficient data that will be required for investigation after a security breach.

STRIDE Category – Repudiation

Risk Rating - High

Remediation – Applications must log all applicable security events such as success and failure of user authentication requests including administrators, user authorization failures, user on-boarding, user profile changes, and off-boarding, session management failures, number of failed login attempts, locking and unlocking of user account, application errors, configuration, and connectivity changes, starting and stopping of application services and components, input and output validation failures and use of all higher-risk functionalities. Applications logs must capture minimum details like user identifier, timestamp, source IP address (this must be the true source IP address and not that of a load balancer or other application or networking component), event name, result of an event: success or failure and admin functionality access or changes. Applications must not log sensitive information, e.g., passwords, secret keys, tokens, etc. All logs must be consumed into the organization's central SIEM for proper log retention and monitoring. Also, ensure that application security log files are retained for at least one year and that retention follows the corporate retention policy.

T07 – The AWS RDS database may not be encrypted

Description – An attacker can gain unauthorized access and compromise sensitive data stored in RDS.

STRIDE Category – Information Disclosure

Risk Rating - High

Remediation – All data at rest must be encrypted. Additional column-level encryption should be implemented for restricted data. The encryption keys must be securely stored in AWS Secrets Manager or AWS KMS.

T08 – The AWS RDS authentication may not be securely implemented.

Description – Developers may use connection strings or username passwords for database authentication. These credentials may be hardcoded in cleartext as part of configuration files and can be easily compromised.

STRIDE Category – Spoofing, Information Disclosure

Risk Rating - High

Remediation – Do not use AWS root accounts to manage RDS instances. Instead, create IAM users with only the required permissions granted. For service-to-service connections use IAM roles with minimal required permissions. All authentication credentials should be stored securely in AWS Secrets Manager and rotated regularly based on organization policies.

T09 – The AWS RDS may be exposed to the internet.

Description – If the RDS database is exposed to the internet without any restrictions, any malicious user can access and steal the data stored.

STRIDE Category – Information disclosure.

Risk Rating - High

Remediation – Make sure RDS is not exposed to the internet. It should be accessible only within the VPC. Implement proper network segmentation.

T10 – The AWS EC2 metadata may not be protected

Description – Sometimes EC2s are deployed in public subnets exposing it to the internet. It may not have adequate security groups defined to control access.

STRIDE Category – Information disclosure, Denial of Service

Risk Rating - High

Remediation – EC2 instances must only reside in private subnets. Direct invocation should be prevented by placing them behind API gateways and WAF to protect against denial-of-service attacks. Direct RDP and SSH connection to EC2 instances should be blocked. EC2 administration should be done through SSM sessions or from a bastion host within the internal network. AWS inspector for EC2 instances should be used to scan regularly to detect any vulnerabilities and insecure configurations.

T11 – The AWS EC2 API gateways may not be implemented

Description – If EC2 instances are exposed to the internet without any restrictions, hackers can launch distributed denial of service attacks on the server and bring it down. Also, they can perform other exploits like SQL injection, XSS, and remote code executions.

STRIDE Category –Denial of Service

Remediation – AWS API gateway must be implemented to protect EC2 instances from DDoS attacks. They also provide rate limiting and authentication as a service capability.

T12 – An attacker can intercept and tamper with data in transit

Description – If encryption in transit is not enabled, malicious users can sniff or intercept cleartext traffic and steal data. Also, they can tramper or add payloads to launch further exploits.

STRIDE Category – Tampering, Information Disclosure

Risk Rating - High

Remediation – For all connections encryption in transit should be enabled. HTTPS with TLS version 1.2 or above with strong ciphers should be used.

T13 – AWS VPC network access may not be restricted.

Description – If VPC network access is not securely configured, malicious users can access the internally hosted AWS services and components.

STRIDE Category – Spoofing, Elevation of privilege

Risk Rating - High

Remediation – AWS VPC access control lists (ACLs) should have a deny by default policy so that all external and internal connections are blocked. Only required connections should be whitelisted.

T14 – AWS IAM policies and permissions may be insecurely defined

Description **–** AWS Identity and Access Management (IAM) is used for all users and services authentication and authorization validation. If IAM user permissions are not properly defined, it may lead to privilege escalations. A malicious low-privilege user can access higher-privilege user features and compromise the deployment.

STRIDE Category – Spoofing, Elevation of privilege

Risk Rating - High

Remediation – Do not use AWS root accounts. Individual IAM users should be created for administration. Use groups to assign permissions to IAM users. Follow least privilege principles while defining IAM users and roles. Enable AWS Access Analyzer to track and manage all the IAM users and roles.

T15 – AWS Trust Advisor may not be enabled.

Description **–** AWS Trust Advisor is a security tool that verifies AWS account security such as security group misconfigurations allowing unrestricted ports, IAM user and role policies, authentication, and MFA usage, and optimizes best practices.

STRIDE Category – Spoofing, Elevation of privilege

Risk Rating - Moderate

Remediation – Make sure the AWS Trust Advisor tool is enabled and regularly review the reports generated.

T16 – AWS WAF may not be enabled.

Description **–** AWS Web Application Firewalls monitor and inspect HTTP traffic between the web applications and the internet. It helps in preventing web-based exploits like cross-site scripting, SQL injection, XML external entity attacks, remote code execution, file inclusion, and cross-site forgery attacks.

STRIDE Category – Tampering, Elevation of privilege, Information Disclosure

Risk Rating - High

Remediation – Ensure AWS WAF is implemented for all externally exposed APIs and web-based applications.

T17 – AWS cloud logging and monitoring may not be enabled

Description **–** Security monitoring must be enabled to detect any malicious behaviors in the traffic. Logging should include sufficient data for investigation after a security incident. AWS Cloud provides several services like CloudWatch and Cloud Trail for logging and monitoring cloud services.

STRIDE Category – Tampering, Information Disclosure

Risk Rating - Moderate

Remediation – Use AWS CloudWatch to log all API requests. Implement CloudTrail to record all actions of a user, role, or service hosted. Enable AWS Config to get a detailed view of the configurations of all resources with the AWS account.

T18 – AWS EC2 instance hardening may not be performed.

Description **–** It is very important to install only approved AMIs on the EC2 instances. If older versions of AMIs are installed it may include pre-existing security vulnerabilities. Security agents like anti-virus, SIEM agents, and SSM agents should be installed on EC2 instances to prevent security breaches.

STRIDE Category – Tampering, Information Disclosure

Risk Rating - Moderate

Remediation – Only approved latest AMIs should be installed on EC2 instances. All industry-standard security agents and antivirus scanners should be installed. SSM agents must be installed for remote administration instead of connecting through SSH. AWS inspector for EC2 must be enabled to frequently scan EC2 instances for security vulnerabilities.

T19 – AWS S3 buckets may be exposed to the internet

Description – AWS S3 is used to store objects. It is important to restrict access to S3 so that malicious users cannot access and steal the stored objects.

STRIDE Category – Tampering, Information Disclosure, Spoofing

Risk Rating - Moderate

Remediation – Use IAM roles to restrict access to S3 buckets. Do not expose S3 to the internet. If external exposure is required, signed URLs should be used.

T20 – An advisory can get unauthorized access to secrets, credentials, and keys

Description – Sometimes developers hardcode unencrypted cleartext user/service credentials, private keys, IAM credentials, and database username passwords in configuration files. Malicious users can gain unauthorized access to these secrets and launch further exploits.

STRIDE Category – Tampering, Information Disclosure, Spoofing

Risk Rating - High

Remediation – All credentials, secrets, and keys must be stored in AWS Secrets Manager. Also, these secrets should be rotated regularly as per industry policies.

T21 – An advisory may exploit unprotected APIs

Description – Application Programming Interfaces (APIs) are used for communicating between components, microservices, and applications. If API authorization is not properly validated on the server side, malicious users can gain access and further exploit the endpoints. APIs can be used to transmit sensitive data like user credentials, credit card details, and other personal information. Thus, it is important to implement proper security controls to prevent information leakage. Also, API calls are susceptible to Denial-of-Service attacks as any user can flood the API with a large number of requests and consume all the resources so that legitimate users are denied access (Security Compass, 2022).

STRIDE Category – Tampering, Information Disclosure, Spoofing

Risk Rating - High

Remediation – APIs should always use secure protocols like HTTPs with TLS version 1.2 or above and strong cipher suits. APIs should use strong authentication and authorization methods like OAuth2, SAML, and mutual TLS. JWT Tokens must be signed and should have a short expiry time. APIs must include rate-limiting features to prevent DoS attacks.

T22 – An advisory can perform web-based exploits due to insecure coding

Description – Web application-based exploits like SQL injection, cross-site scripting, cross-site forgery, redirection attacks, session fixation, authentication bypass, privilege escalations, parameter manipulation, XML external entity attacks, server-side request forgery, and other OWASP Top 10 exploits are possible if secure coding practices are not followed.

STRIDE Category – Tampering, Information Disclosure, Spoofing, Information Disclosure

Risk Rating - High

Remediation – Secure coding practices should always be followed by developers. The use of open-source components with known vulnerabilities must be prevented.

CONCLUSION

As most of the companies have already migrated to the cloud or will be migrating within the next couple of years, it is very important to understand the cloud security risks involved and ways to mitigate them. Threat modeling is one of the crucial processes to be conducted to proactively identify security threats in the initial stages of implementation. There are several threat modeling frameworks that architects and security teams can refer to while performing threat analysis. Today, to scale threat modeling efforts, several automated tools are available. Initial scans are launched in the cloud environments to detect all the cloud services used and the type of connections configured. These tools then analyze all the information gathered and generate the list of security threats identified and ways to remediate the identified risks. These tools also perform periodic scans to detect the changes implemented. After identifying security threats through threat modeling, it is important to plan and prioritize remediation efforts. Application teams should mitigate the identified security risks by incorporating Security-as-a-Service solutions like intrusion detection, security information and event management (SIEM), WAF, network security, IAM policies, logging and monitoring, application security, encryption of data at rest and in transit, business continuity and disaster recovery. Since the shared responsibility model is followed in the cloud environments it is very important for customer organizations to take the initiative to secure their cloud deployments.

REFERENCES

Amini, A., Jamil, N., Ahmad, A. R., & Z'aba, M. R. (2015). *Threat Modeling Approaches for Securing Cloud Computing*. https://docsdrive.com/pdfs/ansinet/jas/2015/953-967.pdf doi:10.3923/jas.2015.953.967

Cloud, A. W. S., & Whitepaper, A. W. S. (2021). *Web Application Hosting in the AWS Cloud*. AWS Whitepaper. https://docs.aws.amazon.com/whitepapers/latest/web-application-hosting-best-practices/an-aws-cloud-architecture-for-web-hosting.html

Cloud Security Alliance – Top Threats Working Group. (2022). *Top Threats to Cloud Computing*. Cloud Security Alliance. https://cloudsecurityalliance.org/artifacts/top-threats-to-cloud-computing-pandemic-eleven/

Hewko Alex. (2021). *STRIDE Threat Modeling: What You Need to Know*. Software Secured. https://www.softwaresecured.com/stride-threat-modeling/

Security Compass. (2022). *How to Best Threat Model Cloud-Native Applications*. Security Compass. https://www.securitycompass.com/blog/threat-modeling-cloud-native-applications/

Shea Tally. (2023). *The Shared Responsibility Model in the Cloud*. Sonrai Security. https://sonraisecurity.com/blog/the-shared-responsibility-model-in-the-cloud/

Tony UcedaVelez & Marco M. Morana. (2015). *"Intro to Pasta," in Risk Centric Threat Modeling: Process for Attack Simulation and Threat Analysis*. Wiley. https://ieeexplore.ieee.org/document/9821030 doi:10.1002/9781118988374.ch6

Vincent, Van Leeuwen, Stout, & Lin. (2018). *Applying a Threat Model to Cloud Computing*. IEEE. https://www.osti.gov/servlets/purl/1594657

APPENDIX

Figure 2. Security risk matrix

Security Risk Matrix

Impact	Insignificant	Negligible	Moderate	Extensive	Significant
People	Minor injury or first aid treatment	Injury requiring treatment by medical practitioner.	Major Injury/ hospitalization.	Single death and/or multiple major injuries.	Multiple deaths
Information	Compromise of information otherwise available in the public domain.	Minor compromise of information sensitive to internal or sub-unit interests.	Compromise of information sensitive to this organization operations.	Compromise of information sensitive to organizational interests.	Compromise of information with significant ongoing impact.
Assets/ Property/ Equipment	Minor damage to assets.	Minor damage or loss of < 5% of total assets.	Damage or loss of <20% of total assets.	Extensive damage or loss <50% of total assets	Destruction or complete loss of >50% of assets.
Company and Brand Reputation	Local mention only. Can operate unaffected. Self-improvement review required.	Scrutiny by Executive, internal committees or internal audit to prevent escalation. Short term local media concern.	Persistent national concern. Scrutiny required by external agencies. Long term brand impact.	Persistent intense national public, political and media scrutiny. Long term brand impact.	International concern. Government inquiry or sustained adverse national/international media. Brand significantly affects organizational abilities.
Financial	1% of project or organizational annual budget. Minor effects on annual profit.	2-5% of project or organizational annual budget.	5-10% of project or organizational annual budget. Significant effects on annual	>10% project or organizational annual budget.	>30% pf project or organizational annual budge or bankruptcy.
Technical Impact Factors	Minimal Slightly corrupt Data. Minimal secondary service interrupted. Fully traceable.	Minimal seriously corrupt data. Extensive secondary service interrupted. Possibly traceable.	Extensive slightly corrupt data. Minimal primary and extensive secondary service interrupted. Possibly traceable.	Extensive seriously corrupt data. Extensive primary services interrupted. Not completely traceable.	All data totally corrupted. All services completed lost. Completely anonymous.

Vulnerability Factors	Threat Agent Factors	Qualitative Factors	Quantitative Factors	Likelihood	Insignificant	Negligible	Moderate	Extensive	Significant
Automated tools can be used to discover. Public knowledge available.	No technical skills required. No access or resources required. Anonymous internet users have access.	Is expected to occur in most circumstances	Has occurred on an annual basis in the past or circumstances are that will cause it to happen.	Almost Certain	6	7	8	9	10
Easy to discover and exploit. May require minimal efforts.	Some technical skills required. Very less access and resources involved. Only authenticated users have access.	Will probably occur in most circumstances.	Has occurred in the last few years or circumstances have occurred that will cause it happen in the next several years.	Likely	5	6	7	8	9
Less efforts required to discover. Lot of information and gidelines available.	Advanced computer user. Some access and resources required. Only authenticated partners have	Might occur at some time.	Has occurred at least once in the history or is considered to have a chance of occuring in the near future.	Possible	4	5	6	7	8
Difficult to discover and exploit. Hidden factors involved.	Network and programing skills required. Special access and resources required. Only intranet users have access.	Could occur at some time.	Has never occurred or is considered to have less chance of occuring in the future.	Unlikely	3	4	5	6	7
Practically impossible to discover. Only theoretical and no awareness.	Security pentesting skills required. Full access and extensive resource required. Only developers and administrators have	May occur only in exeptional circumstances	Is possible but has not occurred to date and is considered to have very much less chance in the future.	Rare	2	3	4	5	6

Chapter 9
Service Level Agreements (SLAs) and Their Role in Establishing Trust

Rajeshwari Sissodia
H.N.B. Garhwal University, India

ManMohan Singh Rauthan
H.N.B. Garhwal University, India

Varun Barthwal
H.N.B. Garhwal University, India

ABSTRACT

In the ever-evolving landscape of modern business, the cultivation of trust between service providers and their clients stands as a linchpin for sustainable success. This chapter seeks to explore the pivotal role played by service level agreements (SLAs) in establishing and fortifying this essential trust. In essence, this chapter aims to provide a comprehensive understanding of SLAs as more than contractual obligations, positioning them as instrumental tools for navigating the complex terrain of modern business relationships. Through insightful analyses and practical insights, the chapter will contribute to the discourse on trust-building mechanisms, underscoring the indispensable role of SLAs in shaping the dynamics of contemporary business interactions.

DOI: 10.4018/979-8-3693-3249-8.ch009

1. INTRODUCTION

In the transformative landscape of cloud computing, where digital connectivity and reliance on external services have become intrinsic to modern business operations, the establishment of trust between service providers and users is fundamental. At the heart of this trust-building endeavor lies the nuanced and critical framework known as Service Level Agreements (SLAs). This chapter embarks on an exploration of the profound role that SLAs play in shaping and sustaining trust within the dynamic ecosystem of cloud computing.

Cloud services have revolutionized the way organizations operate, offering scalable solutions, flexibility, and accessibility. However, this paradigm shift brings forth a unique set of challenges, chief among them being the assurance of reliable and secure service delivery. In this context, SLAs emerge as indispensable instruments that go beyond mere contractual agreements. They serve as dynamic tools that delineate expectations, delineate performance metrics, and provide a structured framework for accountability.

This chapter endeavors to dissect the multifaceted nature of SLAs in the realm of cloud computing, dissecting their application in the face of rapidly evolving technological landscapes. As businesses increasingly migrate to cloud environments, the need for a clear and mutual understanding of service parameters becomes paramount. SLAs, as we will uncover, act as the linchpin in this understanding, offering a roadmap for collaboration, risk mitigation, and dispute resolution.

The exploration will not only navigate the technical intricacies of SLAs but also underscore their broader significance in fostering a culture of trust. Through real-world examples and practical insights, we aim to highlight the pivotal role of SLAs in promoting transparency, reliability, and accountability, ultimately contributing to the cultivation of enduring relationships between cloud service providers and their users. Join us on this journey as we unravel the layers of trust within the intricate tapestry of cloud computing, where SLAs emerge as the guiding thread.

2. LITERATURE SURVEY

Dib et al. (1998) describes and analyses SLAs from an overview of the idea to the particular implementation to date at the Huddersfield NHS Trust. SLAs have been negotiated between the Directorate of Clinical Support and its customers, and these are supported by computerised measurement and reporting tools.

Le Sun et al. (2012) conducted a survey in cloud SLA assurance from two aspects -- pre- and post-interaction phases, based on which research gaps in existing approaches are identified. New research requirements for SLA assurance are then presented.

Walayat Hussain et al. (2022) to present an overview of the literature and make a comparative analysis of SLA monitoring in respect of trust maintenance in cloud computing.

Lu Kuan et al. (2016) introduces a utility architecture designed for optimal resource deployment aligned with business policies. It also presents a mechanism for enhancing Service Level Agreement (SLA) negotiation through optimization. Going a step further, the paper employs actor systems as a theoretical model, enabling fine-grained yet practical monitoring of extensive SLA sets. The approach proves realistic for automating the entire SLA lifecycle, particularly emphasizing monitoring as pivotal for contemporary scalability needs. The proposed work strategically separates fault-tolerance concerns within agreements, employing autonomous layers that hierarchically combine for an intuitive, parallelized, and efficient management structure.

Yudhistira Nugraha et al. (2017) focuses on the integration of security considerations into Service Level Agreements (SLAs). It begins by presenting an overview of system assurance, positioning trustworthy SLAs as a viable assurance technique in service provisioning. The concept of trustworthy SLAs is then explored, examining potential security properties applicable in SLA contexts. The paper concludes by outlining open research problems related to incorporating security capabilities into SLAs, aiming to foster trust between customers and service providers. The study underscores the necessity for a framework that ensures trustworthy SLA capabilities, establishing discrete assurance levels to safeguard data confidentiality, integrity, and availability within SLAs, thereby enhancing trust.

Sabra ben Saad et al. (2021) develop a trust architecture to automatically manage the SLAs and apply penalties and compensations if the SLAs are not respected by one of the involved actors.

Muralidharan et al. (2022) introduced a trusted third party called a trusted cloud broker (TCB) for managing the services. The service level agreements (SLA) management and reputation estimation framework is proposed, which includes three phases such as (i) SLA establishment between the three parties, (ii) violation detection by comparing the observed value of the TCB and (iii) the reputation and penalty estimation of the service. The novel TCB is created to monitor the deployed services, ensuring the achievement of SLA. The TCB observes the values and estimates the reputation value for each service. It is compared with the provider log-based reputation value and found that the proposed model provides a more precise reputation value for the service providers.

Guo Lu et al. (2023) introduces a novel approach to enhance the accuracy of trust evaluations in the context of service transactions. The first innovation involves incorporating the cost deviation trust and service quality coefficient, enabling a simultaneous consideration of common and characteristic factors influencing trust evaluations. This dual-factor consideration aims to improve the precision of trust assessments.

The second key contribution is the establishment of a negotiation and monitoring mechanism. Prior to trade, both parties sign a Service Level Agreement (SLA), and services are monitored by SLA agents. This dual-layered approach not only enhances the accuracy of service cost and quality evaluations but also increases the efficiency of identifying malicious entities.

Lastly, the study proposes a comprehensive evaluation framework incorporating agreement quality, experience quality, and monitoring quality. By accurately assessing these parameters, the study aims to refine the judgment of trade results. The recognition degree, a pivotal factor in trust evaluation, is then updated, leading to an overall enhancement in the accuracy of trust evaluations and, consequently, an improvement in the trade success rate.

3. CLOUD SERVICE MODELS

a) Infrastructure as a Service (IaaS): IaaS provides virtualized computing resources over the internet. It includes virtual machines, storage, and networks, allowing users to deploy and run applications. Well-suited for businesses that require scalable and flexible infrastructure without the need to invest in physical hardware. It's often used for development and testing environments (Sun et al., 2022).

b) Platform as a Service (PaaS): PaaS offers a platform allowing customers to develop, run, and manage applications without dealing with the complexity of underlying infrastructure. It typically includes development frameworks, databases, and other tools. Ideal for application development and deployment, as it streamlines the development process by providing a pre-configured environment (Johnson et al., 2019).

c) Software as a Service (SaaS): SaaS delivers software applications over the internet on a subscription basis. Users can access the software through a web browser without worrying about installation or maintenance. Commonly used for email, customer relationship management (CRM), and collaboration tools. It's convenient for users who want ready-to-use applications without managing the underlying infrastructure (Garcia et al., 2020).

4. CLOUD DEPLOYMENT MODELS

a) Public Cloud: Public cloud services are provided by third-party vendors and are available to anyone over the internet. Resources are shared among multiple users and organizations. Well-suited for scalable applications with variable workloads. Cost-effective as users pay for the resources they consume.

b) Private Cloud: Private clouds are operated solely for a single organization. They can be hosted on-premises or by a third-party provider. Ideal for organizations with specific security, compliance, or performance requirements. Offers greater control over resources.

c) Hybrid Cloud: Hybrid clouds combine public and private cloud services, allowing data and applications to be shared between them. It offers greater flexibility and optimization of existing infrastructure. Useful for businesses with varying workloads, providing the ability to scale resources dynamically between the public and private clouds. Understanding the combination of these service and deployment models enables organizations to tailor their cloud strategy to meet specific business requirements, balancing factors such as cost, performance, security, and scalability.

5. ADVANTAGES OF CLOUD COMPUTING

a) Cost Efficiency: Cloud computing eliminates the need for organizations to invest in and maintain physical hardware. Users can pay for resources on a consumption basis, optimizing costs and reducing capital expenditures.

b) Scalability and Flexibility:

Cloud services allow businesses to scale up or down based on demand. This flexibility ensures that organizations can adapt to changing workloads without over-provisioning resources.

c) Accessibility and Remote Collaboration: Cloud services enable users to access applications and data from anywhere with an internet connection. This fosters remote collaboration, making it easier for distributed teams to work together.

d) Automatic Updates and Maintenance: Cloud service providers handle system updates and maintenance, ensuring that users always have access to the latest features and security patches without the need for manual intervention.

e) Global Reach: Cloud computing facilitates global expansion by providing the infrastructure and services necessary to reach a worldwide audience. This is particularly beneficial for businesses with an international presence.
f) Disaster Recovery and Business Continuity: Cloud services often include robust backup and recovery options, making it easier for organizations to implement effective disaster recovery plans. This contributes to business continuity in the face of unexpected disruptions.
g) Innovation and Time-to-Market: Cloud computing accelerates the development and deployment of applications. Organizations can leverage ready-made services and focus on innovation, reducing time-to-market for new products and features.

6. CHALLENGES OF CLOUD COMPUTING

a) Security Concerns: Storing sensitive data in the cloud raises security concerns. Organizations must ensure robust security measures, including encryption and access controls, to protect data from unauthorized access.
b) Compliance and Legal Issues: Meeting regulatory requirements and industry-specific compliance standards can be challenging in a cloud environment. Organizations need to navigate legal issues related to data privacy and residency.
c) Downtime and Service Outages: Reliance on cloud service providers introduces the risk of downtime and service outages. Organizations must carefully choose providers with strong service level agreements (SLAs) to minimize disruptions.
d) Data Transfer Bottlenecks: Transferring large volumes of data to and from the cloud can be time-consuming, leading to performance bottlenecks. This is particularly relevant for applications that require rapid data access.
e) Limited Customization and Control: Some cloud services may limit customization options, leading to a lack of control over certain aspects of the infrastructure. This can be a concern for organizations with specific requirements.
f) Dependency on Internet Connectivity: Cloud services rely on internet connectivity. In regions with unreliable or slow internet connections, users may experience challenges in accessing cloud resources.

7. UNDERSTANDING SERVICE LEVEL AGREEMENTS (SLAS)

In the intricate landscape of cloud computing, Service Level Agreements (SLAs) stand as pivotal documents shaping the relationship between service providers and users. At its core, an SLA is a formalized agreement that outlines the terms, conditions, and expectations governing the delivery of services. Understanding SLAs is essential for both providers and users, as they serve as a roadmap for defining, measuring, and ensuring the quality of services offered.

8. COMPONENTS OF AN SLA

a) Service Scope and Objectives: Clearly delineate the scope of services provided, outlining the objectives and deliverables expected from the service provider.

b) Quantifiable Benchmarks: Specify the measurable metrics that define the performance standards, such as uptime, response times, and throughput.

c) Availability and Downtime: Detail the level of availability expected and the compensation or penalties in case of service downtime falling below agreed-upon thresholds.

d) Security and Data Protection: Address the security measures in place, ensuring compliance with data protection regulations and guaranteeing the confidentiality of user data.

e) Responsibilities and Roles: Clearly outline the responsibilities of both the service provider and the user, defining roles, communication channels, and escalation procedures.

f) Scalability and Flexibility: Specify how the services can scale in response to changing user needs, ensuring the flexibility to accommodate growth or fluctuations in demand.

Incident Response and Resolution:

g) Framework for Resolution: Establish a structured framework for incident response, detailing the procedures for reporting, investigating, and resolving service disruptions or issues.

h) Termination and Exit Strategy: Include clauses addressing termination conditions, transition plans, and data ownership in the event of the termination of the service agreement.

Understanding these components is crucial for all parties involved, as they form the basis for a clear and mutual understanding of service expectations. Service providers use SLAs to showcase the quality and reliability of their offerings, while users rely on them to ensure that the services align with their business needs and standards.

9. SLAS AS PERFORMANCE METRICS

In the ever-evolving landscape of cloud computing, Service Level Agreements (SLAs) serve as more than contractual commitments; they are dynamic instruments that define, measure, and assure the quality of services provided. Central to this multifaceted role is the concept of SLAs as performance metrics, establishing clear benchmarks and standards that delineate the excellence of service delivery.

a) Quantifiable Benchmarks: SLAs act as the compass guiding service providers and users toward success by setting quantifiable benchmarks. These metrics, whether related to response times, system availability, or other performance indicators, provide a tangible measure of service excellence.
b) Uptime and Availability: A cornerstone of SLAs as performance metrics is the commitment to uptime. Service providers specify the level of availability users can expect, with high-performing SLAs often guaranteeing a certain percentage of uptime, ensuring services are consistently accessible.
c) Response Times and Throughput: SLAs meticulously outline expectations regarding response times and data throughput. These metrics directly impact user experience, emphasizing the provider's commitment to delivering services in a timely and efficient manner.
d) Quality of Service (QoS):QoS metrics within SLAs address the overall quality and reliability of services. This includes parameters such as network performance, latency, and data integrity, ensuring a consistent and satisfactory user experience.
e) Performance Monitoring and Reporting: SLAs often incorporate mechanisms for performance monitoring and reporting. Service providers commit to transparently tracking and sharing performance data, fostering accountability and demonstrating a commitment to continuous improvement.
f) Load Balancing and Scalability: SLAs as performance metrics extend beyond static measures, encompassing the ability of services to scale dynamically. This adaptability to changing workloads ensures that users receive optimal performance even during periods of increased demand.
g) Compliance with Service Levels: crux of SLAs lies in the commitment to meeting or exceeding defined service levels. Service providers use these metrics to showcase their dedication to delivering a high standard of service that aligns with user expectations.
h) Continuous Improvement Strategies: SLAs as performance metrics are not stagnant; they embody a commitment to continuous improvement. Providers often include clauses detailing their strategies for enhancing performance

over time, ensuring the evolution of services to meet emerging challenges and technological advancements.

10. MITIGATING RISKS AND DISPUTES

In the intricate dance of cloud computing, the relationship between service providers and users is not immune to uncertainties and challenges. Addressing these challenges head-on, Service Level Agreements (SLAs) emerge as powerful tools, not only for mitigating risks but also for cultivating collaboration in the face of potential disputes.

a) **Roadmap for Incident Response:**
   - *Anticipating Challenges:* One of the primary roles of SLAs is to provide a structured roadmap for incident response. By clearly defining the procedures for reporting, investigating, and resolving service disruptions or issues, SLAs act as a proactive strategy for mitigating risks.

b) **Guarantees and Compensation:**
   - *Aligning Interests:* SLAs often include clauses specifying the level of availability expected and the compensation or penalties in case of service downtime falling below agreed-upon thresholds. These guarantees align the interests of service providers and users, encouraging a commitment to reliable service.

c) **Security Measures and Compliance:**
   - *Building Trust through Compliance:* SLAs address security concerns by outlining the security measures in place and ensuring compliance with data protection regulations. This not only mitigates the risk of data breaches but also builds trust by demonstrating a commitment to safeguarding user data.

d) **Clear Roles and Responsibilities:**
   - *Defining Boundaries:* By clearly outlining the roles and responsibilities of both the service provider and the user, SLAs mitigate the risk of misunderstandings. This clarity establishes a foundation for collaboration, minimizing the potential for disputes arising from unmet expectations.

11. BUILDING TRUST THROUGH SLAS

a) Clarity and Transparency

Transparency is a cornerstone of trust. SLAs provide a transparent framework by clearly articulating the terms and conditions of service. This transparency eliminates ambiguity and ensures that both parties have a shared understanding of expectations, reducing the likelihood of disputes.

b) Aligning Expectations
Effective communication is essential for trust-building. SLAs facilitate this by aligning the expectations of both parties. When expectations are well-defined and agreed upon, clients are more likely to trust that their needs will be met, and providers can confidently commit to delivering quality services.
c) Measurable Performance
By establishing measurable performance metrics, SLAs enable objective assessments of service delivery. This transparency allows clients to evaluate whether the service provider is meeting agreed-upon standards, reinforcing trust through accountability and tangible evidence of performance.

12. COLLABORATIVE DEVELOPMENT

The collaborative development of SLAs involves engaging clients in the process. This approach fosters collaboration, ensuring that the agreement reflects the unique needs and expectations of the client. The result is a sense of partnership and mutual understanding, contributing to a stronger foundation of trust.

a) Regular Review and Adaptation Trust is not static, and neither should be SLAs. Regular reviews and, when necessary, adaptations of SLAs based on changing business needs, technological advancements, or external factors are crucial. This iterative process demonstrates a commitment to continuous improvement and client satisfaction.
b) Communication and Accessibility Open communication channels and easy accessibility to SLAs are vital for building trust. Ensuring that clients can readily access and comprehend the SLA reinforces the commitment to openness and builds trust over time. It also provides a mechanism for addressing any concerns or clarifying ambiguities promptly.

CONCLUSION

In conclusion, this chapter has underscored the pivotal role that Service Level Agreements (SLAs) play in establishing and fostering trust within the dynamic landscape of cloud computing. As businesses increasingly rely on digital interactions and cloud services for their operations, the need for robust mechanisms to ensure transparency, reliability, and accountability becomes paramount. SLAs, as explored in this chapter, emerge as indispensable instruments that transcend mere contractual obligations, evolving into key drivers of quality assurance and trust-building in the realm of cloud services.

The unique attributes of SLAs in the context of cloud computing were thoroughly examined, revealing their capacity to define, measure, and assure the quality of services. Through real-world scenarios and industry best practices, it became evident that well-constructed SLAs contribute significantly to the transparency of service providers, giving users clear guidelines for performance expectations, uptime, and data security. This transparency, in turn, forms the foundation for building trust between service providers and users.

One of the notable aspects discussed was the dynamic nature of cloud services and how SLAs adapt to address evolving user needs. This adaptability not only reflects the agility of SLAs but also ensures that they remain relevant and effective in guiding cloud relationships. By serving as dynamic frameworks, SLAs help navigate the complexities inherent in cloud computing, providing a roadmap for both service providers and users to understand their respective responsibilities and expectations.

Furthermore, the chapter delved into the crucial role of SLAs in mitigating risks and uncertainties associated with cloud computing. It was demonstrated that SLAs offer a structured approach to dispute resolution and incident response, providing a level of assurance and clarity that is essential in the ever-changing landscape of digital services. Through concise analyses and practical insights, the chapter emphasized how well-constructed SLAs contribute not only to optimizing the performance of cloud services but also to cultivating a culture of trust.

In essence, this chapter has brought to light the multifaceted significance of SLAs in the era of cloud computing. It has showcased how these agreements go beyond being contractual documents, becoming strategic tools that shape the quality of cloud services and the relationships between service providers and users. As businesses continue to rely on cloud technologies, understanding and implementing effective SLAs will be imperative in fostering a culture of trust, reliability, and accountability in the digital landscape.

REFERENCES

Dib, N., Freer, J., & Gray, C. (1998). Service-level agreements at the Huddersfield NHS Trust. *International Journal of Health Care Quality Assurance*, *11*(3), 96–101.

Garcia, R., & Kim, Y. (2020). Understanding the Dynamics of Software as a Service (SaaS) Models. *International Journal of Cloud Applications and Services*, *12*(1), 45–68.

Guo, L., Yang, H., Luan, K., Luo, Y., & Sun, L. (2023). A Trust Model Based on Characteristic Factors and SLAs for Cloud Environments. *IEEE Transactions on Network and Service Management.*

Hussain, W., Hussain, F. K., & Hussain, O. K. (2014). Maintaining trust in cloud computing through SLA monitoring. *Neural Information Processing: 21st International Conference, ICONIP 2014, Kuching, Malaysia, November 3-6, 2014 Proceedings*, *21*, 690–697.

Johnson, M., & White, L. (2019). Platform as a Service (PaaS) Adoption: Challenges and Opportunities. *Cloud Computing Research*, *8*(4), 567–589.

Lu, K., Yahyapour, R., Wieder, P., Yaqub, E., Abdullah, M., Schloer, B., & Kotsokalis, C. (2016). Fault-tolerant service level agreement lifecycle management in clouds using actor system. *Future Generation Computer Systems*, *54*, 247–259.

Muralidharan, C., Shitharth, S., Alhebaishi, N., Mosli, R. H., & Alhelou, H. H. (2022). Three-phase service level agreements and trust management model for monitoring and managing the services by trusted cloud broker. *IET Communications*, *16*(19), 2309–2320.

Nugraha, Y., & Martin, A. (2017). Understanding trustworthy service level agreements: Open problems and existing solutions. In *International Workshop on Open Problems in Network Security (iNetSec)* (pp. 54-70). Academic Press.

Saad, S. B., Ksentini, A., & Brik, B. (2021, June). A Trust architecture for the SLA management in 5G networks. In *ICC 2021-IEEE International Conference on Communications* (pp. 1-6). IEEE.

Smith, J., & Brown, A. (2021). Exploring Infrastructure as a Service (IaaS) in Cloud Computing. *Journal of Cloud Computing (Heidelberg, Germany)*, *5*(2), 123–145.

Sun, L., Singh, J., & Hussain, O. K. (2012, December). Service level agreement (SLA) assurance for cloud services: A survey from a transactional risk perspective. In *Proceedings of the 10th International Conference on Advances in Mobile Computing & Multimedia* (pp. 263-266). Academic Press.

Chapter 10
Threat Landscape and Common Security Challenges in Cloud Environments

J. Jeyalakshmi
https://orcid.org/0000-0001-7545-6449
Amrita VishwaVidhyapeetham, India

S. Gnanavel
https://orcid.org/0000-0003-2344-0482
Department of Computing Technologies, SRM Institute of Science and Technology-Kattankulathur, India

K. Vijay
Rajalakshmi Engineering College, India

I. Eugene Berna
https://orcid.org/0000-0002-3066-6511
Bannari Amman Institute of Technology, India

ABSTRACT

Because of the proliferation of cloud computing, the security landscape in these settings presents a unique set of difficulties and risks. The benefits and game-changing consequences of cloud apps make them essential in the digital era. The ability to scale up or down helps organizations maximize their time and money commitments. They enable remote work and cooperation by letting users access their data and apps from anywhere. Cloud services save money by reducing hardware, software, and maintenance costs. But the security threats are deterring their performance. Data breaches are caused by, for example, insufficient encryption or slack access controls, interface and API vulnerabilities that can be exploited, insider threats caused by the misuse of privileges, identity and access management flaws, poor configuration and security practices, DoS attacks, shared technology flaws, data privacy and compliance concerns, a lack of oversight and control, and new, unknown threats.

DOI: 10.4018/979-8-3693-3249-8.ch010

1. INTRODUCTION

With the rise of remote work over the past year, cloud adoption has become a particularly hot issue. Businesses have been progressively preparing cloud migrations over the past decade. The cloud has several benefits, including better productivity, lower costs, and greater ease of use. Inadequate management, however, leaves your company vulnerable to a wide variety of sophisticated cyber threats. Expert Insight portal brings a summary of cloud based breaches. It states that about half of all hacks occur on the cloud. Eighty percent of businesses have had at least one cloud security event in the past year, and twenty-seven percent of businesses have had a public cloud security problem, which is ten percent more than in 2016. Since most modern firms have been compromised, it's no surprise that 72% of them are turning to cloud-based services first when making technology upgrades or purchases (Ma et al., 2023).

Part of the issue is that many companies have rushed into adopting the cloud in an attempt to allow their staff to work remotely in the wake of the COVID-19 epidemic. Many businesses felt compelled to compromise on safety in order to speed up the process of supplying their staff. Since these tools and apps weren't designed specifically for the cloud, they lacked the necessary level of security to scale to meet the needs of a cloud infrastructure. In reality, the same survey cited above found that while 46% of businesses employ cloud-based apps designed specifically for the cloud, 54% have instead migrated them from an on-premises setting. Small and medium-sized businesses (SMBs) are more likely to have adopted a cloud-native strategy, whereas enterprises are more likely to have transferred on-premises apps. Organisations in the government and financial sectors were far more likely to transfer on-premises applications to the cloud, while those in the technology and education sectors were just as likely to use migrated on-premises programmes as they were purpose-built cloud apps (Babu & Jayashree, 2015).

Securing a heterogeneous cloud system presents a number of obstacles, which leads us to the following part. But there are lot of challenges for cloud services. About 96% of organisations have faced substantial obstacles while executing their cloud strategy, despite the fact that putting IT on the cloud provides several benefits such as better flexibility, cost savings, and enhanced continuity (Abdulsalam & Hedabou, 2022; Balani & Varol, 2020).

The cloud skills gap, the need to manage costs, and security are the three biggest obstacles here. Concerns over data privacy and security are reported by 35% of IT decision-makers, while 34% cite concerns over a lack of cloud security skills and knowledge, and 25% cite concerns over the inability to secure cloud resources. Hence this is becoming a major security issue (Shahid et al., 2023).

2. SECURITY THREATS IN CLOUD ENVIRONMENT

Every business has unique security concerns, risks, and threats every day. Many people confuse these concepts, although there is nuance between them. Protecting your cloud resources is easier if you grasp the nuances between them.

Data loss or other vulnerabilities are examples of risks. A threat is any potential danger or enemy. Organizational difficulties in enforcing reasonable cloud security measures constitute a difficulty.There are several challenges in effectively protecting public APIs while keeping them available for legitimate users or customers who need them. The risk is an API endpoint hosted in the cloud and exposed to the public Internet; the attacker who attempts to access sensitive data using that API is the threat.

Access permissions are another misconfiguration problem. 83% of organisations report at least one access-related cloud data breach, and 50% report at least 25%. This is probable because 52% of organisations lack visibility into user resource access and permissions (Alrassan & Alqahtani, 2023).

One of the major objectives for identity- and access-related fraudsters is privileged accounts. Based on greater permissions, privileged accounts allow administrative access to "high-tier" organisational systems with serious implications if violated. Cybercriminals seeking sensitive company data find privileged accounts profitable and appealing.

Unfortunately, 50% of major organisations who try to deploy least-privilege access in their cloud settings fail. The challenge of uniformly controlling access across many clouds, lack of visibility into cloud architecture, and implementation time and difficulties are the biggest impediments to least-privilege access.

Attackers can access crucial data unnoticed by security teams using accounts with improper permissions. This is a typical AWS cloud service issue. More than half of AWS companies have IDs with super admin access. Hidden privilege escalation identities can award themselves admin credentials without consent and access important data, allowing attackers to access vital systems using user-level accounts. Over 40% of machine identities are inactive and over-permissioned, like user identities.

Many data breaches include human mistake, credential theft, or social engineering like phishing. Phishing is when a bad actor emails a target as a reputable source. The attacker manipulates their target during communication. The attacker can share confidential information like login passwords to access and take over their target's account, click on a malicious link or file to download malware to the target's device allows the attacker to spy or take over the account.The attacker can steal company data and do more phishing assaults to access higher-privileged accounts (Gupta & Vashisth, 2023).

Cybercriminals exploit legal domain names like docs.google.com, my-sharepoint.com, and cloudfront.net to lure users to phishing pages. material delivery networks and cloud file share services let their "customers" host material on valid domains. This provides customers more file storage, but it also allows thieves a place to put dangerous files masquerading as genuine domains.

Attackers do this for two reasons. First, people are more inclined to click on trustworthy domain links. Second, security firms can't restrict these sites without blocking all their material, even excellent things.

Data breaches cost money in downtime, reputational harm, compliance fines, and legal expenditures. IBM reports that data breaches cost $4.35 million on average. The survey demonstrates a growing disparity between organisations with effective security measures and those without. This means formal security architecture reduces expenses tremendously.

Public cloud breaches cost more than hybrid ones. Additionally, mature cloud security organisations had a reduced data breach cost of 3.87 million dollars, 15.7% less than early-stage maturity companies, who had initiated certain security practises. This is likely because more developed security can discover and contain a compromise faster.The list of security threats in cloud environment are summarized in table 1.

Table 1. Summary of security threats in cloud environment

Security Challenge	Description
Data Breaches and Loss	Unauthorized access to sensitive data, inadequate encryption, accidental deletion or corruption.
Insecure Interfaces and APIs	Exploitation of poorly designed or insecure APIs, insufficient authentication and authorization.
Insider Threats	Malicious actions or data theft by authorized personnel, privilege misuse, abuse of credentials.
Access Management Issues	Weak or compromised user credentials, insufficient access controls, unauthorized privilege escalation.
Misconfiguration	Improperly configured resources exposing data, failure to follow security best practices.
Denial of Service Attacks	Overloading services to make them unavailable, resource exhaustion attacks.
Shared Technology Vulnerabilities	Exploiting weaknesses in shared components or infrastructure affecting multiple tenants.
Data Privacy and Compliance	Non-compliance with regulations, challenges in meeting data residency and sovereignty requirements.
Lack of Visibility and Control	Limited insight into underlying infrastructure security, monitoring and auditing difficulties.
Emerging Threats and Zero-Day Exploits	Targeting new vulnerabilities, evolving attack techniques leveraging cloud weaknesses.
Cloud Service Provider Risks	Varying security responsibility between customer and CSP based on deployment type.
Data Migration and Transfer Vulnerabilities	Insecure data transfer processes during migration, leading to data interception or leakage.

They are briefed in detail as below:

- Data Breaches and Loss
- Insecure Interfaces and APIs
- Insider Threats
- Access Management Issues
- Misconfiguration
- Denial of Service Attacks
- Shared Technology Vulnerabilities
- Data Privacy and Compliance
- Lack of Visibility and Control
- Emerging Threats and Zero-Day Exploits
- Cloud Service Provider Risks
- Data Migration and Transfer Vulnerabilities

2.1 Data Breaches and Loss

There are several potential causes of data loss in cloud computing, such as human mistake, natural catastrophes, security breaches, etc. Client organisations may suffer significant losses in the form of money, reputation, compliance breaches, regulatory implications, and the loss of vital information in the case of such calamities. A data breach occurs when sensitive information is accessed or shared without proper authorization, such as during a cyber assault. Any company, no matter how large or little, is susceptible to data breaches. Medical records, social security numbers, credit card numbers, and passwords are just few examples of the kinds of private information that could be included. Examples of personally identifiable information and business-critical data that could be compromised in a data breach include credit card details, Social Security numbers, driver's licence numbers, and medical records (M. M. R & A. T. P, 2023).

Possible solutions can be regular backups, developing manpower skilled to thwart breaches, preparing snapshot of the system state.

2.2 Insecure Interfaces and APIs

The proliferation of mobile internet and app use has spurred widespread adoption of application programming interfaces. While financial institutions are the early adopters of cloud APIs, other sectors including retail, transportation, and government agencies are quickly catching up. However, as API's popularity grows, so do the number of cyber threat actors seeking for ways to abuse it for harm.

In light of this increased risk, businesses must implement more severe rules and safeguards to keep cloud APIs from being used in cyber attacks. Recently, the Personal Data Protection Commission (PDPC) of Singapore imposed a steep fine to a ride-sharing company that compromised driver and passenger information due to an API update that was not tested before its roll out. A strict security procedure should be in place to prevent unauthorised access to data while updating a system that might be compromised.

With more and more services dependent on APIs, hackers have discovered two popular exploits.

According to the Open Web Application Security Project's (OWASP) 2019 report, weak user authentication is one of API's major security vulnerabilities. Sometimes developers build APIs that don't require a login. Because of this, these interfaces are public on the internet and may be used by anybody to get access to internal business systems and data. It's like going door-to-door in a new area, hoping one of them will be unlocked.

In today's IT industry, it's usual practise to build programmes using modular components. Many programmers choose open source tools because of the time savings they provide. As a result, many applications may be vulnerable to supply chain assaults. A developer may, for instance, obtain code for bitcoin mining from one of the many public Docker hubs available online. There are certain measures that can help in this direction. OAuth 2.0 and OpenID Connect are two examples of secure authentication mechanisms that should be used. To limit who may access what, use access control lists (ACLs).Use HTTPS for all API traffic to encrypt it. Keep an eye out for any unusual activities via the API.Keep API keys safe and change them frequently. Leverage industry-standard API frameworks that were built with safety in mind. Invest in tools that reveal the whole security landscape of the company.

2.3 Insider Threats

Those with authorised access to your network who maliciously exploit that access are considered insider risks. Oftentimes, insider threats go undetected for quite some time—sometimes even years. Any insider threat, whether from a hostile employee or a contractor with compromised credentials, necessitates a swift and effective response from the security team.

User Behaviour Analysis can be very helpful in this problem. Ransomware protection and access privilege control are other related solutions (Vyas et al., 2023).

2.4 Access Management Issues

While there are obstacles in managing user identities and rights in the cloud, they are not insurmountable. Navigating these challenges and improving identity and access management (IAM) calls for an approach combining real solutions. Lack of a centralised perspective and difficulty in user lifecycle management are major obstacles in IAM for cloud and on-premises system security. The first problem is the need for distributed identity management, which occurs when data moves to the cloud and gets more dispersed.

However, Software as a Service (SaaS) management platform provides a consolidated perspective, using single sign-on and identity providers to monitor app consumption and reveal actionable data in real time. The second difficulty is in managing the whole user lifetime, from onboarding to access provisioning through deprovisioning. Risk is heightened by the use of manual processes and third-party programme administrators. Zluri streamlines and automates these procedures for maximum productivity and safety, including onboarding, job changes, and offboarding.

In order to facilitate the administration of digital identities, businesses have developed a collection of procedures, guidelines, and technology known as identity and access management (IAM). IT departments may regulate who has access to sensitive data by using an IAM architecture. A variety of authentication techniques, including single sign-on, two-factor and multi-factor authentication, and privileged access control, are in use today.

2.5 Misconfiguration

Any problems, omissions, or mistakes in cloud configuration that leave your environment vulnerable are known as cloud misconfiguration. Security flaws, hackers from the outside, ransomware, malware, and malicious insiders are all examples of cyber risks.

According to the NSA, one of the biggest threats to a secure cloud infrastructure is improper setup. While the sophistication of these threats is often lower, their incidence is skyrocketing.

Due to the complexity of multi-cloud settings, it might be difficult to discover and manually correct misconfigurations in the cloud. Gartner found that these problems account for 80% of all data security breaches, and that up to 99% of cloud environment failures would be traced back to human error through 2025.

This is difficult because problems caused by incorrect cloud settings, such as cloud leaks, cannot be fixed with a single command. The construction phase is an ideal time to introduce security measures. Therefore, cooperation between DevOps and security groups is essential (Sharma et al., 2023).

The ways to overcome misconfiguration issues can be to keep an eye out for any storage nodes that have the "public" designation. o keep an eye on how people are accessing internal storage to close down any superfluous or too permissive ports. Secure data stored in the cloud should be encrypted with regularly changing keys.

2.6 Denial of Service Attacks

A Denial-of-Service (DoS) attack is one that intentionally crashes a system or network by sending too much data or traffic to it. This prevents the intended service or resource from being made available to the intended audience, which might include workers or members. DoS assaults frequently target prominent institutions in spheres including banking, trade, media, and government. While denial-of-service attacks seldom result in permanent loss of data or assets, they can nonetheless cost victims a lot of money and effort. DoS attacks may either flood a service or cause it to crash. Inundating a system to the point of delay or stoppage is what we mean when we talk about flooding.

Attacks like ICMP floods, SYN floods, and buffer overflows are only a few examples. Still others use security holes to bring down a computer system. DDoS assaults, which involve several systems working together to disrupt a single service, are notoriously difficult to identify and counteract. While most distributed denial of service (DDoS) assaults may be mitigated with today's security tools, enterprises still need to take precautions lest they fall victim to a Distributed Denial of Service (DDoS). Methods to prevent DDoS attacks are given as below in Table 2.

Table 2. Methods to prevent DDoS attacks in cloud computing

Prevention Step	Description
Configure Network Filtering	Use firewalls and security tools to filter and block traffic from known malicious sources.
Use Content Delivery Networks	CDNs distribute traffic across multiple servers, making it harder for DDoS attacks to overwhelm.
Monitor for Unusual Traffic	Regularly watch for unusual traffic patterns like sudden traffic spikes indicating a DDoS attack.
Prevent Account Takeover	Utilize cloud providers' built-in account takeover and mitigation features. Implement MFA and rate limiting.
Cloud-Based DDoS Protection	Employ cloud-based DDoS protection services to absorb and mitigate attacks before they reach your network.
Develop DDoS Response Plan	Have a plan in place for how to respond to a DDoS attack, including contact points and mitigation steps.

2.7 Shared Technology Vulnerabilities

Risks associated with cloud computing infrastructure include circumvention of administrative controls, exposure of sensitive data during backup or recovery, and circumvention of invoicing and measurement systems. The on-demand features of cloud computing necessitate a management interface. Management interface unauthorised access is a problem. Such shared vulnerabilities are overcome using Service Level Agreements(SLA). Propose a security issue that should be covered by the SLA (Veena et al., 2023).

In cloud computing, data security is an issue since the consumer or client does not have access to their private information. The location of data storage and processing is hidden from the client. In a service level agreement, the provider gives only limited guarantees. Because of this contract, the client will feel more comfortable with the service provider. When a client abuses the service they get, what legal recourse is available is also part of SLA. Propose a security issue that should be covered by the SLA. In cloud computing, data security is an issue since the consumer or client does not have access to their private information.

2.8 Data Privacy and Compliance

Laws controlling the collecting, processing, storage, and transmission of data inside and across borders are often adopted to protect the personal information of a country's inhabitants. For example, even if a Mexican national is employed in Canada and their communications are held by a cloud service in Brazil, the legal systems in all three nations would be triggered. The legal department of a company must keep a close eye on all the company's electronic data transfers to guarantee compliance. Employers are required to seek the approval of individuals (data owners) before processing their personal information, making consent a prominent issue in these rules.

This necessitates familiarity with the legal processes involved in requesting and withdrawing consent in all applicable jurisdictions. Some laws make an exemption for processing personal information in the course of judicial proceedings or to fulfil legal responsibilities. There are frequently strict requirements for transferring data over international borders, and the receiving country must meet those same standards. Understanding security and reporting requirements is also essential. Data privacy rules require the use of basic security protocols and the immediate reporting of data breach victims. Cloud service users should have clear channels of communication in place for reporting security incidents to their staff and the owners of the data they store.

2.9 Lack of Visibility and Control

The most typical reasons for privacy leaks in the Cloud include improper Cloud configuration, a lack of identity access management, data abuse, and a lack of visibility and control mechanisms. Cloud data management has its share of issues, including insecure APIs, hostile insiders, and accidental or careless mistakes. To make the move to the cloud, businesses must give up some control over their IT and put it in the hands of cloud service providers. You have lost control of the data centres housing your information. The network via which your data travels is likewise outside your control. There may be an interruption in visibility if control is lost (Tarahomi et al., 2023).

It is possible to put all trust on a third-party service to fix performance problems. With sufficient oversight, issues may be addressed immediately, bypassing the need for assistance from customer support. Firewalls and other threat detection systems may be effective for on-premises installations, but they won't cut it in the cloud. The elastic and decentralised nature of cloud infrastructure is to blame for this. As a result, you can have trouble following its developments. If it can be seen how your cloud operates, it is possible to can fix any security issues immediately after discovering them.

The more one can see into cloud deployment, the easier it will be to spot unused resources and waste. It's possible, for instance, that you're spending a lot of money on underutilised capacity that's not helping your business expand. With more information at disposal, one can fine-tune operations to maximise productivity and expand as needed. Time and money are both spared as a result.

2.10 Emerging Threats and Zero-Day Exploits

The phrase "zero-day" refers to any newly found security flaw that may be exploited by hackers. Since the manufacturer or developer recently found out about the vulnerability, they have "zero days" to remedy it, hence the name "zero-day." In a zero-day attack, hackers take advantage of a vulnerability before the issue can be fixed.

It's possible to see zero-day spelt as 0-day. When discussing zero-day, it's important to differentiate between vulnerability, exploit, and attack. The term "zero-day vulnerability" refers to a flaw in software that has been found by attackers before the vendor is aware of it. Zero-day vulnerabilities are particularly dangerous because there is no fix available and the vendors are in the dark about them.

A zero-day exploit is a hacking technique used to target systems using a flaw that has not yet been discovered by security researchers. Using a zero-day exploit to harm or steal information from a system that is vulnerable is known as a zero-day attack.

Vulnerabilities in computer programmes allow malicious users to wreak damage. While patches are being developed, vulnerabilities still exist that hackers may use. This is known as exploit code. Cybercrimes like identity theft can result from this code. Attackers take advantage of "zero-day vulnerabilities," loopholes that engineers aren't aware of. They utilise deception and persuasion to trick people into performing harmful behaviours, such as downloading and opening files or visiting malicious websites. Data is stolen when the infection sneaks in. In the while that developers are working to patch vulnerabilities, attackers can take advantage of them. The dark web is a rich market for exploits. When these vulnerabilities are patched, they are no longer considered "zero-day," but they remain dangerous since only attackers have access to this information. Since criminals may launch zero-day attacks whenever they see fit, they pose a significant threat.

Organisations vulnerable to zero-day attacks may detect suspicious scanning activities or unusual client or service behaviour. Various methods exist for detecting such vulnerabilities:

- Existing Malware Databases: While often updated and helpful, these databases have their limits due to the novelty and unknown nature of zero-day vulnerabilities.
- Instead of just analysing incoming file code, behavioural analysis looks at how zero-day malware interacts with the target system. It analyses the malware's behaviours within the context of the host application to determine whether or not they are harmful.
- In order to establish a standard for typical system behaviour based on previous and present interactions, machine learning is increasingly being used. More information means more precise detection.

2.11 Cloud Service Provider Risks

Cloud Service provider takes the following risks when offering a service on cloud. When businesses move their operations, assets, and workloads to the cloud, they often outsource management of key infrastructure components to third-party providers. Data Sovereignty, Insecure Integration, and APIs, and Loss of Control Over Data in the Cloud (Jaeyalakshmi & Kumar, 2016).

These issues are fixed with Service Level Agreements and Security enforcement process.

2.12 Data Migration and Transfer Vulnerabilities

There are several potential security issues when moving data to the cloud, including human error, external assaults, malware, incorrectly setup servers, cloud provider issues, unsecured APIs, violations of contracts and regulations, and so on.

Cloud migration has many benefits, but there are also hazards that firms should be aware of. These risks include data loss, security breaches, and a lack of visibility. The following threats must be mitigated to guarantee the security of cloud-based application and data transfers.

Complexity of existing IT infrastructures might impede easy transition to the cloud due to incompatibility. To reduce this danger, businesses must form an IT department with the expertise to modify the system's design for use in the cloud. Resolving technological debt, evaluating existing architecture, documenting thoroughly, and managing dependent parts are all essential.

Accessing databases,programmes, and services in the cloud may have performance concerns due to the additional latency. This is a major issue for programmes that need instant feedback. Understanding the root causes of latency, optimising networks, segmenting traffic flows, and, if all else fails, contemplating hybrid solutions are all important steps in reducing or eliminating it.

While many businesses are moving to the cloud, security remains a top worry. There are several potential security issues when moving data to the cloud, including human error, hacking, and breach of contract. There is a need for better cloud security training and people since many businesses lack the expertise to deal with these problems (Saxena et al., 2023).

Companies are aware of the hazards, but many are unprepared, according to the reports. A proactive strategy and investment in experts with the necessary skills to properly manage security problems are needed to meet these difficulties.

The following methods can help reduce potential dangers during a cloud migration:

- Top cloud service providers include security features to prevent hackers from gaining access to sensitive information and hardware. While they do provide security solutions, it is wise to staff up with a seasoned security team and DevOps experts. Multi-factor authentication, data encryption, access restrictions, firewall setup, employee training, and the implementation of controls are all important.
- Inadequate Control and Visibility: Moving to the public cloud might lessen your ability to manage resources and monitor how your networks and apps are performing. Invest in app and network performance monitoring tools to solve this problem. Cloud service providers and other third-party security suppliers

supply answers. Automatic threat response, analytics, simple integration, and effective monitoring are all features that should be available in the right tools.

- Cloud cost complexity might lead to unnecessary spending if management strategies aren't optimised. There is a possible 70% waste of cloud expenditures. Get the most out of your budget by taking advantage of deals, removing unused instances, raising spot instances for less important work, balancing workloads, making use of reserved instances, relying on autoscaling, and even thinking about using a different location to host your data.
- Failure to Select an Appropriate Cloud Migration Strategy: Determine if a Single Cloud Provider or Multiple Cloud Platforms will best meet your objectives. There are benefits and drawbacks to every approach. Choose which data to move and which to stay where it is now stored. Use of hybrid models is advised, as is refraining from storing critical information on the cloud.
- Loss of Data: Make sure you have a backup of your data before moving it to the cloud so you don't lose anything. There might be problems with files being damaged, partial, or missing. Data loss may be avoided using preventative measures like frequent backups and distributed replicas across various providers. Set up and regularly check your backups to avoid any delays in recovering lost data.

3. CLOUD SERVICE SECURITY

The term "cloud security" refers to a set of protocols and tools developed to protect businesses from both external and internal dangers. As businesses adopt a digital transformation plan and begin using cloud-based applications and services, they must ensure their data is safe on the cloud (Nguyen et al., 2019).

In recent years, the phrases "digital transformation" and "cloud migration" have become commonplace in business contexts. While the precise meaning of each phrase may vary from organisation to institution, the yearning for improvement is consistent across all settings. Enterprises that adopt these ideas and work to optimise their operational approach face additional problems in striking a good balance between production and safety. Transitioning predominantly to cloud-based settings has a number of ramifications if it is not done safely, despite the fact that newer technologies allow organisations expand capabilities outside the constraints of on-premise infrastructure. To find that sweet spot, you'll need some familiarity with how modern businesses may take use of linked cloud technology while still implementing top-notch cloud security measures. Some of the techniques for security offerings are summarized in Table 3.

Table 3. Cloud security strategies

Security Solution	Description
Cloud Access Security Brokers (CASBs)	Monitor and enforce security regulations for cloud data, provide compliance and encryption features.
Multi-Factor Authentication (MFA)	Requires users to authenticate with multiple factors, preventing unauthorized access even if passwords are compromised.
Privileged Access Management (PAM)	Controls and monitors privileged user access in the cloud, improves governance and compliance.
Endpoint Antivirus and Security Software	Detects and prevents harmful files, with antivirus suitable for SMBs and endpoint security for larger organizations.

These are explained in detail as below:

- Cloud Access Security Brokers (CASBs)
- Multi-Factor Authentication (MFA)
- Privileged Access Management (PAM)
- Endpoint Antivirus and Security Software

3.1 Cloud Access Security Brokers (CASBs)

To facilitate communication between an organization's internal resources (its data centres, servers, endpoints, users, etc.) and the cloud environment (its platforms, software, and infrastructure "as a service"), a cloud access security broker (CASB) may be deployed. Between cloud service users and cloud service providers, cloud access security brokers (CASBs) aggregate and insert enterprise security policies throughout the access process for cloud-based resources. CASBs can be hosted on-premises or in the cloud. The use of several security policies is simplified by CASBs. Possible security policies include things like authentication, single sign-on, authorization, credential mapping, device profiling, encryption, tokenization, logging, alerting, malware detection/prevention, etc. The framework for the cloud security broker architecture is discussed in Figure 2.

Figure 1. Cloud security broker
Source: https://www.spiceworks.com/it-security/cloud-security/articles/what-is-casb/

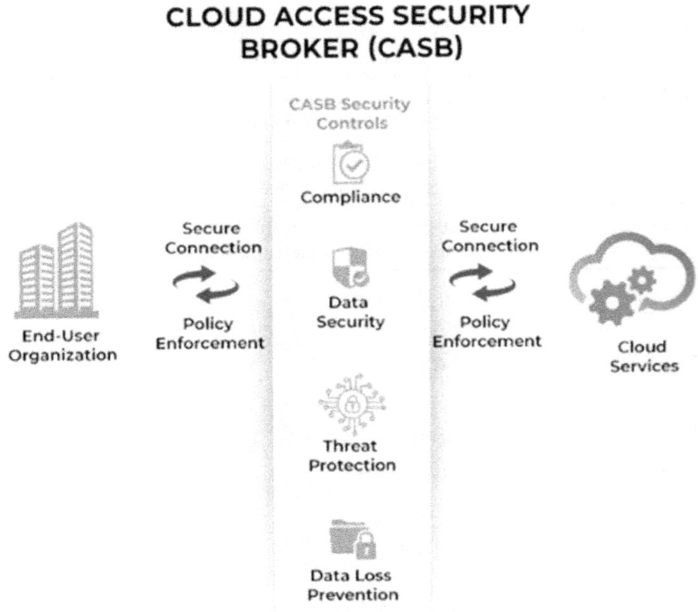

3.2 Multi-Factor Authentication (MFA)

Access to resources like apps, online accounts, or VPNs may need users to give additional verification information in the form of multi-factor authentication (MFA). Important for effective IAM (identity and access management). Multi-factor authentication (MFA) requires additional verification factors beyond usernames and passwords, drastically lowering the possibility of successful cyber assaults (Yan et al., 2013).

Multi-factor authentication is critical because it strengthens the security of an organisation by making it so that users must provide more evidence of their identity than simply a username and password. These common credentials are vulnerable to brute force assaults and theft. Implementing multi-factor authentication (MFA) with a method like a fingerprint or hardware key boosts faith in the security of the business network.

Additional verification variables are required for MFA to work. The use of one-time passwords (OTPs), which are commonly 4-digit to 8-digit numbers sent through email, SMS, or applications, is widespread. These codes are created using a seed value supplied to the user upon registration and another component, such as a counter or time value, and are refreshed at regular intervals or in response to authentication requests (Jaeyalakshmi et al., 2023).

There are three main types of MFA authentication methods:

- Factors dependent on what you know, such as passwords and personal identification numbers.
- Things you have in your possession, like badges or a smartphone, have a role.
- Things you have or are by nature, such as fingerprint or voice recognition technology.

3.3 Privileged Access Management (PAM)

Privilege Access Management (PAM) is an essential method for reducing the likelihood of security breaches, exploits, and mistakes. It reduces the chances of a breach occurring and the damage it may do to an organization's IT infrastructure. Default credentials are removed, least privilege is applied, and admin privileges are revoked when using PAM, all of which improve security. Notably, PAM can thwart assaults at several levels, protecting networks from both external and internal threats. Important advantages include lessening the likelihood of malware infection, boosting productivity, simplifying compliance, minimising the cost of cyber insurance, and reducing attack surfaces. PAM is compatible with regulatory frameworks and laws such as HIPAA, PCI DSS, and the zero trust principles. Best practises for Privileged Account Management (PAM) consist of comprehensive policies, the identification and management of privileged accounts, the enforcement of least privilege, the separation of duties, the segmentation of networks, the enforcement of password security, the monitoring of privileged activity, the implementation of dynamic access, the security of privileged task automation, and the use of privileged threat/user analytics. These methods improve safety, lessen vulnerabilities, and keep organisations in compliance (Ramgovind et al., 2010).

3.4 Endpoint Antivirus and Security Software

Endpoint security is a method that utilises threat information to identify, prevent, and eliminate cybersecurity threats in your network and on end-user devices. Traditional antivirus software offers insufficient protection against modern malware, zero-day threats, and sophisticated cyberattacks.

The term "endpoint protection platform" (EPP) is used to describe a kind of security software that includes next-generation antivirus programmes that are hosted in the cloud and include several capabilities for sharing data across various endpoint security tools. Modern endpoint security solutions protect your company from harmful attacks before they may cause data loss or disruption to operations (Sabahi, 2011). Complete endpoint security safeguards your network's endpoints from potential threats in advance, allowing your team to keep working without interruption.

3.5 NIST Security Policy

The National Institute of Standards and Technology (NIST) has established best practises for setting up a reliable and long-lasting cloud computing infrastructure. The NIST has published recommendations to aid firms in conducting risk assessments and enacting corrective and preventative measures. These standards are based on a cybersecurity framework created by the National Institute of Standards and Technology (NIST) (Nagarajan et al., 2022).

The National Institute of Standards and Technology (NIST) recommends analysing, mitigating, and managing risks at the organisational, mission, and information system levels as part of cloud security risk management processes. The management of cloud security risks is simplified by including risk management procedures into a system development life cycle (SDLC). Effective cloud security deployment and risk management may be aided by developing a risk management framework and following the procedures outlined in the NIST Cloud Security RMF (Risk Management Framework). Consumers of cloud services must specify what services they need, who is responsible for security, and what controls should be in place as a minimum. Cloud service providers must prioritise both regulatory compliance and the enhancement of security measures. Generally speaking, organisations may improve their cloud security by adhering to NIST's guidelines for cloud security policies (Antony Kumar et al., 2018).

3.6 Security as a Code

The best method for rapidly and nimbly safeguarding cloud workloads is "security as code" (SaC). Most industry experts in the cloud now believe that infrastructure as code (IaC) is the best way to eliminate manual, error-prone configuration when developing cloud-based solutions. Cloud-based systems can be compared with security policies to prevent "drift," and SaC takes this a step further by establishing cybersecurity policies and standards in code that can be referenced automatically in the configuration scripts used to create cloud platforms. By submitting code, developers put the company's regulations into effect, such as the mandate that sensitive data be secured while stored. Any programme that doesn't follow the PII policy is immediately disapproved (Narayana & Jayashree, 2017).

Figure 2. McKinsey & Company security framework as code
Source: https://www.mckinsey.com/capabilities/mckinsey-digital/our-insights/security-as-code-the-best-and-maybe-only-path-to-securing-cloud-applications-and-systems

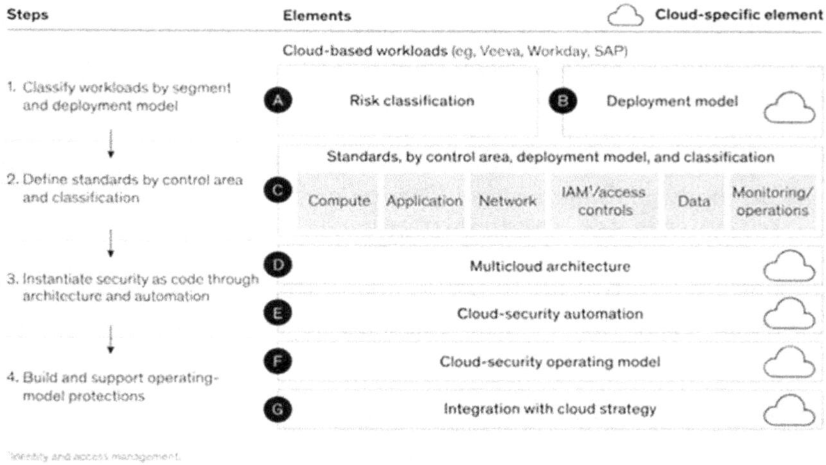

4. CONCLUSION

There is lot of ease with which applications can be offered at a low cost and wide range of users using cloud technology. Inspite of all the security risks and challenges the cloud security policy ideologies of NIST and Security as a code frameworks are offering security and privacy to the users involved. New threats keep evolving and new security paradigms like blockchain are also evolving. In near future more secure and safe cloud applications will continue to serve mankind with much ease and cost.

REFERENCES

Abdulsalam, Y. S., & Hedabou, M. (2022). Security and Privacy in Cloud Computing: Technical Review. *Future Internet, 14*(1), 11. doi:10.3390/fi14010011

Alrassan, & Alqahtani. (2023). Detection of DDoS Attacks on Clouds Computing Environments Using Machine Learning Techniques. *2023 International Conference on Intelligent Computing, Communication, Networking and Services (ICCNS),* 190-196. 10.1109/ICCNS58795.2023.10193141

Antony Kumar, Neeba, Durai, & Ravikumar. (2018). Secured Cryptographic Data Model for Cloud. *International Journal of Engineering and Technology, 7*(7), 128–31.

Babu & Jayashree. (2015). A Survey on the Role of IoT and Cloud in Health Care. *International Journal of Scientific, Engineering and Technology Research, 4*(12), 2217-2219.

Balani, Z., & Varol, H. (2020). Cloud Computing Security Challenges and Threats. *2020 8th International Symposium on Digital Forensics and Security (ISDFS)*, 1-4. 10.1109/ISDFS49300.2020.9116266

Gupta, Y., & Vashisth, R. (2023). Cyber Threats in Cloud Computing Environment. *2023 4th International Conference on Electronics and Sustainable Communication Systems (ICESC),* 548-555. 10.1109/ICESC57686.2023.10193701

Jaeyalakshmi, M., & Kumar, P. (2016). Task scheduling using meta-heuristic optimization techniques in cloud environment. *IJ Intelligent Systems and Applications, 5.*

Jaeyalakshmi, Vijay, Jayashree, & Vijay. (2023). A Cloud Based Healthcare Data Storage System Using Encryption Algorithm. In *Recent Trends in Computational Intelligence and Its Application* (pp. 486-491). CRC Press.

M. M. R. & A. T. P. (2023). Enhancing the Detection of DDoS Attacks in Cloud using Linear Discriminant Algorithm. *2023 8th International Conference on Communication and Electronics Systems (ICCES),* 505-509. 10.1109/ICCES57224.2023.10192657

Ma, M., Yu, Z., & Liu, B. (2023). Automatic Generation of Network Micro-Segmentation Policies for Cloud Environments. *2023 4th International Seminar on Artificial Intelligence, Networking and Information Technology (AINIT),* 1-5. 10.1109/AINIT59027.2023.10212857

Narayana, K. E., & Jayashree, K. (2017). A Overview on Cloud Computing Platforms and Issues. *International Journal of Advanced Research in Computer Science and Software Engineering*, *7*(1), 238–22. doi:10.23956/ijarcsse/V7I1/0162

Nguyen, D. C., Pathirana, P. N., Ding, M., & Seneviratne, A. (2019). Blockchain for Secure EHRs Sharing of Mobile Cloud Based E-Health Systems. *IEEE Access : Practical Innovations, Open Solutions*, *7*, 66792–66806. doi:10.1109/ACCESS.2019.2917555

Prithi, S., Sumathi, D., Poongodi, T., & Suresh, P. (2022). Trust Management Framework for Handling Security Issues in Multi-cloud Environment. In R. Nagarajan, P. Raj, & R. Thirunavukarasu (Eds.), *Operationalizing Multi-Cloud Environments. EAI/Springer Innovations in Communication and Computing*. Springer. doi:10.1007/978-3-030-74402-1_16

Ramgovind, S., Eloff, M. M., & Smith, E. (2010). The management of security in Cloud computing. *Information Security for South Africa, Johannesburg, South Africa, 2010*, 1–7. doi:10.1109/ISSA.2010.5588290

Sabahi, F. (2011). Cloud computing security threats and responses. *2011 IEEE 3rd International Conference on Communication Software and Networks*, 245-249. 10.1109/ICCSN.2011.6014715

Saxena, D., Gupta, I., Gupta, R., Singh, A. K., & Wen, X. (2023, November). An AI-Driven VM Threat Prediction Model for Multi-Risks Analysis-Based Cloud Cybersecurity. *IEEE Transactions on Systems, Man, and Cybernetics. Systems*, *53*(11), 6815–6827. Advance online publication. doi:10.1109/TSMC.2023.3288081

Shahid, V., Nayyer, M. Z., & Ahmed, U. (2023). Trust-aware Cloudlet Federation Model for Secure Service Selection. *2023 International Conference on Energy, Power, Environment, Control, and Computing (ICEPECC)*, 1-5. 10.1109/ICEPECC57281.2023.10209493

Sharma, Sharma, Kumar, Kelkar, & Deshmukh. (2023). Cloud Top Management Role in Reducing Mobile Broadband Transmission Hazards and Offering Safety. *2023 3rd International Conference on Advance Computing and Innovative Technologies in Engineering (ICACITE)*, 1064-1068. 10.1109/ICACITE57410.2023.10182893

Tarahomi, S., Holz, R., & Sperotto, A. (2023). Quantifying Security Risks in Cloud Infrastructures: A Data-driven Approach. *2023 IEEE 9th International Conference on Network Softwarization (NetSoft)*, 346-349. 10.1109/NetSoft57336.2023.10175501

Veena, S., Mallikarjun, C. J. T., Adiga, S. V., Reddy, B. C. V., & Yogish, P. D. (2023). Cloud Security Using The Smart Contracts. *2023 International Conference on Computational Intelligence and Sustainable Engineering Solutions (CISES)*, 312-316. 10.1109/CISES58720.2023.10183573

Vyas, P., Bhavani, G. L., Gairola, N., Ranjith, D., Ibrahim, W. K., & Alazzam, M. B. (2023). Machine Learning Approaches for Security Detection in Cloud Web Applications. *2023 3rd International Conference on Advance Computing and Innovative Technologies in Engineering (ICACITE)*, 1195-1199. 10.1109/ICACITE57410.2023.10183265

Yan, G., Wen, D., Olariu, S., & Weigle, M. C. (2013, March). Security challenges in vehicular cloud computing. *IEEE Transactions on Intelligent Transportation Systems*, *14*(1), 284–294. doi:10.1109/TITS.2012.2211870

Chapter 11
Strengthening Security, Privacy, and Trust in Artificial Intelligence Drones for Smart Cities

R. Sonia
Department of Computer Applications, B.S. Abdur Rahman Crescent Institute of Science and Technology, India

R. Hemalatha
Department of Computer Science and Engineering, St. Joseph's College of Engineering, India

Neha Gupta
Department of Computer Science, ABES Engineering College, India

M. Jogendra Kumar
Department of Computer Science and Engineering, Koneru Lakshmaiah Education Foundation, India

K. P. Manikandan
https://orcid.org/0000-0003-4685-1751
Department of CSE (Cyber Security), Madanapalle Institute of Technology and Science, India

Sampath Boopathi
https://orcid.org/0000-0002-2065-6539
Department of Mechanical Engineering, Muthayammal Engineering College, India

ABSTRACT

Smart cities are transforming by integrating artificial intelligence (AI) drones for various applications, including traffic monitoring, public space management, and surveillance. However, the increasing reliance on AI drones raises concerns about the security, privacy, and trust of both the technology and the data it collects and processes. Ensuring these factors is crucial for the success of these smart cities. The chapter explores the challenges and strategies for improving security, privacy, and trust in AI drones in smart cities. It emphasizes the role of AI drones in urban

DOI: 10.4018/979-8-3693-3249-8.ch011

innovation, the evolving threat landscape, and the importance of robust security measures. Privacy considerations are also discussed, along with transparency, accountability, ethical use, and public engagement. Technical solutions include AI algorithms, secure communication protocols, and trusted hardware and software components. The chapter also explores future trends and emerging technologies in AI drones and the evolving regulatory landscape.

INTRODUCTION

Smart cities are integrating AI drones into traffic management, urban planning, goods delivery, surveillance, and public safety. However, security, privacy, and trust are crucial. This chapter explores strategies to protect security, privacy, and trust in AI drones. The integration of AI drones is essential for creating efficient, sustainable, and livable environments in smart cities. Smart cities, driven by rapid urbanization and technological advancements, aim to improve quality of life for residents by integrating advanced technologies. Artificial Intelligence (AI) drones are a key component of this vision, revolutionizing urban management, public safety, and other services. However, addressing security, privacy, and trust issues is crucial as they are inextricably linked to the deployment of AI drones in smart cities (Bhati et al., 2017; Kaldate et al., 2022; Kalra & Pradhan, 2021).

AI drones, equipped with advanced sensors and machine learning, can improve urban surveillance, traffic management, disaster response, and environmental monitoring. They can reduce traffic congestion, improve public safety, and make cities more sustainable. However, ethical and secure use of these technologies is crucial, as they capture high-resolution imagery and sensitive data. Misuse can lead to unwarranted surveillance, invasion of privacy, and eroded trust between citizens and government authorities. AI drones pose a significant threat to public safety, infrastructure, and personal privacy due to their vulnerability to cyberattacks and unauthorized access. In urban airspace, accidents and collisions are common, necessitating robust security measures. Trust in the technology and its deploying institutions is crucial for public acceptance and successful integration into smart cities (Butler et al., 2021; Saleem et al., 2020). Building and maintaining this trust requires transparency, accountability, and ethical practices.

This paper explores the challenges and opportunities in ensuring the security, privacy, and trustworthiness of AI drones in smart cities. It discusses the existing landscape of AI drone technology, privacy implications, security vulnerabilities, and strategies for building trust among citizens (Ajchariyavanich et al., 2019; Perera et al., 2017). The goal is to harness AI drones responsibly and sustainably, prioritizing the welfare and interests of residents in smart cities.

Background and Context: Smart cities are transforming our lives and work by utilizing technology and data to enhance efficiency and sustainability. AI drones, equipped with advanced sensors, are a key component in this evolution, enabling real-time data collection and analysis, enabling informed decisions and improved quality of life for residents.

Importance of Security, Privacy, and Trust in Smart Cities: Smart city development is a complex process requiring security, privacy, and trust. AI drones can pose risks to public safety and personal privacy. The success of smart cities depends on their technological prowess, perception of safety, and respect for individual privacy. Addressing these concerns is crucial for global smart city growth.

Scope and Objectives of the Chapter: This chapter delves into the challenges of securing, preserving, and fostering trust in AI drones in smart cities. It covers threat landscape, data protection, ethical considerations, and technology's role in mitigating these issues. The aim is to provide readers with a deep understanding of securing AI drone technology and strategies to navigate the complex interplay of technology, privacy, and public trust in smarter, safer, and more sustainable urban environments.

SMART CITIES AND AI DRONES

This chapter explores the potential of smart cities and AI drones in improving urban living through advanced technologies, data analytics, and connectivity (Abualigah et al., 2021; Billah et al., 2022). It highlights their transformative potential, applications, and challenges, while also highlighting their key applications.

The Role of AI Drones in Smart Cities: AI drones are essential tools in smart cities, providing real-time data on traffic flow, air quality, and environmental conditions. They enable city planners to make informed decisions, optimize resource use, and enhance urban environments (Figure 1). They can also be deployed for surveillance, public safety, and disaster response, enhancing security and minimizing risks. Additionally, they facilitate the delivery of goods, medical supplies, and services, making urban life more convenient and responsive to residents' needs.

Figure 1. Roles of AI drones in smart cities

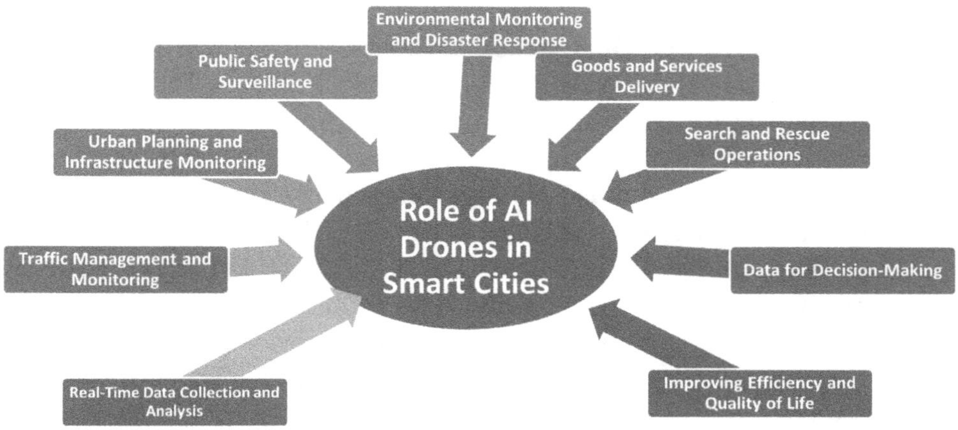

- **Real-Time Data Collection and Analysis:** AI drones serve as valuable tools for real-time data collection in smart cities. They can capture a wide range of data, such as traffic patterns, air quality, weather conditions, and more. This data is essential for city planners and decision-makers to gain insights into the dynamic urban environment.
- **Traffic Management and Monitoring:** AI drones are used to monitor and manage traffic congestion in real time. They can help identify traffic bottlenecks, accidents, and other disruptions, enabling authorities to take immediate actions to alleviate congestion and improve traffic flow.
- **Urban Planning and Infrastructure Monitoring:** AI drones provide a bird's-eye view of the city, making them indispensable for urban planning and infrastructure monitoring. They can assess the condition of roads, bridges, buildings, and other critical infrastructure, aiding in maintenance and development efforts.
- **Public Safety and Surveillance:** AI drones are employed for public safety and surveillance purposes. They can be used to monitor public events, crowd management, and emergency response. AI drones equipped with thermal cameras can detect anomalies and potential security threats.
- **Environmental Monitoring and Disaster Response:** AI drones are instrumental in monitoring environmental conditions and natural disasters. They can assess air quality, detect pollution sources, and provide valuable information during emergencies like wildfires, floods, and earthquakes.
- **Goods and Services Delivery:** Drones are increasingly used for the delivery of goods, medical supplies, and services in smart cities. They offer a more

efficient and environmentally friendly mode of transportation for last-mile deliveries.

- **Search and Rescue Operations:** AI drones are employed in search and rescue operations, especially in challenging urban terrains. They can quickly locate missing persons or provide critical data to first responders in emergency situations.
- **Data for Decision-Making:** The data collected by AI drones is instrumental for data-driven decision-making in smart cities. This data helps city officials and policymakers understand trends, optimize resource allocation, and plan for the future.
- **Improving Efficiency and Quality of Life:** By providing real-time data and actionable insights, AI drones contribute to increased operational efficiency in various aspects of urban life. This, in turn, improves the quality of life for residents, as cities become more responsive to their needs.

AI drones are crucial for smart cities to improve efficiency, sustainability, and resilience, but they pose challenges like privacy, security, and public trust. Addressing these issues is essential for successful adoption, ensuring residents' protection and fostering trust in AI drone technology.

Benefits and Challenges: AI drones are playing a crucial role in smart cities, improving operational efficiency, reducing emergency response times, and enhancing public services quality. They contribute to sustainability by monitoring environmental conditions and supporting clean energy solutions. AI drones also create new business opportunities and employment in the drone industry, addressing challenges and opportunities in urban development.

The Future of Smart Cities and AI Drones: AI drones are set to significantly impact smart cities due to advancements in algorithms, communication protocols, and hardware. However, ethical considerations and regulatory frameworks will need to balance technological innovation with safeguarding individual rights and privacy in smart cities (Gadekallu et al., 2021; Yazdinejad et al., 2021).

The integration of AI drones in smart cities is a significant technological advancement, improving efficiency, safety, and convenience. However, challenges like privacy, security, and public trust must be addressed to fully realize its potential. Strategies for enhancing security, privacy, and trust will be discussed in subsequent chapters.

SECURITY IN AI DRONES

The security of AI drones, particularly in smart cities, is crucial due to their extensive data collection and communication capabilities. Understanding and mitigating threats is essential for their safe and effective use. The threat landscape for AI drones in smart cities includes various threats (Alarcón et al., 2020; Al-Quraan et al., 2023; Zeng et al., 2023).

- **Data Interception and Eavesdropping:** Malicious actors may attempt to intercept the data transmitted by AI drones. This data could include sensitive information, such as surveillance footage or real-time monitoring data, making it a valuable target for interception and eavesdropping.
- **Unauthorized Access and Control:** Unauthorized individuals or entities may attempt to gain control over AI drones, potentially using them for malicious purposes. This could involve hacking into the drone's communication systems or exploiting vulnerabilities in its software.
- **Physical Attacks:** AI drones are susceptible to physical attacks, such as being shot down or physically damaged. These attacks can disrupt drone operations and pose risks to public safety if drones are used in critical functions like emergency response.
- **Malware and Cyberattacks:** Drones can be vulnerable to malware and cyberattacks, including viruses and ransomware. These attacks can compromise the integrity of the drone's software and data, leading to operational disruptions.
- **Frequency Jamming:** Jamming the communication frequencies used by AI drones can disrupt their control and data transmission. This can render drones inoperable or cause them to lose contact with their operators.
- **Privacy Concerns:** Drones equipped with cameras and sensors raise privacy concerns. Unauthorized or intrusive surveillance can infringe on the privacy of residents and citizens, leading to legal and ethical issues.
- **Geofencing Violations:** Many drones are programmed with geofencing capabilities to prevent them from flying in restricted areas. However, determined individuals may attempt to override these geofencing restrictions, potentially leading to security breaches or safety hazards.
- **Data Storage and Retention:** The way AI drones store and retain data can be a security concern. Data stored on drones can be vulnerable to theft or tampering if proper security measures are not in place.
- **Counter-Drone Measures:** Counter-drone technologies can pose a security threat when used to neutralize AI drones, especially in critical applications like law enforcement or military operations.

- **Legal and Regulatory Compliance:** The evolving landscape of drone regulations and compliance adds another layer of security concern. Ensuring that AI drones meet legal requirements and adhere to privacy regulations is vital to maintaining security.

To protect AI drones in smart cities, a comprehensive security strategy including encryption, access control, regular software updates, physical security measures, and privacy regulations is crucial. Public awareness and education on responsible drone use are also essential components. The Figure 2 depicts the various security aspects of AI Drones.

Figure 2. The various aspects of AI drones in the security aspects

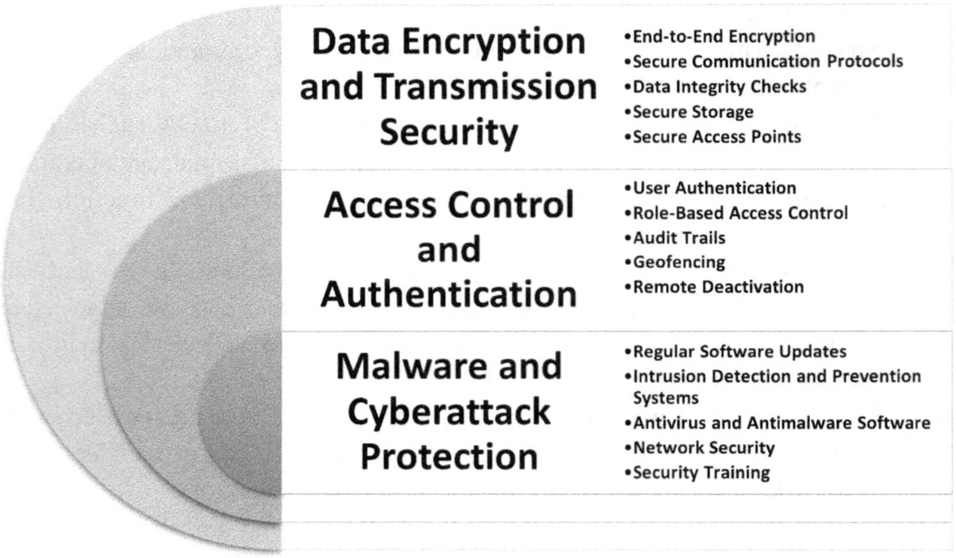

Data Encryption and Transmission Security

Encryption and transmission security measures are essential for safeguarding the data collected and transmitted by AI drones (Salama et al., 2023).

- **End-to-End Encryption:** Implementing strong end-to-end encryption for all data transmitted between the drone and its control center or remote operators ensures that data remains confidential and is protected from interception during transmission.

- **Secure Communication Protocols:** The use of secure communication protocols, such as SSL/TLS, ensures that data is securely transmitted over networks. These protocols help safeguard data against eavesdropping and man-in-the-middle attacks.
- **Data Integrity Checks:** Employing cryptographic techniques to verify data integrity during transmission helps detect any unauthorized tampering with the data.
- **Secure Storage:** Ensuring that data stored on the drone is also encrypted helps protect against physical theft and unauthorized access to the data.
- **Secure Access Points:** Securing the communication channels between the drone and its operators, including remote command centers, ensures that only authorized individuals can access and control the drone.

Access Control and Authentication

The control and verification of AI drone access is crucial for preventing unauthorized use and enhancing security, with measures including (Asaamoning et al., 2021; Everson et al., 2019).

- **User Authentication:** Implementing strong user authentication methods, such as multi-factor authentication (MFA), to ensure that only authorized personnel can access and control the drone.
- **Role-Based Access Control:** Assigning specific roles and permissions to users based on their responsibilities helps limit their access to drone functions and data, reducing the risk of misuse.
- **Audit Trails:** Maintaining detailed audit logs of drone operations and access helps track and investigate any unauthorized or suspicious activities.
- **Geofencing:** Setting up geofencing boundaries to restrict the drone's operational area helps prevent accidental or intentional breaches of restricted zones.
- **Remote Deactivation:** Implementing the ability to remotely deactivate the drone in case of unauthorized access or security threats can be a valuable security feature.

Malware and Cyberattack Protection

The use of AI drones is becoming increasingly important due to their potential vulnerability to malware and cyberattacks (Alarcón et al., 2020; Shukla et al., 2021).

- **Regular Software Updates:** Keeping the drone's software and firmware up to date helps patch known vulnerabilities and enhance security.
- **Intrusion Detection and Prevention Systems:** Employing intrusion detection and prevention systems can help identify and thwart cyberattacks in real time.
- **Antivirus and Antimalware Software:** Installing antivirus and antimalware solutions on the drone's onboard systems can help detect and remove malicious software.
- **Network Security**: Protecting the drone's network connections and communication channels with firewalls and network security measures helps thwart cyberattacks.
- **Security Training:** Providing security training to personnel who operate and maintain AI drones is essential for raising awareness and ensuring responsible use.

Implementing a comprehensive security strategy for AI drones in smart cities can enhance their security and prepare them to mitigate potential threats and vulnerabilities.

PRIVACY CONSIDERATIONS

The deployment of AI drones in smart cities requires careful privacy considerations, as these devices, equipped with cameras and sensors, can capture vast amounts of data, including personal and sensitive information (Billah et al., 2022; Reus-Muns & Chowdhury, 2021). The use of AI drones in smart cities raises significant privacy concerns.

- **Data Collection and Purpose Limitation:** Define clear guidelines for what data the AI drones can collect and the purposes for which it can be used. Ensure that data collection is limited to what is necessary for the intended functions, and avoid collecting excessive or irrelevant information.
- **Informed Consent:** In situations where individuals might be subject to drone surveillance, such as public events or monitoring in residential areas, consider obtaining informed consent from those being observed. Transparency about the use of drones and the data collected is critical.
- **Anonymization and Pseudonymization:** Implement techniques to anonymize or pseudonymize data collected by the drones. This helps protect the privacy of individuals by making it more difficult to identify specific individuals from the data.

- **Data Retention and Deletion:** Establish clear data retention and deletion policies. Data should only be retained for as long as necessary and should be securely deleted when no longer needed.
- **Geofencing and No-Fly Zones:** Implement geofencing to prevent drones from flying in restricted or sensitive areas, such as private properties or areas with a reasonable expectation of privacy.
- **Facial Recognition and Biometric Data:** Exercise caution when using facial recognition or biometric technologies with drones, as these can pose significant privacy risks. Compliance with relevant laws and regulations, such as GDPR, is essential.
- **Privacy Impact Assessments (PIAs):** Conduct privacy impact assessments to identify and address potential privacy risks associated with drone operations. This helps in ensuring that privacy considerations are thoroughly evaluated and mitigated.
- **Encryption and Data Security:** Implement strong encryption for data storage and transmission to safeguard it from unauthorized access. Protect the data against breaches and cyberattacks.
- **Compliance with Data Protection Regulations:** Ensure compliance with data protection regulations applicable in the region or jurisdiction where the drones are deployed. For example, in Europe, GDPR (General Data Protection Regulation) imposes strict requirements on data handling and privacy.
- **Public Awareness and Education:** Educate the public about the use of AI drones in smart cities, their data collection practices, and the measures in place to protect privacy. Public awareness can help build trust and understanding.
- **Transparent Policies and Accountability:** Establish clear and transparent privacy policies regarding the operation of AI drones. Hold those responsible for drone operations accountable for ensuring privacy protection.
- **Privacy by Design:** Incorporate privacy principles into the design and development of AI drone systems from the outset. This approach, known as "privacy by design," ensures that privacy considerations are integral to the technology.

The ethical deployment of AI drones in smart cities requires a balance between their potential benefits and the privacy concerns of residents, ensuring responsible and ethical use of this technology.

Data Collection and Privacy Concerns

- **Scope of Data Collection:** Define the scope of data that AI drones can collect. Ensure that the data collected is relevant to the drone's intended purpose and doesn't intrude on individuals' privacy. Avoid collecting unnecessary or overly sensitive information.

- **Consent and Notification:** In situations where individuals may be subject to drone surveillance, such as public events or residential areas, consider obtaining informed consent or providing clear notification. Transparency and consent are critical to respecting individual privacy.
- **Anonymization and Pseudonymization:** Implement techniques to anonymize or pseudonymize data collected by the drones. This helps protect individuals' privacy by making it more difficult to identify specific individuals from the data.
- **Data Minimization:** Collect only the data that is necessary for the drone's mission. Avoid collecting more data than needed, and delete data that is no longer required.
- **Encryption:** Use strong encryption to protect the data both during storage and transmission. Encryption helps safeguard data from unauthorized access and breaches.
- **Data Security:** Implement robust data security measures to protect the data against unauthorized access or cyberattacks. Ensure that the data is stored securely and that access is restricted to authorized personnel.

Compliance with Privacy Regulations

- **Know Applicable Laws:** Familiarize yourself with the privacy regulations and laws relevant to your jurisdiction. In the European Union, this may include the General Data Protection Regulation (GDPR), while other regions have their own privacy regulations.
- **Data Protection Impact Assessments (DPIAs):** Conduct Data Protection Impact Assessments to evaluate and mitigate the privacy risks associated with drone operations. DPIAs help identify and address potential privacy issues.
- **Data Protection Officers (DPOs):** Appoint a Data Protection Officer or designate someone responsible for ensuring compliance with privacy regulations. DPOs play a crucial role in data protection and privacy management.
- **Consent Management:** If required by privacy regulations, implement a consent management system to obtain and manage consent from individuals whose data is being collected by the drones.
- **Privacy by Design:** Incorporate privacy principles into the design and development of AI drone systems from the outset. This approach, known as

"privacy by design," ensures that privacy considerations are an integral part of the technology.

- **Data Subject Rights:** Be prepared to respect data subject rights, which may include the right to access, correct, or delete their personal data. Ensure processes are in place to respond to data subject requests.
- **Record Keeping:** Maintain records of data processing activities and any consents obtained. Documentation is a key aspect of demonstrating compliance with privacy regulations.
- **Security Audits and Assessments:** Regularly audit and assess the security and privacy measures in place for AI drone operations to ensure ongoing compliance.
- **Privacy Training:** Provide privacy training for personnel involved in drone operations to ensure that they understand and adhere to privacy regulations and best practices.
- **Collaborate with Regulators:** Establish lines of communication and collaboration with relevant privacy regulators to ensure transparency and compliance with regulations.

Privacy regulations are crucial for responsible and legal drone operations in smart cities, safeguarding individual privacy rights and enabling the ethical and lawful utilization of AI drones.

Anonymization

Anonymization is the process of transforming sensitive data into a form that cannot be used to identify individuals, crucial for protecting privacy in AI drone operations. The important considerations for anonymization in the context of AI drones in smart cities are discussed as given below (Al-Quraan et al., 2023; Iversen et al., 2021; Zeng et al., 2023).

- **Data De-Identification:** Anonymization involves removing or obfuscating direct identifiers (e.g., names, addresses) and potentially also transforming quasi-identifiers (e.g., birthdates) to prevent re-identification.
- **Aggregate Data:** Aggregate data whenever possible to prevent the disclosure of individual information. This reduces the risk of privacy breaches.
- **Data Masking:** Mask or truncate specific data elements that could lead to the identification of individuals, such as hiding the last few digits of a phone number or email address.

- **Differential Privacy:** Consider applying differential privacy techniques to add noise to the data, making it harder to identify specific individuals while still providing valuable insights.
- **Data Separation:** Separate sensitive data from non-sensitive data and apply anonymization techniques to the sensitive data, ensuring that non-sensitive data remains intact and useful.
- **Continuous Review:** Regularly review and update anonymization techniques to stay ahead of evolving privacy risks and threats.

Data Minimization

Data minimization is the practice of collecting only the data that is necessary for a specific purpose and avoiding the collection of excessive or irrelevant information. This principle helps reduce the risks associated with data breaches and unauthorized access (Gadekallu et al., 2021; Jackisch et al., 2019). Considerations for data minimization in the context of AI drones include:

- **Purpose-Limited Data Collection:** Clearly define the purpose for collecting data and limit the collection to what is strictly needed to achieve that purpose.
- **Avoid Overcollection:** Do not collect data beyond what is required for the drone's mission. For example, if a drone is monitoring air quality, it doesn't need to collect personal information about individuals in the area.
- **Regular Data Purging:** Implement policies for regular data purging or deletion, ensuring that data is not retained longer than necessary.
- **Data Lifecycle Management:** Establish a data lifecycle management process that includes data collection, storage, retention, and destruction phases. Ensure that data is managed throughout its entire lifecycle.
- **Data Mapping:** Create a data map to identify and track the flow of data within the organization and ensure that data minimization practices are consistently applied.
- **Consent and Transparency:** Clearly inform individuals about the data that will be collected by AI drones and obtain their consent when necessary. Transparency helps build trust and ensures that individuals are aware of data collection practices.

BUILDING TRUST

Trust in AI drone use in smart cities is crucial for successful integration and acceptance, and significant strategies include building trust through transparency and accountability (Donevski et al., 2021; Shukla et al., 2022; Wu et al., 2021).

Figure 3. Trust in AI drone use in smart cities by successful integration

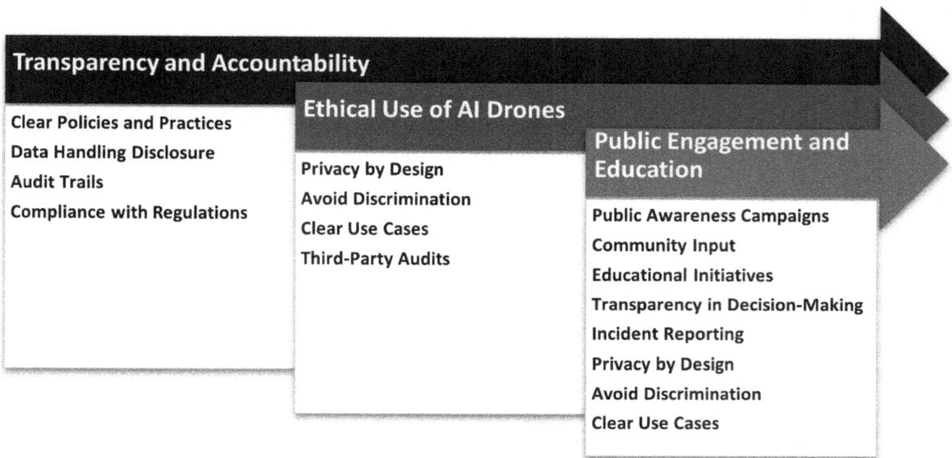

Transparency and Accountability

- **Clear Policies and Practices:** Maintain transparent and well-defined policies regarding the use of AI drones in smart cities. These policies should detail how data is collected, used, and protected. Make them easily accessible to the public.
- **Data Handling Disclosure:** Clearly disclose how data collected by AI drones is handled, including data storage, retention, and deletion policies. Be open about who has access to the data and why.
- **Audit Trails:** Implement audit trails that track the actions taken by operators and the data accessed. These logs can be used for accountability and transparency.
- **Compliance with Regulations:** Ensure strict compliance with relevant privacy regulations and adhere to ethical guidelines for AI drone usage.

Ethical Use of AI Drones

- **Privacy by Design:** Integrate privacy and ethical considerations into the design and development of AI drone systems from the outset. Ensure that privacy and ethical principles are core components of the technology.
- **Avoid Discrimination:** Ensure that AI algorithms used in drones do not discriminate against certain individuals or groups. Implement regular audits and tests to identify and mitigate biases.
- **Clear Use Cases:** Clearly define and communicate the acceptable and ethical use cases for AI drones. Avoid applications that could lead to privacy violations or harm to individuals.
- **Third-Party Audits:** Consider third-party audits of AI drone systems to assess their ethical use, data handling practices, and compliance with regulations.

Public Engagement and Education

- **Public Awareness Campaigns:** Launch public awareness campaigns to educate residents about the benefits of AI drones in smart cities, their rights regarding data privacy, and the safeguards in place to protect their privacy.
- **Community Input:** Involve the community and stakeholders in discussions about AI drone deployments. Solicit their input, listen to concerns, and take their feedback into account.
- **Educational Initiatives:** Implement educational programs and initiatives to inform the public, local businesses, and relevant organizations about the responsible use of AI drones.
- **Transparency in Decision-Making:** Be open about the decision-making processes related to AI drone deployments. Share information about where, why, and how drones are being used, and explain the benefits and safeguards in place.
- **Incident Reporting:** Set up clear channels for reporting any incidents, concerns, or privacy breaches related to AI drones. Ensure that these reports are promptly addressed and investigated.

To build trust in AI drones in smart cities, a combination of technical and ethical measures, community engagement, transparency, accountability, ethical use, and public education is needed, ensuring residents can enjoy drones while respecting privacy and ethical standards.

Trust in artificial intelligence drones encompasses various components that collectively contribute to the overall confidence and reliability of these technologies. These components include:

- **Transparency and Explain-ability:** Transparency involves making the operation and decision-making of AI drones understandable to the public. Explain-ability is the ability to provide clear and comprehensible explanations for the actions and decisions made by AI drones. Transparency and explain-ability are essential for building trust as they ensure that the technology's functioning is not hidden or opaque.
- **Data Privacy and Security:** Trust in AI drones depends on robust data privacy and security measures. This includes the protection of data collected by drones, adherence to privacy regulations, and secure data transmission. Individuals need assurance that their personal data is handled responsibly and securely.
- **Accountability and Responsibility:** Ensuring accountability and responsibility in the use of AI drones is vital. This involves clearly defining roles and responsibilities for their operation and establishing accountability for any misuse or ethical violations. People need to know who is responsible for the actions of these technologies.
- **Ethical Use and Bias Mitigation:** Trust is bolstered when AI drones are used ethically, with a focus on avoiding biases and discrimination. This includes addressing potential biases in AI algorithms, ensuring fairness, and adhering to ethical guidelines. Fair and unbiased use of AI drones is critical for public acceptance.
- **Public Engagement and Involvement:** Trust is fostered when the public is actively engaged and involved in discussions and decisions related to AI drones. This can include seeking public input, conducting public awareness campaigns, and involving stakeholders in the development and deployment of AI drone systems.
- **Regulatory Compliance:** Compliance with relevant laws and regulations is paramount. Trust is built when AI drones adhere to legal requirements and follow data protection and privacy regulations, as well as other applicable rules and standards.
- **Technical Reliability:** The technical reliability of AI drones, including their hardware and software components, is crucial for trust. Reliability ensures that the drones perform their functions accurately and consistently, reducing the risk of accidents or operational failures.
- **Emergency Response and Safety Measures:** Trust in AI drones for public safety is built through effective emergency response capabilities.

The technology must demonstrate its ability to assist in emergencies, such as search and rescue operations, and to ensure the safety of individuals in various scenarios.

- **Public Education and Awareness:** Providing education and increasing public awareness about AI drones is key to building trust. Informing the public about how these technologies work, their benefits, and the safeguards in place can help demystify them and promote understanding.
- **Ethical Oversight and Audits:** Establishing ethical oversight bodies and conducting regular audits can help ensure that AI drones are used ethically and responsibly. External audits can provide an additional layer of accountability and transparency.

These components collectively contribute to the development of trust in AI drones, making them more acceptable to the public and stakeholders. Building trust is an ongoing process that requires a combination of technical, ethical, and communication strategies to address public concerns and foster confidence in the technology.

TECHNICAL SOLUTIONS

Technical solutions are essential for improving the security, privacy, and trust of AI drones in smart cities through technical measures as shown in Figure 4. Technical solutions are essential for improving the security, privacy, and trust of AI drones in smart cities through technical measures (Maguluri et al., 2023; Reddy et al., 2023).

Figure 4. Technical measures for improving security, privacy, and trust

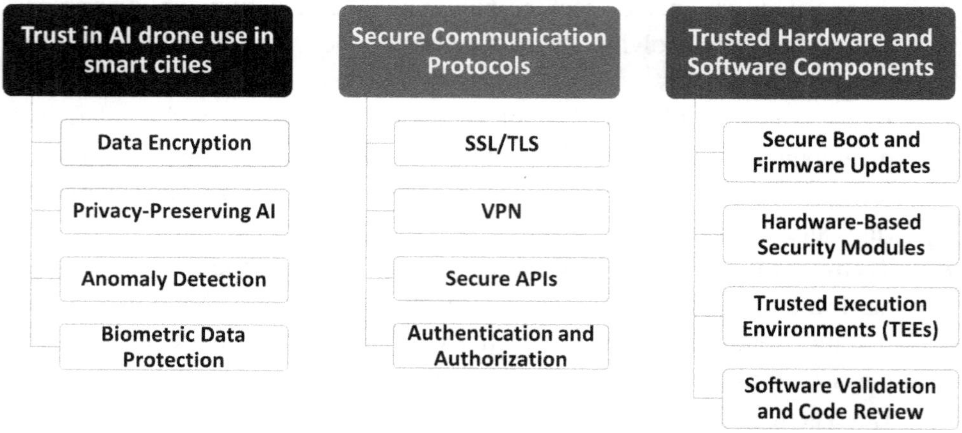

AI Algorithms for Security and Privacy

AI algorithms enhance drone security and privacy by protecting data collected and transmitted, ensuring ethical use of the technology, and play a crucial role in drone technology development (Agrawal et al., 2023; Karthik et al., 2023; Rahamathunnisa et al., 2023).

- **Data Encryption:** AI algorithms can implement strong encryption techniques to protect data both at rest (stored on the drone) and in transit (during communication). Encryption ensures that even if data is intercepted, it remains unintelligible to unauthorized users.
- **Privacy-Preserving AI:** Techniques like federated learning and homomorphic encryption allow AI drones to analyze data without exposing sensitive information. This helps protect individual privacy while still gaining insights from the data.
- **Anomaly Detection:** AI algorithms can be used to detect anomalies in drone behavior or data patterns, which can indicate potential security breaches. For example, they can identify unauthorized access attempts or unexpected changes in data.
- **Biometric Data Protection:** If drones collect biometric data (such as facial images), AI algorithms can be used to protect and anonymize this data to prevent re-identification and unauthorized access.

Secure Communication Protocols

Secure communication protocols are crucial for protecting data transmitted between AI drones and control centers, operators, or remote servers, ensuring confidentiality and protection against eavesdropping and interception.

- **SSL/TLS (Secure Sockets Layer/Transport Layer Security):** These protocols are commonly used to encrypt data during transmission, preventing unauthorized access to the data as it travels over networks.
- **VPN (Virtual Private Network):** VPNs can be used to create secure, encrypted tunnels for data transfer, which protects the data as it moves between the drone and its control center.
- **Secure APIs (Application Programming Interfaces):** Secure APIs facilitate data exchange between the drone and external systems while maintaining data integrity and confidentiality.

- **Authentication and Authorization:** These protocols ensure that only authorized personnel or systems can access and interact with the drone's data and control systems.

Trusted Hardware and Software Components

Trustworthiness of hardware and software components is crucial for AI drone reliability and security, which can be achieved through various measures.

- **Secure Boot and Firmware Updates:** Implement a secure boot process that verifies the integrity of the drone's software during startup. Secure firmware updates can ensure that the drone is running the latest, most secure software.
- **Hardware-Based Security Modules:** Hardware security modules (HSMs) can be integrated into the drone to protect cryptographic keys and perform secure operations, reducing the risk of key compromise.
- **Trusted Execution Environments (TEEs):** TEEs, such as ARM TrustZone or Intel SGX, provide isolated environments for executing sensitive operations, ensuring that critical data is protected from potential software vulnerabilities.
- **Software Validation and Code Review:** Regularly review and validate the drone's software code to identify and address vulnerabilities. Ensure that secure coding practices are followed.

The implementation of technical solutions in AI drones enhances security, privacy, and trust, protecting data, communication, and hardware and software integrity, crucial for responsible use in smart cities, thereby enhancing the overall safety of drones.

CASE STUDIES

Traffic Management in a Smart City

The case study explores the use of AI drones for real-time traffic monitoring and management in a smart city, aiming to improve transportation efficiency. It focuses on how AI drones are deployed for real-time traffic monitoring and management in a smart city. The study aims to enhance transportation efficiency, reduce traffic congestion, and improve urban mobility by using AI drones equipped with sensors and cameras to gather data on traffic flow, congestion, and incidents (Maguluri et al., 2023; Venkateswaran, Kumar, et al., 2023). The case study will evaluate the effectiveness of these drones in achieving these objectives and potentially optimizing traffic management strategies.

Public Safety and Emergency Response

In this case study, the use of AI drones in various emergency response scenarios is investigated. AI drones are employed for tasks such as search and rescue operations, disaster management, and public safety initiatives. The study examines the impact of AI drones on emergency response times, outcomes, and public safety effectiveness, while also assessing their cost-effectiveness and potential for life-saving in critical situations, particularly in disaster-stricken areas, where they can locate missing individuals.

Environmental Monitoring and Pollution Control

This case study delves into the application of AI drones for environmental monitoring and pollution control in a smart city. AI drones equipped with sensors and cameras are used to collect data related to air quality, pollution sources, and environmental conditions. The collected data is then analyzed to identify pollution hotspots and assess the overall environmental health of the city. The study aims to promote sustainable urban development by guiding environmental policy and promoting public health by examining how AI drones can improve city residents' quality of life by addressing environmental concerns and providing data-driven insights (Arunprasad & Boopathi, 2019; Boopathi, 2022; Hanumanthakari et al., 2023; Sengeni et al., 2023).

FUTURE TRENDS

Emerging Technologies

Emerging technologies and trends are expected to significantly shape the future of AI drones in smart cities, transforming their capabilities and applications.

- **5G Connectivity:** The rollout of 5G networks will significantly enhance the real-time communication capabilities of AI drones. This ultra-fast, low-latency connectivity will enable drones to transmit data and receive commands with minimal delay, making them more responsive and suitable for a wider range of applications (Agrawal et al., 2024; Venkateswaran, Vidhya, Ayyannan, et al., 2023).

- **Edge Computing:** Edge computing allows AI drones to process data closer to the source, reducing latency and the need to transmit large amounts of data to centralized servers. This enables faster decision-making and more efficient operation, particularly in real-time tasks like surveillance and emergency response (Kumar et al., 2023; Syamala et al., 2023; Venkateswaran, Vidhya, Naik, et al., 2023).
- **AI and Machine Learning Advancements:** Ongoing advancements in AI and machine learning algorithms will make AI drones smarter and more capable of autonomous decision-making. This will improve their ability to analyze data, identify objects, and adapt to changing environments (Boopathi & Kanike, 2023; Veeranjaneyulu et al., 2023; Zekrifa et al., 2023).
- **Swarming Technology:** Swarming technology involves the coordination of multiple drones to work together as a cohesive unit. This enables collaborative tasks such as search and rescue operations, environmental monitoring, and large-scale data collection with improved efficiency and redundancy.
- **Longer Flight Durations and Battery Technology:** Advances in battery technology and energy efficiency will extend the flight duration of AI drones. This will allow them to cover larger areas and undertake longer missions, such as aerial inspections, without frequent recharging.
- **Advanced Sensors and Cameras:** Improved sensor technology, including LiDAR, multispectral cameras, and thermal imaging, will enhance the capabilities of AI drones for various applications, such as precision agriculture, environmental monitoring, and infrastructure inspections.
- **Urban Air Mobility (UAM):** The development of UAM systems, including passenger-carrying drones and flying taxis, will revolutionize urban transportation and mobility in smart cities. UAM will require sophisticated traffic management systems to ensure safety and efficiency.
- **Blockchain for Data Security:** The integration of blockchain technology can enhance data security and privacy by providing an immutable and transparent ledger for tracking data provenance and access. This is particularly important in applications involving sensitive data.
- **Drone Traffic Management:** The proliferation of drones in urban airspace will necessitate the development of drone traffic management systems (UTM). These systems will regulate drone flight paths, prevent collisions, and ensure safe integration with other air traffic.
- **AI-Enhanced Disaster Response:** AI drones equipped with advanced sensors and AI algorithms will play a crucial role in disaster response and recovery efforts, rapidly assessing damage, identifying survivors, and delivering supplies to affected areas.

- **Green and Sustainable Drones:** As environmental concerns grow, there will be an increased focus on developing environmentally friendly and sustainable drones, including electric and solar-powered models (B et al., 2024; Venkateswaran, Kumar, et al., 2023; Venkateswaran, Vidhya, Ayyannan, et al., 2023).
- **Regulatory Frameworks:** Governments and regulatory bodies will continue to develop and refine regulations to ensure safe and responsible drone operations in smart cities. These regulations will address issues related to privacy, safety, and airspace management.

The future of AI drones in smart cities is promising, driven by emerging technologies and trends. However, challenges related to privacy, safety, and ethical use will need to be addressed as these technologies evolve.

Evolving Threats

- **Security Vulnerabilities:** With the increasing reliance on AI drones for various applications, they become more attractive targets for cyberattacks. Threat actors may attempt to hack into drone systems, intercept data, or disrupt their operation.
- **Privacy Concerns:** As the amount of data collected by AI drones grows, so do concerns about privacy. Unauthorized data collection, facial recognition, and invasive surveillance could lead to public backlash and regulatory restrictions.
- **Airspace Congestion:** The proliferation of AI drones in urban areas may lead to congestion in airspace, increasing the risk of mid-air collisions and accidents. Effective traffic management and integration with other air traffic will be crucial.
- **Technological Advancements in Threats:** As AI drone technology evolves, so do the capabilities of malicious actors. For example, drones could be used for more sophisticated cyberattacks or physical threats, such as delivering malicious payloads.

Regulatory Challenges

- **Privacy Regulations:** Governments are likely to enact or strengthen privacy regulations to protect citizens from intrusive surveillance and data collection. Striking a balance between public safety and individual privacy will be a significant regulatory challenge.

- **Airspace Regulations:** As urban airspace becomes more congested with drones, regulatory bodies will need to establish and enforce rules for safe drone operations, including altitude restrictions, no-fly zones, and collision avoidance systems.
- **Data Handling and Storage:** Regulations concerning the handling, storage, and retention of data collected by AI drones will continue to evolve. Compliance with data protection laws, such as GDPR, will be a priority.
- **Certification and Standards:** Regulatory bodies will need to define certification and safety standards for AI drones, including hardware, software, and communication systems. This ensures the reliability and security of drone operations.

The Road Ahead

- **Collaboration and Standardization:** Collaboration among governments, industry stakeholders, and drone manufacturers will be crucial in developing common standards and best practices for AI drones. This will help create a more consistent and secure environment for their deployment.
- **Improved Security Measures:** The development of more robust cybersecurity measures and practices will be essential to protect AI drones from evolving threats. This includes advanced encryption, intrusion detection systems, and regular security audits.
- **Public Awareness and Education:** Increasing public awareness of the benefits and potential risks of AI drones, as well as educating the public about their rights and options, will be an important part of building public trust and engagement.
- **Ethical Considerations:** Ethical discussions surrounding the use of AI drones, especially in areas like public surveillance and law enforcement, will continue. These discussions will inform the development of guidelines and policies that align with societal values.
- **Research and Development:** Investment in research and development of AI drone technology will drive innovation and the development of more reliable and secure systems. Research should also focus on making drones more environmentally friendly and energy-efficient.
- **Regulatory Agility:** Regulatory bodies will need to maintain agility and adaptability to respond to the rapidly changing landscape of AI drone technology and its applications. Regulations should support responsible and safe usage while promoting innovation.

AI drones in smart cities are promising, but they require a balance between technological advancement, security, privacy, and ethical considerations. Collaboration, education, and ethical practices will be crucial in shaping this future, ensuring safer, more efficient, and sustainable smart cities.

CONCLUSION

The integration of AI drones in smart cities offers a promising solution for urban transformation. These drones can be used for traffic management, public safety, and environmental monitoring. However, challenges such as security, privacy, and trust need to be addressed. To ensure responsible use, it is crucial to prioritize security measures, protect data privacy, and build trust among residents and stakeholders. Key components include transparency, ethical use, public engagement, and compliance with regulations. These elements are essential for fostering public acceptance and support for AI drone technology. Emerging technologies like 5G, edge computing, and AI will enhance the capabilities of AI drones in urban applications like traffic management and emergency response. However, they also present cybersecurity risks and privacy concerns, necessitating ongoing attention. The future of AI drones in smart cities requires collaboration, standardization, improved security measures, public awareness, and ethical considerations. Regulatory agility is also necessary to adapt to the rapidly changing landscape of AI drone technology. By addressing these challenges, smart cities can harness AI drones to create sustainable, innovative urban environments while upholding security, privacy, and trust values.

ABBREVIATIONS

AI: Artificial Intelligence

5G: Fifth Generation (of wireless communication)

IoT: Internet of Things

UAV: Unmanned Aerial Vehicle (commonly known as a drone)

UAS: Unmanned Aircraft System

GDPR: General Data Protection Regulation

HSMs: Hardware Security Modules

TEE: Trusted Execution Environment

UTM: Unmanned Traffic Management

REFERENCES

Abualigah, L., Diabat, A., Sumari, P., & Gandomi, A. H. (2021). Applications, deployments, and integration of internet of drones (iod): A review. *IEEE Sensors Journal, 21*(22), 25532–25546. doi:10.1109/JSEN.2021.3114266

Agrawal, A. V., Magulur, L. P., Priya, S. G., Kaur, A., Singh, G., & Boopathi, S. (2023). Smart Precision Agriculture Using IoT and WSN. In *Handbook of Research on Data Science and Cybersecurity Innovations in Industry 4.0 Technologies* (pp. 524–541). IGI Global. doi:10.4018/978-1-6684-8145-5.ch026

Agrawal, A. V., Shashibhushan, G., Pradeep, S., Padhi, S. N., Sugumar, D., & Boopathi, S. (2024). Synergizing Artificial Intelligence, 5G, and Cloud Computing for Efficient Energy Conversion Using Agricultural Waste. In Practice, Progress, and Proficiency in Sustainability (pp. 475–497). IGI Global. doi:10.4018/979-8-3693-1186-8.ch026

Ajchariyavanich, C., Limpisthira, T., Chanjarasvichai, N., Jareonwatanan, T., Phongphanpanya, W., Wareechuensuk, S., Srichareonkul, S., Tachatanitanont, S., Ratanamahatana, C., Prompoon, N., & ... (2019). Park king: An IoT-based smart parking system. *2019 IEEE International Smart Cities Conference (ISC2)*, 729–734. 10.1109/ISC246665.2019.9071721

Al-Quraan, M., Mohjazi, L., Bariah, L., Centeno, A., Zoha, A., Arshad, K., Assaleh, K., Muhaidat, S., Debbah, M., & Imran, M. A. (2023). Edge-native intelligence for 6G communications driven by federated learning: A survey of trends and challenges. *IEEE Transactions on Emerging Topics in Computational Intelligence, 7*(3), 957–979. doi:10.1109/TETCI.2023.3251404

Alarcón, V., García, M., Alarcón, F., Viguria, A., Martínez, Á., Janisch, D., Acevedo, J. J., Maza, I., & Ollero, A. (2020). Procedures for the integration of drones into the airspace based on U-space services. *Aerospace (Basel, Switzerland), 7*(9), 128. doi:10.3390/aerospace7090128

Arunprasad, R., & Boopathi, S. (2019). Chapter-4 Alternate Refrigerants for Minimization Environmental Impacts: A Review. In Advances in Engineering Technology (p. 75). AkiNik Publications.

Asaamoning, G., Mendes, P., Rosário, D., & Cerqueira, E. (2021). Drone swarms as networked control systems by integration of networking and computing. *Sensors (Basel), 21*(8), 2642. doi:10.339021082642 PMID:33918696

B, M. K., K, K. K., Sasikala, P., Sampath, B., Gopi, B., & Sundaram, S. (2024). Sustainable Green Energy Generation From Waste Water. In *Practice, Progress, and Proficiency in Sustainability* (pp. 440–463). IGI Global. doi:10.4018/979-8-3693-1186-8.ch024

Bhati, A., Hansen, M., & Chan, C. M. (2017). Energy conservation through smart homes in a smart city: A lesson for Singapore households. *Energy Policy*, *104*, 230–239. doi:10.1016/j.enpol.2017.01.032

Billah, M., Mehedi, S. T., Anwar, A., Rahman, Z., & Islam, R. (2022). *A systematic literature review on blockchain enabled federated learning framework for internet of vehicles.* arXiv Preprint arXiv:2203.05192.

Boopathi, S. (2022). An investigation on gas emission concentration and relative emission rate of the near-dry wire-cut electrical discharge machining process. *Environmental Science and Pollution Research International*, *29*(57), 86237–86246. doi:10.100711356-021-17658-1 PMID:34837614

Boopathi, S., & Kanike, U. K. (2023). Applications of Artificial Intelligent and Machine Learning Techniques in Image Processing. In *Handbook of Research on Thrust Technologies' Effect on Image Processing* (pp. 151–173). IGI Global. doi:10.4018/978-1-6684-8618-4.ch010

Butler, L., Yigitcanlar, T., & Paz, A. (2021). Barriers and risks of Mobility-as-a-Service (MaaS) adoption in cities: A systematic review of the literature. *Cities (London, England)*, *109*, 103036. doi:10.1016/j.cities.2020.103036

Donevski, I., Nielsen, J. J., & Popovski, P. (2021). On addressing heterogeneity in federated learning for autonomous vehicles connected to a drone orchestrator. *Frontiers in Communications and Networks*, *2*, 709946. doi:10.3389/frcmn.2021.709946

Everson, L. R., Sapatnekar, S. S., & Kim, C. H. (2019). 2.5 A 40\times 40 four-neighbor time-based in-memory computing graph ASIC chip featuring wavefront expansion and 2D gradient control. *2019 IEEE International Solid-State Circuits Conference-(ISSCC)*, 50–52. 10.1109/ISSCC.2019.8662455

Gadekallu, T. R., Pham, Q.-V., Huynh-The, T., Bhattacharya, S., Maddikunta, P. K. R., & Liyanage, M. (2021). *Federated learning for big data: A survey on opportunities, applications, and future directions.* arXiv Preprint arXiv:2110.04160.

Hanumanthakari, S., Gift, M. M., Kanimozhi, K., Bhavani, M. D., Bamane, K. D., & Boopathi, S. (2023). Biomining Method to Extract Metal Components Using Computer-Printed Circuit Board E-Waste. In *Handbook of Research on Safe Disposal Methods of Municipal Solid Wastes for a Sustainable Environment* (pp. 123–141). IGI Global. doi:10.4018/978-1-6684-8117-2.ch010

Iversen, N., Schofield, O. B., Cousin, L., Ayoub, N., Vom Bögel, G., & Ebeid, E. (2021). Design, integration and implementation of an intelligent and self-recharging drone system for autonomous power line inspection. *2021 IEEE/RSJ International Conference on Intelligent Robots and Systems (IROS)*, 4168–4175. 10.1109/IROS51168.2021.9635924

Jackisch, R., Madriz, Y., Zimmermann, R., Pirttijärvi, M., Saartenoja, A., Heincke, B. H., Salmirinne, H., Kujasalo, J.-P., Andreani, L., & Gloaguen, R. (2019). Drone-borne hyperspectral and magnetic data integration: Otanmäki Fe-Ti-V deposit in Finland. *Remote Sensing (Basel)*, *11*(18), 2084. doi:10.3390/rs11182084

Kaldate, A., Kanase-Patil, A., & Lokhande, S. (2022). Artificial Intelligence Based Integrated Renewable Energy Management in Smart City. In Energy Storage Systems: Optimization and Applications (pp. 1–20). Springer.

Kalra, D., & Pradhan, M. R. (2021). Enduring data analytics for reliable data management in handling smart city services. *Soft Computing*, *25*(18), 12213–12225. doi:10.100700500-021-05892-1

Karthik, S., Hemalatha, R., Aruna, R., Deivakani, M., Reddy, R. V. K., & Boopathi, S. (2023). Study on Healthcare Security System-Integrated Internet of Things (IoT). In Perspectives and Considerations on the Evolution of Smart Systems (pp. 342–362). IGI Global.

Kumar, P. R., Meenakshi, S., Shalini, S., Devi, S. R., & Boopathi, S. (2023). Soil Quality Prediction in Context Learning Approaches Using Deep Learning and Blockchain for Smart Agriculture. In R. Kumar, A. B. Abdul Hamid, & N. I. Binti Ya'akub (Eds.), (pp. 1–26). Advances in Computational Intelligence and Robotics. IGI Global. doi:10.4018/978-1-6684-9151-5.ch001

Maguluri, L. P., Arularasan, A. N., & Boopathi, S. (2023). Assessing Security Concerns for AI-Based Drones in Smart Cities. In R. Kumar, A. B. Abdul Hamid, & N. I. Binti Ya'akub (Eds.), Advances in Computational Intelligence and Robotics (pp. 27–47). IGI Global. doi:10.4018/978-1-6684-9151-5.ch002

Perera, C., Qin, Y., Estrella, J. C., Reiff-Marganiec, S., & Vasilakos, A. V. (2017). Fog computing for sustainable smart cities: A survey. *ACM Computing Surveys*, *50*(3), 1–43. doi:10.1145/3057266

Rahamathunnisa, U., Subhashini, P., Aancy, H. M., Meenakshi, S., Boopathi, S., & ... (2023). Solutions for Software Requirement Risks Using Artificial Intelligence Techniques. In *Handbook of Research on Data Science and Cybersecurity Innovations in Industry 4.0 Technologies* (pp. 45–64). IGI Global.

Reddy, M. A., Gaurav, A., Ushasukhanya, S., Rao, V. C. S., Bhattacharya, S., & Boopathi, S. (2023). Bio-Medical Wastes Handling Strategies During the COVID-19 Pandemic. In Multidisciplinary Approaches to Organizational Governance During Health Crises (pp. 90–111). IGI Global. doi:10.4018/978-1-7998-9213-7.ch006

Reus-Muns, G., & Chowdhury, K. R. (2021). Classifying UAVs with proprietary waveforms via preamble feature extraction and federated learning. *IEEE Transactions on Vehicular Technology*, *70*(7), 6279–6290. doi:10.1109/TVT.2021.3081049

Salama, R., Al-Turjman, F., & Culmone, R. (2023). AI-Powered Drone to Address Smart City Security Issues. *International Conference on Advanced Information Networking and Applications*, 292–300. 10.1007/978-3-031-28694-0_27

Saleem, A. A., Siddiqui, H. U. R., Shafique, R., Haider, A., & Ali, M. (2020). A review on smart IOT based parking system. *Recent Advances on Soft Computing and Data Mining: Proceedings of the Fourth International Conference on Soft Computing and Data Mining (SCDM 2020)*, 264–273.

Sengeni, D., Padmapriya, G., Imambi, S. S., Suganthi, D., Suri, A., & Boopathi, S. (2023). Biomedical Waste Handling Method Using Artificial Intelligence Techniques. In *Handbook of Research on Safe Disposal Methods of Municipal Solid Wastes for a Sustainable Environment* (pp. 306–323). IGI Global. doi:10.4018/978-1-6684-8117-2.ch022

Shukla, P., Muralidhar, A., Iliev, N., Tulabandhula, T., Fuller, S. B., & Trivedi, A. R. (2021). Ultralow-power localization of insect-scale drones: Interplay of probabilistic filtering and compute-in-memory. *IEEE Transactions on Very Large Scale Integration (VLSI) Systems*, *30*(1), 68–80.

Shukla, P., Nasrin, S., Darabi, N., Gomes, W., & Trivedi, A. R. (2022). MC-CIM: Compute-in-Memory With Monte-Carlo Dropouts for Bayesian Edge Intelligence. *IEEE Transactions on Circuits and Systems. I, Regular Papers*, *70*(2), 884–896. doi:10.1109/TCSI.2022.3224703

Syamala, M., Komala, C., Pramila, P., Dash, S., Meenakshi, S., & Boopathi, S. (2023). Machine Learning-Integrated IoT-Based Smart Home Energy Management System. In *Handbook of Research on Deep Learning Techniques for Cloud-Based Industrial IoT* (pp. 219–235). IGI Global. doi:10.4018/978-1-6684-8098-4.ch013

Veeranjaneyulu, R., Boopathi, S., Kumari, R. K., Vidyarthi, A., Isaac, J. S., & Jaiganesh, V. (2023). Air Quality Improvement and Optimisation Using Machine Learning Technique. *IEEE Explore*, 1–6.

Venkateswaran, N., Kumar, S. S., Diwakar, G., Gnanasangeetha, D., & Boopathi, S. (2023). Synthetic Biology for Waste Water to Energy Conversion: IoT and AI Approaches. In M. Arshad (Ed.), (pp. 360–384). Advances in Bioinformatics and Biomedical Engineering. IGI Global. doi:10.4018/978-1-6684-6577-6.ch017

Venkateswaran, N., Vidhya, K., Ayyannan, M., Chavan, S. M., Sekar, K., & Boopathi, S. (2023). A Study on Smart Energy Management Framework Using Cloud Computing. In 5G, Artificial Intelligence, and Next Generation Internet of Things: Digital Innovation for Green and Sustainable Economies (pp. 189–212). IGI Global. doi:10.4018/978-1-6684-8634-4.ch009

Venkateswaran, N., Vidhya, R., Naik, D. A., Raj, T. M., Munjal, N., & Boopathi, S. (2023). Study on Sentence and Question Formation Using Deep Learning Techniques. In *Digital Natives as a Disruptive Force in Asian Businesses and Societies* (pp. 252–273). IGI Global. doi:10.4018/978-1-6684-6782-4.ch015

Wu, S., Wang, J., Yan, Z., Song, G., Chen, Y., Ma, Q., Deng, M., Wu, Y., Zhao, Y., Guo, Z., Yuan, Z., Dai, G., Xu, X., Yang, X., Su, Y., Liu, L., & Wu, J. (2021). Monitoring tree-crown scale autumn leaf phenology in a temperate forest with an integration of PlanetScope and drone remote sensing observations. *ISPRS Journal of Photogrammetry and Remote Sensing*, *171*, 36–48. doi:10.1016/j.isprsjprs.2020.10.017

Yazdinejad, A., Parizi, R. M., Dehghantanha, A., & Karimipour, H. (2021). Federated learning for drone authentication. *Ad Hoc Networks*, *120*, 102574. doi:10.1016/j.adhoc.2021.102574

Zekrifa, D. M. S., Kulkarni, M., Bhagyalakshmi, A., Devireddy, N., Gupta, S., & Boopathi, S. (2023). Integrating Machine Learning and AI for Improved Hydrological Modeling and Water Resource Management. In *Artificial Intelligence Applications in Water Treatment and Water Resource Management* (pp. 46–70). IGI Global. doi:10.4018/978-1-6684-6791-6.ch003

Zeng, S., Li, Z., Yu, H., Zhang, Z., Luo, L., Li, B., & Niyato, D. (2023). Hfedms: Heterogeneous federated learning with memorable data semantics in industrial metaverse. *IEEE Transactions on Cloud Computing*, 1–15. doi:10.1109/TCC.2023.3254587

Compilation of References

Aarts, J., Hannink, J., & Olde Keizer, M. (2016). The Internet of Things in Industry: A Survey. *IEEE Transactions on Industrial Informatics*, *12*(6), 2233–2243.

Abdulsalam, Y. S., & Hedabou, M. (2022). Security and Privacy in Cloud Computing: Technical Review. *Future Internet*, *14*(1), 11. doi:10.3390/fi14010011

Abualigah, L., Diabat, A., Sumari, P., & Gandomi, A. H. (2021). Applications, deployments, and integration of internet of drones (iod): A review. *IEEE Sensors Journal*, *21*(22), 25532–25546. doi:10.1109/JSEN.2021.3114266

Agrawal, A. V., Shashibhushan, G., Pradeep, S., Padhi, S. N., Sugumar, D., & Boopathi, S. (2024). Synergizing Artificial Intelligence, 5G, and Cloud Computing for Efficient Energy Conversion Using Agricultural Waste. In Practice, Progress, and Proficiency in Sustainability (pp. 475–497). IGI Global. doi:10.4018/979-8-3693-1186-8.ch026

Agrawal, A. V., Magulur, L. P., Priya, S. G., Kaur, A., Singh, G., & Boopathi, S. (2023). Smart Precision Agriculture Using IoT and WSN. In *Handbook of Research on Data Science and Cybersecurity Innovations in Industry 4.0 Technologies* (pp. 524–541). IGI Global. doi:10.4018/978-1-6684-8145-5.ch026

Ajchariyavanich, C., Limpisthira, T., Chanjarasvichai, N., Jareonwatanan, T., Phongphanpanya, W., Wareechuensuk, S., Srichareonkul, S., Tachatanitanont, S., Ratanamahatana, C., Prompoon, N., & ... (2019). Park king: An IoT-based smart parking system. *2019 IEEE International Smart Cities Conference (ISC2)*, 729–734. 10.1109/ISC246665.2019.9071721

Alarcón, V., García, M., Alarcón, F., Viguria, A., Martínez, Á., Janisch, D., Acevedo, J. J., Maza, I., & Ollero, A. (2020). Procedures for the integration of drones into the airspace based on U-space services. *Aerospace (Basel, Switzerland)*, *7*(9), 128. doi:10.3390/aerospace7090128

Alheeti, K. M. A., Al-Ani, M. S., Al-Aloosy, A. K. N., Alzahrani, A., & Rukan, D. A. S. (2022). Intelligent mobile detection of cracks in concrete utilising an unmanned aerial vehicle. *Bulletin of Electrical Engineering and Informatics*, *11*(1), 176–184. doi:10.11591/eei.v11i1.2987

Ali, Khan, Riaz, Kwak, & Abuhmed. (2017). A Fuzzy Ontology and SVM–Based Web Content Classification System. *IEEE Access*. doi:10.1109/ACCESS.2017.2768564

Alien4Cloud. (2020). https://alien4cloud.github.io/

Aljawarneh, S., Aldwairi, M., & Seassein, M. B. (2019). Secure data sharing in the cloud: a systematic literature review. *IEEE Introduction, 7*, 1003-1012.

Alkahtani, H., & Aldhyani, T. H. (2021). Intrusion detection system to advance internet of things infrastructure-based deep learning algorithms. *Complexity, 2021*, 1–18. doi:10.1155/2021/5579851

Alléaume, R., Branciard, C., Bouda, J., Debuisschert, T., Dianati, M., Gisin, N., Godfrey, M., Grangier, P., Länger, T., Lütkenhaus, N., Monyk, C., Painchault, P., Peev, M., Poppe, A., Pornin, T., Rarity, J., Renner, R., Ribordy, G., Riguidel, M., ... Zeilinger, A. (2014). Using quantum key distribution for cryptographic purposes: A survey. *Theoretical Computer Science, 560*, 62–81. doi:10.1016/j.tcs.2014.09.018

Allouch, A., Cheikhrouhou, O., Koubâa, A., Khalgui, M., & Abbes, T. (2019, June). MAVSec: Securing the MAVLink protocol for ardupilot/PX4 unmanned aerial systems. In 2019 15th International Wireless Communications & Mobile Computing Conference (IWCMC) (pp. 621-628). IEEE.

Almahmoud, S., Hammo, B., Al-Shboul, B., & Obeid, N. (2022). A hybrid approach for identifying non-human traffic in online digital advertising. *Multimedia Tools and Applications, 81*(2), 1–34. doi:10.100711042-021-11533-4

Al-Quraan, M., Mohjazi, L., Bariah, L., Centeno, A., Zoha, A., Arshad, K., Assaleh, K., Muhaidat, S., Debbah, M., & Imran, M. A. (2023). Edge-native intelligence for 6G communications driven by federated learning: A survey of trends and challenges. *IEEE Transactions on Emerging Topics in Computational Intelligence, 7*(3), 957–979. doi:10.1109/TETCI.2023.3251404

Alrassan, & Alqahtani. (2023). Detection of DDoS Attacks on Clouds Computing Environments Using Machine Learning Techniques. *2023 International Conference on Intelligent Computing, Communication, Networking and Services (ICCNS),* 190-196. 10.1109/ICCNS58795.2023.10193141

Alsafi, T., & Fan, I. S. (2020, June). Cloud computing adoption barriers faced by Saudi manufacturing SMEs. In *2020 15th Iberian Conference on Information Systems and Technologies (CISTI)* (pp. 1-6). IEEE. 10.23919/CISTI49556.2020.9140940

Amazon. (2020). *Aws cloudformation: Speed up cloud provisioning with infrastructure as code.* https://aws.amazon.com/cloudformation/

Ambika, N. (2019). Energy-Perceptive Authentication in Virtual Private Networks Using GPS Data. In Security, privacy and trust in the IoT environment (pp. 25-38). Cham: Springer. doi:10.1007/978-3-030-18075-1_2

Aminanto, M. E., Choi, R., Tanuwidjaja, H. C., Yoo, P. D., & Kim, K. (2017). Deep abstraction and weighted feature selection for Wi-Fi impersonation detection. *IEEE Transactions on Information Forensics and Security, 13*(3), 621–636. doi:10.1109/TIFS.2017.2762828

Amini, A., Jamil, N., Ahmad, A. R., & Z'aba, M. R. (2015). *Threat Modeling Approaches for Securing Cloud Computing*. https://docsdrive.com/pdfs/ansinet/jas/2015/953-967.pdf doi:10.3923/jas.2015.953.967

Antony Kumar, Neeba, Durai, & Ravikumar. (2018). Secured Cryptographic Data Model for Cloud. *International Journal of Engineering and Technology, 7*(7), 128–31.

Aravindhan, R., Shanmugalakshmi, R., Ramya, K., & Selvan, C. (2016). Certain investigation on web application security: Phishing detection and phishing target discovery. *3rd International Conference on Advanced Computing and Communication Systems (ICACCS).*

Armbrust, M., Fox, A., Griffith, R., Joseph, A. D., Katz, R. H., Konwinski, A., Lee, G., Patterson, D. A., Rabkin, A., Stoica, I., & Zaharia, M. (2009). *Above the clouds: A berkeley view of cloud computing*. Technical Report UCB/EECS-2009-28.

Armbrust, M., Fox, A., Griffith, R., Joseph, A. D., Katz, R., Konwinski, A., Lee, G., Patterson, D., Rabkin, A., Stoica, I., & Zaharia, M. (2010). A view of cloud computing. *Communications of the ACM*, *53*(4), 50–58. doi:10.1145/1721654.1721672

Arunprasad, R., & Boopathi, S. (2019). Chapter-4 Alternate Refrigerants for Minimization Environmental Impacts: A Review. In Advances in Engineering Technology (p. 75). AkiNik Publications.

Asaamoning, G., Mendes, P., Rosário, D., & Cerqueira, E. (2021). Drone swarms as networked control systems by integration of networking and computing. *Sensors (Basel)*, *21*(8), 2642. doi:10.339021082642 PMID:33918696

Aslan, M. F., Durdu, A., Yusefi, A., & Yilmaz, A. (2022). HVIOnet: A deep learning based hybrid visual–inertial odometry approach for unmanned aerial system position estimation. *Neural Networks*, *155*, 461–474. doi:10.1016/j.neunet.2022.09.001 PMID:36152378

Avram, M. G. (2014). Advantages and challenges of adopting cloud computing from an enterprise perspective. *Procedia Technology*, *12*, 529–534. doi:10.1016/j.protcy.2013.12.525

Awad, A., & Ali, M. (2015). Cloud Computing: A Survey. *Journal of Grid Computing*, *13*(3), 331–355.

B, M. K., K, K. K., Sasikala, P., Sampath, B., Gopi, B., & Sundaram, S. (2024). Sustainable Green Energy Generation From Waste Water. In *Practice, Progress, and Proficiency in Sustainability* (pp. 440–463). IGI Global. doi:10.4018/979-8-3693-1186-8.ch024

Babu & Jayashree. (2015). A Survey on the Role of IoT and Cloud in Health Care. *International Journal of Scientific, Engineering and Technology Research, 4*(12), 2217-2219.

Babu, C. V., & Srisakthi, S. (2023). Cyber Physical Systems and Network Security: The Present Scenarios and Its Applications. In R. Thanigaivelan, S. Kaliappan, & C. Jegadheesan (Eds.), Cyber-Physical Systems and Supporting Technologies for Industrial Automation (pp. 104–130). Academic Press.

Babu, C. V., & Yadav, S. (2023). Cyber Physical Systems Design Challenges in the Areas of Mobility, Healthcare, Energy, and Manufacturing. In R. Thanigaivelan, S. Kaliappan, & C. Jegadheesan (Eds.), Cyber-Physical Systems and Supporting Technologies for Industrial Automation (pp. 131–151). Academic Press.

Bagui, S., Nandi, D., Bagui, S., & White, R. J. (2021). Machine learning and deep learning for phishing email classification using one-hot encoding. *Journal of Computational Science*, *17*(7), 610–623. doi:10.3844/jcssp.2021.610.623

Balani, Z., & Varol, H. (2020). Cloud Computing Security Challenges and Threats. *2020 8th International Symposium on Digital Forensics and Security (ISDFS)*, 1-4. 10.1109/ISDFS49300.2020.9116266

Balogh, S., Gallo, O., Ploszek, R., Špaček, P., & Zajac, P. (2021). IoT security challenges: Cloud and blockchain, postquantum cryptography, and evolutionary techniques. *Electronics (Basel)*, *10*(21), 2647. doi:10.3390/electronics10212647

Bellendorf, J., & Mann, Z. Á. (2018). Cloud topology and orchestration using TOSCA: A systematic literature review. In: Lecture Notes in Computer Science (including subseries Lecture Notes in Artificial Intelligence and Lecture Notes in Bioinformatics). doi:10.1007/978-3-319-99819-0_16

Beloglazov, A., & Buya, R. (2010). Energy-efficient resource management in virtualized cloud data centers. In *2010 10th IEEE / ACM International Conference on Cluster, Cloud and Grid Computing* (pp. 826-831). IEEE. 10.1109/CCGRID.2010.46

Bennett, C. H., & Brassard, G. (2014). Quantum cryptography: Public key distribution and coin tossing. *Theoretical Computer Science*, *560*, 7–11. doi:10.1016/j.tcs.2014.05.025

Bhati, A., Hansen, M., & Chan, C. M. (2017). Energy conservation through smart homes in a smart city: A lesson for Singapore households. *Energy Policy*, *104*, 230–239. doi:10.1016/j.enpol.2017.01.032

Bhattacharjee, R., & Siwa, S. (2016). Internet of Life: Securing the Cloud. In *IoT and big data technologies for next generation healthcare* (pp. 97–112). Springer.

Billah, M., Mehedi, S. T., Anwar, A., Rahman, Z., & Islam, R. (2022). *A systematic literature review on blockchain enabled federated learning framework for internet of vehicles*. arXiv Preprint arXiv:2203.05192.

Böhm, S., & Wirtz, G. (2022). Cloud-edge orchestration for smart cities: A review of kubernetes-based orchestration architectures. *EAI Endorsed Trans Smart Cities*, *6*(18), e2–e2. doi:10.4108/eetsc.v6i18.1197

Boopathi, S. (2022). An investigation on gas emission concentration and relative emission rate of the near-dry wire-cut electrical discharge machining process. *Environmental Science and Pollution Research International*, *29*(57), 86237–86246. doi:10.100711356-021-17658-1 PMID:34837614

Boopathi, S., & Kanike, U. K. (2023). Applications of Artificial Intelligent and Machine Learning Techniques in Image Processing. In *Handbook of Research on Thrust Technologies' Effect on Image Processing* (pp. 151–173). IGI Global. doi:10.4018/978-1-6684-8618-4.ch010

Buhari, A., Zukarnain, Z. A., Subramaniam, S. K., Zainuddin, H., & Saharudin, S. (2012). A Quantum Based Challenge Response User authentication Scheme Over Noiseless. *International Journal of Network Security & its Applications*, *4*(6), 67–79. doi:10.5121/ijnsa.2012.4605

Bu, S. J., & Kim, H. J. (2022). Optimized URL feature selection based on genetic-algorithm-embedded deep learning for phishing website detection. *Electronics (Basel)*, *11*(7), 1090. doi:10.3390/electronics11071090

Butler, L., Yigitcanlar, T., & Paz, A. (2021). Barriers and risks of Mobility-as-a-Service (MaaS) adoption in cities: A systematic review of the literature. *Cities (London, England)*, *109*, 103036. doi:10.1016/j.cities.2020.103036

Cai. (2009). *Customer Centric Cloud Service Model and a Case Study on Commerce as a Service.* Academic Press.

Chen. (2009). *What's New About Cloud Computing Security?* Academic Press.

Chen, D., & Zhao, H. (2012). Data Security and Privacy Protection Issues in Cloud Computing. *International Conference on Computer Science and Electronics Engineering*, 647-651. 10.1109/ICCSEE.2012.193

Chen, M., Ma, Y., Song, J., Lai, C. F., & Hu, B. (2019). Edge computing in the Internet of Things. In *Internet of Things* (pp. 1–16). Springer.

Chow, R., Golle, P., Jakobsson, M., Shi, E., Staddon, J., Masuoka, R., ... Devadas, S. (2009). Controlling data in the cloud: outsourcing computation without outsourcing control. In *Proceedings of the 2009 ACM workshop on Cloud computing security* (pp. 85-90). 10.1145/1655008.1655020

Cloud Security Alliance – Top Threats Working Group. (2022). *Top Threats to Cloud Computing.* Cloud Security Alliance. https://cloudsecurityalliance.org/artifacts/top-threats-to-cloud-computing-pandemic-eleven/

Cloud, A. W. S., & Whitepaper, A. W. S. (2021). *Web Application Hosting in the AWS Cloud.* AWS Whitepaper. https://docs.aws.amazon.com/whitepapers/latest/web-application-hosting-best-practices/an-aws-cloud-architecture-for-web-hosting.html

Curty & Santos. (2001). Quantum authentication of classical messages. *Physical Review A, 64*(6).

Davis, F. D. (1985). *A technology acceptance model for empirically testing new end-user information systems: Theory and results* [Doctoral dissertation]. Massachusetts Institute of Technology.

Decker, C., & Chiambaretto, P. (2022). Economic policy choices and trade-offs for Unmanned aircraft systems Traffic Management (UTM): Insights from Europe and the United States. *Transportation Research Part A, Policy and Practice*, *157*, 40–58. doi:10.1016/j.tra.2022.01.006

Depietro, R., Wiarda, E., & Fleischer, M. (1990). The context for change: Organization, technology and environment. *The Processes of Technological Innovation, 199*(0), 151-175.

Devare, M. H. (2019). Cloud Computing and Innovations. In G. Kecskemeti (Ed.), *Applying Integration Techniques and Methods in Distributed Systems and Technologies* (pp. 1–33). IGI Global. doi:10.4018/978-1-5225-8295-3.ch001

Dewar, R. D., & Dutton, J. E. (1986). The adoption of radical and incremental innovations: An empirical analysis. *Management Science, 32*(11), 1422–1433. doi:10.1287/mnsc.32.11.1422

Dib, N., Freer, J., & Gray, C. (1998). Service-level agreements at the Huddersfield NHS Trust. *International Journal of Health Care Quality Assurance, 11*(3), 96–101.

Dillon. (2010). *Cloud Computing: Issues and Challenges.* Academic Press.

DiPetro, J. (2014). Cloud computing security. *Journal of Computer Information Systems, 54*(1), 1–10.

Donevski, I., Nielsen, J. J., & Popovski, P. (2021). On addressing heterogeneity in federated learning for autonomous vehicles connected to a drone orchestrator. *Frontiers in Communications and Networks, 2*, 709946. doi:10.3389/frcmn.2021.709946

Duncan, D. B. (2020). *Certified Cloud Security Professional (CCSP).* All-in-One Exam Guide. McGraw-Hill Education.

El-Gazzar, R. F. (2014). A literature review on cloud computing adoption issues in enterprises. In *Creating Value for All Through IT: IFIP WG 8.6 International Conference on Transfer and Diffusion of IT, TDIT 2014, Aalborg, Denmark, June 2-4, 2014. Proceedings* (pp. 214-242). Springer Berlin Heidelberg. 10.1007/978-3-662-43459-8_14

Erl, T., Puttini, R., & Mahmood, Z. (2013). *Cloud computing: Concepts, technology & architecture.* Pearson Education.

Esposito, C., De Santis, A., Tortora, G., Chang, H., & Choo, K. K. (2018). Blockchain: A panacea for healthcare cloud-based data security and privacy? *IEEE Cloud Computing, 5*(1), 31-37.

Everson, L. R., Sapatnekar, S. S., & Kim, C. H. (2019). 2.5 A 40\times 40 four-neighbor time-based in-memory computing graph ASIC chip featuring wavefront expansion and 2D gradient control. *2019 IEEE International Solid-State Circuits Conference-(ISSCC)*, 50–52. 10.1109/ISSCC.2019.8662455

Faughnan, M. S., Hourican, B. J., MacDonald, G. C., Srivastava, M., Wright, J. P. A., Haimes, Y. Y., Andrijcic, E., Guo, Z., & White, J. C. (2013, April). *Risk analysis of unmanned aerial vehicle hijacking and methods of its detection. In 2013 IEEE systems and information engineering design symposium.* IEEE.

Fisher, C. (2018). Cloud versus on-premise computing. *American Journal of Industrial and Business Management, 8*(09), 1991–2006. doi:10.4236/ajibm.2018.89133

Frambach, R. T., & Barkema, H. G. (1998). Adoption of a service innovation in the business market: An empirical test of supply-side variables. *Journal of Business Research*. https://www.sciencedirect.com/science/article/abs/pii/S0148296397000052

Frambach, R. T., Barkema, H. G., Nooteboom, B., & Wedel, M. (1998). Adoption of a service innovation in the business market: An empirical test of supply-side variables. *Journal of Business Research*, *41*(2), 161–174. doi:10.1016/S0148-2963(97)00005-2

Fujitsu, S. (2011). *Cloud Adoption The definitive guide to a business technology revolution.* https://www.fujitsu.com/us/Images/WBOC-1-Adoption-US.pdf

Gadekallu, T. R., Pham, Q.-V., Huynh-The, T., Bhattacharya, S., Maddikunta, P. K. R., & Liyanage, M. (2021). *Federated learning for big data: A survey on opportunities, applications, and future directions.* arXiv Preprint arXiv:2110.04160.

Gaetani, E., Aniello, L., Baldoni, R., Lombardi, F., Margheri, A., & Sassone, V. (2017). Blockchain-based database to ensure data integrity in cloud computing environments. In *Italian Conference on Cybersecurity* (p. 10). University of Southampton.

Garcia, R., & Kim, Y. (2020). Understanding the Dynamics of Software as a Service (SaaS) Models. *International Journal of Cloud Applications and Services*, *12*(1), 45–68.

Goyal, D., Kakkar, P., & Kumar, N. (2020). Information Security in Cloud Computing: Issues, Challenges, and Solutions. In Recent Trends and Future Technologies in Cloud Computing (pp. 1-14). Springer.

Graniszewski & Arciszewski. (2016). Performance analysis of selected hypervisors (virtual machine monitors-vmms). *International Journal of Electronics and Telecommunications, 62.*

Guo, L., Yang, H., Luan, K., Luo, Y., & Sun, L. (2023). A Trust Model Based on Characteristic Factors and SLAs for Cloud Environments. *IEEE Transactions on Network and Service Management.*

Gupta, Y., & Vashisth, R. (2023). Cyber Threats in Cloud Computing Environment. *2023 4th International Conference on Electronics and Sustainable Communication Systems (ICESC),* 548-555. 10.1109/ICESC57686.2023.10193701

Gutierrez, A., & Lumsden, J. R. (2014). *Key management determinants for cloud computing adoption.* Academic Press.

Gu, Y., Zhang, Y., Han, Q., Li, B., & Shu, L. (2019). *Fog Computing in the Internet of Things: A Survey.* Raja Saud University-Journal of Computer and Information Science.

Habib, G., Sharma, S., Ibrahim, S., Ahmad, I., Qureshi, S., & Ishfaq, M. (2022). Blockchain Technology: Benefits, Challenges, Applications, and Integration of Blockchain Technology with Cloud Computing. *Future Internet*, *14*(11), 341. doi:10.3390/fi14110341

Hanumanthakari, S., Gift, M. M., Kanimozhi, K., Bhavani, M. D., Bamane, K. D., & Boopathi, S. (2023). Biomining Method to Extract Metal Components Using Computer-Printed Circuit Board E-Waste. In *Handbook of Research on Safe Disposal Methods of Municipal Solid Wastes for a Sustainable Environment* (pp. 123–141). IGI Global. doi:10.4018/978-1-6684-8117-2.ch010

Hashizume, K., Rosado, D. G., Fernandez-Medina, E., & Fernandez, E. B. (2013). Analysis of security issues for cloud computing. *Journal of Internet Services and Applications*, *4*(1), 5. doi:10.1186/1869-0238-4-5

Heinzl, B., & Kastner, W. (2019). Platform-independent Modeling for Simulation-based Energy Optimization in Industrial Production. *International Journal of Simulation: Systems, Science and Technology*, *20*(6), 10–11.

Hewko Alex. (2021). *STRIDE Threat Modeling: What You Need to Know*. Software Secured. https://www.softwaresecured.com/stride-threat-modeling/

Hildmann, H., & Kovacs, E. (2019). Using unmanned aerial vehicles (UAVs) as mobile sensing platforms (MSPs) for disaster response, civil security and public safety. *Drones (Basel)*, *3*(3), 59. doi:10.3390/drones3030059

Hilley. (2009). *Cloud Computing: A Taxonomy of Platform and Infrastructure-level Offerings*. Academic Press.

Huang, L., & Zhu, Q. (2019). Adaptive strategic cyber defense for advanced persistent threats in critical infrastructure networks. *Performance Evaluation Review*, *46*(2), 52–56. doi:10.1145/3305218.3305239

Hu, C., & Liu, X. (2016). Cloud computing security: A survey. *Security and Privacy*, *14*(3), 5.

Hussain, F., Hussain, R., Hassan, S. A., & Hossain, E. (2020). Machine learning in IoT security: Current solutions and future challenges. *IEEE Communications Surveys and Tutorials*, *22*(3), 1686–1721. doi:10.1109/COMST.2020.2986444

Hussain, W., Hussain, F. K., & Hussain, O. K. (2014). Maintaining trust in cloud computing through SLA monitoring. *Neural Information Processing: 21st International Conference, ICONIP 2014, Kuching, Malaysia, November 3-6, 2014 Proceedings*, *21*, 690–697.

Huth, A., & Cebula, J. (2013). Basics of cloud computing. Academic Press.

Hwang, T., Lee, K.-C., & Li, C.-M. (2007). Provably secure three-party authenticated quantum key distribution protocols. *IEEE Transactions on Dependable and Secure Computing*, *4*(1), 71–80. doi:10.1109/TDSC.2007.13

Illiashenko, O., Kharchenko, V., Babeshko, I., Fesenko, H., & Di Giandomenico, F. (2023). Security-Informed Safety Analysis of Autonomous Transport Systems Considering AI-Powered Cyberattacks and Protection. *Entropy (Basel, Switzerland)*, *25*(8), 1123. doi:10.3390/e25081123 PMID:37628153

Iversen, N., Schofield, O. B., Cousin, L., Ayoub, N., Vom Bögel, G., & Ebeid, E. (2021). Design, integration and implementation of an intelligent and self-recharging drone system for autonomous power line inspection. *2021 IEEE/RSJ International Conference on Intelligent Robots and Systems (IROS)*, 4168–4175. 10.1109/IROS51168.2021.9635924

Jackisch, R., Madriz, Y., Zimmermann, R., Pirttijärvi, M., Saartenoja, A., Heincke, B. H., Salmirinne, H., Kujasalo, J.-P., Andreani, L., & Gloaguen, R. (2019). Drone-borne hyperspectral and magnetic data integration: Otanmäki Fe-Ti-V deposit in Finland. *Remote Sensing (Basel)*, *11*(18), 2084. doi:10.3390/rs11182084

Jadeja, Y., & Modi, K. (2012). *Cloud computing-concepts, architecture and challenges. In 2012 international conference on computing, electronics and electrical technologies (ICCEET)*. IEEE.

Jaeger, P. T. (2008). Cloud computing and information policy: Computing in a policy cloud? *Journal of Information Technology & Politics*, *5*, 269–283.

Jaeyalakshmi, M., & Kumar, P. (2016). Task scheduling using meta-heuristic optimization techniques in cloud environment. *IJ Intelligent Systems and Applications, 5*.

Jaeyalakshmi, Vijay, Jayashree, & Vijay. (2023). A Cloud Based Healthcare Data Storage System Using Encryption Algorithm. In *Recent Trends in Computational Intelligence and Its Application* (pp. 486-491). CRC Press.

Janbi, N., Katib, I., Albeshri, A., & Mehmood, R. (2020). Distributed Artificial Intelligence-as-a-Service (DAIaaS) for Smarter IoE and 6G Environments. *Sensors (Basel)*, *20*(20), 5796. doi:10.339020205796 PMID:33066295

Jansen, W., & Grace, T. (2011). Guidelines for security and privacy in public cloud computing. *NIST Special Publications*, *800*(144), 800–145. doi:10.6028/NIST.SP.800-144

Jha, D., & Buyya, R. (2013). Cloud security: A survey of challenges and solutions. *Journal of Network and Computer Applications*, *36*(1), 388–405.

Jhaveri, R. H., & Patel, R. B. (2017). Objects and Cloud Computing: A Study. In *2017 International Conference on Computing and Communication Methods (ICCMC)* (pp. 1076-1080). IEEE.

Johnson, M., & White, L. (2019). Platform as a Service (PaaS) Adoption: Challenges and Opportunities. *Cloud Computing Research*, *8*(4), 567–589.

Joyner, C. C., & Lotrionte, C. (2017). Information warfare as international coercion: Elements of a legal framework. In *The Use of Force in International Law* (pp. 433–473). Routledge. doi:10.4324/9781315084992-18

Kaldate, A., Kanase-Patil, A., & Lokhande, S. (2022). Artificial Intelligence Based Integrated Renewable Energy Management in Smart City. In Energy Storage Systems: Optimization and Applications (pp. 1–20). Springer.

Kalra, D., & Pradhan, M. R. (2021). Enduring data analytics for reliable data management in handling smart city services. *Soft Computing*, *25*(18), 12213–12225. doi:10.100700500-021-05892-1

Kamra, V., Sonawane, K., & Alappanavar, P. (2012). Cloud computing and its pricing schemes. *International Journal on Computer Science and Engineering*, *4*(4), 577.

Kandias, M., & Gritzalis, D. (2012). Cloud insiders: The threat within. *Computer*, *45*(8), 49–55.

Karthik, S., Hemalatha, R., Aruna, R., Deivakani, M., Reddy, R. V. K., & Boopathi, S. (2023). Study on Healthcare Security System-Integrated Internet of Things (IoT). In Perspectives and Considerations on the Evolution of Smart Systems (pp. 342–362). IGI Global.

Khalid, U., Ghafoor, A., Irum, M., & Shibli, M. A. (2013). Cloud based secure and privacy enhanced authentication & authorization protocol. *Procedia Computer Science*, *22*, 680–688. doi:10.1016/j.procs.2013.09.149

Khalil, I., Khreishah, A., & Azeem, M. C. (2014). Cloud Computing Security: A Survey. *Computers*, *3*(1), 1–35. doi:10.3390/computers3010001

Kirlappos, I., & Sasse, M. A. (2011). Security education against phishing: A modest proposal for a major rethink. *IEEE Security and Privacy*, *10*(2), 24–32. doi:10.1109/MSP.2011.179

Knights, M. (2007). The art of quantum computing. *Engineering and Technology, IEEE*, *2*(1), 30–34. doi:10.1049/et:20070103

Kollu, P. K. (2021). Blockchain techniques for secure storage of data in cloud environment. *Turkish Journal of Computer and Mathematics Education*, *12*(11), 1515–1522.

Kshetri, N. (2017). Will Blockchain Power the Internet of Things? *IT Professional*, *19*(4), 68–72. doi:10.1109/MITP.2017.3051335

Kumar, P. R., Meenakshi, S., Shalini, S., Devi, S. R., & Boopathi, S. (2023). Soil Quality Prediction in Context Learning Approaches Using Deep Learning and Blockchain for Smart Agriculture. In R. Kumar, A. B. Abdul Hamid, & N. I. Binti Ya'akub (Eds.), (pp. 1–26). Advances in Computational Intelligence and Robotics. IGI Global. doi:10.4018/978-1-6684-9151-5.ch001

Kushida, M., O'Leary, D., Le, T., & Paliwal, A. (2020). *Advanced cloud security and application security*. Springer.

Kushwaha, A. (2020). Research Paper on AWS Cloud Infrastructure vs Traditional On-Premises. *International Research Journal of Engineering and Technology (IRJET)*, *7*(1).

Lauwers, C., & Tamburri, D. (n.d.). *OASIS Topology and Orchestration Specification for Cloud Applications*. www.oasis-open.org/committees/tosca

Leavitt, N. (2009). Is cloud computing really ready for prime time. *Growth*, *27*(5), 15–20.

Liu, J., Zhao, T., Zhou, S., Yu, C., & Niu, Z. (2015). CONCERT: A Cloud-based Architecture for Next-Generation Cellular Systems. *IEEE Wireless Communications*, 21.

Liu, Y., Wang, J., Niu, S., & Song, H. (2020). Deep learning enabled reliable identity verification and spoofing detection. *Wireless Algorithms, Systems, and Applications: 15th International Conference, WASA 2020, Qingdao, China, September 13–15, 2020 Proceedings, 15*(Part I), 333–345.

Lo, H., & Lütkenhaus, N. (2007). *Quantum cryptography: from theory to practice*. arXiv preprint quant-ph/0702202.

Lu, K., Yahyapour, R., Wieder, P., Yaqub, E., Abdullah, M., Schloer, B., & Kotsokalis, C. (2016). Fault-tolerant service level agreement lifecycle management in clouds using actor system. *Future Generation Computer Systems, 54*, 247–259.

M. M. R. & A. T. P. (2023). Enhancing the Detection of DDoS Attacks in Cloud using Linear Discriminant Algorithm. *2023 8th International Conference on Communication and Electronics Systems (ICCES),* 505-509. 10.1109/ICCES57224.2023.10192657

Ma, M., Yu, Z., & Liu, B. (2023). Automatic Generation of Network Micro-Segmentation Policies for Cloud Environments. *2023 4th International Seminar on Artificial Intelligence, Networking and Information Technology (AINIT),* 1-5. 10.1109/AINIT59027.2023.10212857

Maguluri, L. P., Arularasan, A. N., & Boopathi, S. (2023). Assessing Security Concerns for AI-Based Drones in Smart Cities. In R. Kumar, A. B. Abdul Hamid, & N. I. Binti Ya'akub (Eds.), Advances in Computational Intelligence and Robotics (pp. 27–47). IGI Global. doi:10.4018/978-1-6684-9151-5.ch002

Manesh, M. R., Kenney, J., Hu, W. C., Devabhaktuni, V. K., & Kaabouch, N. 2019, January. Detection of GPS spoofing attacks on unmanned aerial systems. In 2019 16th IEEE Annual Consumer Communications & Networking Conference (CCNC) (pp. 1-6). IEEE. doi:10.1109/CCNC.2019.8651804

Mather, T., Kumaraswamy, S., & Latif, S. (2009). *Cloud Security and Privacy: An Enterprise Perspective on Risks and Compliance*. O'Reilly Media.

Matsumoto, R. (2007). *Quantum multiparty key distribution protocol without use of entanglement*. arXiv preprint arXiv:0708.0902.

Meidan, Y., Bohadana, M., Mathov, Y., Mirsky, Y., Shabtai, A., Breitenbacher, D., & Elovici, Y. (2018). N-baiot—Network-based detection of iot botnet attacks using deep autoencoders. *IEEE Pervasive Computing, 17*(3), 12–22. doi:10.1109/MPRV.2018.03367731

Mell, P., & Grance, T. (2011). *The NIST definition of cloud computing*. Academic Press.

Microsoft. (2019). *Microsoft Cloud datacenter regions now available in the UAE to help fuel the Middle East's future economic ambitions*. https://news.microsoft.com/en-xm/2019/06/19/microsoft-cloud-datacenter-regions-now-available-in-the-uae-to-help-fuel-the-middle-easts-future-economic-ambitions/

Mourtaji, Y., Bouhorma, M., Alghazzawi, D., Aldabbagh, G., & Alghamdi, A. (2021). Hybrid Rule-Based Solution for Phishing URL Detection Using Convolutional Neural Network. Hindawi Wireless Communications and Mobile Computing. doi:10.1155/2021/8241104

Muralidharan, C., Shitharth, S., Alhebaishi, N., Mosli, R. H., & Alhelou, H. H. (2022). Three-phase service level agreements and trust management model for monitoring and managing the services by trusted cloud broker. *IET Communications*, *16*(19), 2309–2320.

Nagaraj, A. (2021). *Introduction to Sensors in IoT and Cloud Computing Applications*. Bentham Science Publishers. doi:10.2174/97898114793591210101

Narayana, K. E., & Jayashree, K. (2017). A Overview on Cloud Computing Platforms and Issues. *International Journal of Advanced Research in Computer Science and Software Engineering*, *7*(1), 238–22. doi:10.23956/ijarcsse/V7I1/0162

Nguyen, D. C., Pathirana, P. N., Ding, M., & Seneviratne, A. (2019). Blockchain for Secure EHRs Sharing of Mobile Cloud Based E-Health Systems. *IEEE Access : Practical Innovations, Open Solutions*, *7*, 66792–66806. doi:10.1109/ACCESS.2019.2917555

Nichols, R. K., Mumm, H. C., Lonstein, W. D., Ryan, J. J., Carter, C., & Hood, J. P. (2020). *Counter unmanned aircraft systems technologies and operations*. New Prairie Press.

Nielsen & Chuang. (2001). Quantum computation and quantum information. *Phys. Today, 54*(2).

Nugraha, Y., & Martin, A. (2017). Understanding trustworthy service level agreements: Open problems and existing solutions. In *International Workshop on Open Problems in Network Security (iNetSec)* (pp. 54-70). Academic Press.

O'Brien, J. L., Furusawa, A., & Vučković, J. (2009). Photonic quantum technologies. *Nature Photonics*, *3*(12), 687–695. doi:10.1038/nphoton.2009.229

Odun-Ayo, I. (2018). Cloud computing architecture: A critical analysis. In *2018 18th international conference on computational science and applications (ICCSA)*. IEEE. 10.1109/ICCSA.2018.8439638

Oguntala, G. A., Abd-Alhameed, P., Raed, A., Odeyemi, D., & Janet, O. (2017). Systematic analysis of enterprise perception towards cloud adoption in the African states: The Nigerian perspective. *The African Journal of Information Systems*, *9*(4), 1.

Oliveira, T., & Martins, M. F. (2011). Literature review of information technology adoption models at firm level. *Electronic Journal of Information Systems Evaluation, 14*(1), 110-121.

One, Q., Zhang, K., Wang, J., Ma, J., & Yu, S. (2018). Edge computing in the Internet of Things: A new architecture for efficient and real-time data processing. *IEEE Journal of Internet of Things*, *5*(1), 396–405.

Otter, D. W., Medina, J. R., & Kalita, J. K. (2020). A survey of the usages of deep learning for natural language processing. *IEEE Transactions on Neural Networks and Learning Systems*, *32*(2), 604–624. doi:10.1109/TNNLS.2020.2979670 PMID:32324570

Pandey, Gurjar, Nguyen, & Yadav. (n.d.). Security Threats and Mitigation Techniques in UAV Communications: A Comprehensive Survey. *IEEE Access*. doi:10.1109/ACCESS.2022.3215975

Pandit, M., Gupta, D., Anand, D., Goyal, N., Aljahdali, H., Mansilla, A., Kadry, S., & Kumar, A. (2022). Towards Design and Feasibility Analysis of DePaaS: AI Based Global Unified Software Defect Prediction Framework. *Applied Sciences (Basel, Switzerland)*, *12*(1), 493. doi:10.3390/app12010493

Perera, C., Qin, Y., Estrella, J. C., Reiff-Marganiec, S., & Vasilakos, A. V. (2017). Fog computing for sustainable smart cities: A survey. *ACM Computing Surveys*, *50*(3), 1–43. doi:10.1145/3057266

Prasanna, R. (2017). Basics of cloud computing. In *Big data analytics and cloud computing* (pp. 3–11). Springer.

Prithi, S., Sumathi, D., Poongodi, T., & Suresh, P. (2022). Trust Management Framework for Handling Security Issues in Multi-cloud Environment. In R. Nagarajan, P. Raj, & R. Thirunavukarasu (Eds.), *Operationalizing Multi-Cloud Environments. EAI/Springer Innovations in Communication and Computing*. Springer. doi:10.1007/978-3-030-74402-1_16

Qian, L. (2009). Cloud computing: An overview. *Cloud Computing: First International Conference, CloudCom 2009, Beijing, China, December 1-4, 2009. Proceedings 1.*

Rahamathunnisa, U., Subhashini, P., Aancy, H. M., Meenakshi, S., Boopathi, S., & ... (2023). Solutions for Software Requirement Risks Using Artificial Intelligence Techniques. In *Handbook of Research on Data Science and Cybersecurity Innovations in Industry 4.0 Technologies* (pp. 45–64). IGI Global.

Rahman, M. A., Asyhari, A. T., Wen, O. W., Ajra, H., Ahmed, Y., & Anwar, F. (2021). Effective combining of feature selection techniques for machine learning-enabled IoT intrusion detection. *Multimedia Tools and Applications*, *80*(20), 1–19. doi:10.100711042-021-10567-y

Raj, P., & Srinivasan, A. (2019). A Survey of Insider Threats in Cloud Computing. In *2019 International Conference on Machine Learning and Cyber Security (ICMLCS)* (pp. 72-77). IEEE.

Ramgovind, S., Eloff, M. M., & Smith, E. (2010). The management of security in Cloud computing. *Information Security for South Africa, Johannesburg, South Africa, 2010*, 1–7. doi:10.1109/ISSA.2010.5588290

Ranjan, R., Benatallah, B., Dustdar, S., & Papazoglou, M. P. (2015). Cloud Resource Orchestration Programming: Overview, Issues, and Directions. *IEEE Internet Computing*, *19*(5), 46–56. doi:10.1109/MIC.2015.20

Reddy, M. A., Gaurav, A., Ushasukhanya, S., Rao, V. C. S., Bhattacharya, S., & Boopathi, S. (2023). Bio-Medical Wastes Handling Strategies During the COVID-19 Pandemic. In Multidisciplinary Approaches to Organizational Governance During Health Crises (pp. 90–111). IGI Global. doi:10.4018/978-1-7998-9213-7.ch006

Reus-Muns, G., & Chowdhury, K. R. (2021). Classifying UAVs with proprietary waveforms via preamble feature extraction and federated learning. *IEEE Transactions on Vehicular Technology*, *70*(7), 6279–6290. doi:10.1109/TVT.2021.3081049

Rimal, B. P., & Choi, E. (2009). A taxonomy and survey of cloud computing systems. In *Fifth International Joint Conference on INC, IMS and IDC*. IEEE Computer Society. 10.1109/NCM.2009.218

Rios, A., Muppala, J. K., & Van Dijk, M. (2013). Survey of Cloud Computing Security Management. *Journal of Cloud Computing: Advances, Systems, and Applications*, *2*(1), 1–17.

Ristenpart, T., Tromer, E., Shacham, H., & Savage, S. (2009). Hey, You, Get Off of My Cloud: Exploring Information Leakage in Third-Party Compute Clouds. In *Proceedings of the 16th ACM Conference on Computer and Communications Security (CCS '09)* (pp. 199-212). 10.1145/1653662.1653687

Rittinghouse, J. W., & Ransome, J. F. (2016). *Cloud Computing: Implementation, Management, and Security*. CRC Press.

Rizomiliotis, P., Maniatakos, M., & Karatza, H. (2017). Cloud forensic analysis based on virtual machine research. *Next Generation Computer Systems*, *76*, 237–250.

Rizvi, S., Ryoo, J., Kissell, J., & Aiken, B. (n.d.). A stakeholder-oriented assessment index for cloud security auditing. *Proceedings of the 9th International Conference on Ubiquitous Information Management and Communication*, 1-7. 10.1145/2701126.2701226

Rochlin, G. I., La Porte, T. R., & Roberts, K. H. (1987). The self-designing high-reliability organization: Aircraft carrier flight operations at sea. *Naval War College Review*, *40*(4), 76–92.

Rodriguez, V. K. Q., & Guillemin, F. (2016). Performance analysis of resource pooling for network function virtualization. In *2016 17th International Telecommunications Network Strategy and Planning Symposium (Networks)*. IEEE.

Roman, R., Lopez, J., & Mambo, M. (2013). Mobile Edge Computing, Fog, and More: Overview and Analysis of Security Threats and Challenges. *Future Generation Computer Systems*, *78*, 680–698. doi:10.1016/j.future.2016.11.009

Ross, P. K., & Blumenstein, M. (2015). Cloud computing as a facilitator of SME entrepreneurship. *Technology Analysis and Strategic Management*, *27*(1), 87–101. doi:10.1080/09537325.2014.951621

Saad, S. B., Ksentini, A., & Brik, B. (2021, June). A Trust architecture for the SLA management in 5G networks. In *ICC 2021-IEEE International Conference on Communications* (pp. 1-6). IEEE.

Saadon, G., Haddad, Y., & Simoni, N. (2019). A survey of application orchestration and OSS in next-generation network management. *Computer Standards & Interfaces*, *62*, 17–31. doi:10.1016/j.csi.2018.07.003

Sabahi, F. (2011). Cloud computing security threats and responses. *2011 IEEE 3rd International Conference on Communication Software and Networks*, 245-249. 10.1109/ICCSN.2011.6014715

Salama, R., Al-Turjman, F., & Culmone, R. (2023). AI-Powered Drone to Address Smart City Security Issues. *International Conference on Advanced Information Networking and Applications*, 292–300. 10.1007/978-3-031-28694-0_27

Saleem, A. A., Siddiqui, H. U. R., Shafique, R., Haider, A., & Ali, M. (2020). A review on smart IOT based parking system. *Recent Advances on Soft Computing and Data Mining: Proceedings of the Fourth International Conference on Soft Computing and Data Mining (SCDM 2020)*, 264–273.

Santos, N., Gummadi, K. P., & Rodrigues, R. (2009). Towards trusted cloud computing. USENIX Hot Cloud.

Saxena, D., Gupta, I., Gupta, R., Singh, A. K., & Wen, X. (2023, November). An AI-Driven VM Threat Prediction Model for Multi-Risks Analysis-Based Cloud Cybersecurity. *IEEE Transactions on Systems, Man, and Cybernetics. Systems*, *53*(11), 6815–6827. Advance online publication. doi:10.1109/TSMC.2023.3288081

Security Compass. (2022). *How to Best Threat Model Cloud-Native Applications.* Security Compass. https://www.securitycompass.com/blog/threat-modeling-cloud-native-applications/

Sengeni, D., Padmapriya, G., Imambi, S. S., Suganthi, D., Suri, A., & Boopathi, S. (2023). Biomedical Waste Handling Method Using Artificial Intelligence Techniques. In *Handbook of Research on Safe Disposal Methods of Municipal Solid Wastes for a Sustainable Environment* (pp. 306–323). IGI Global. doi:10.4018/978-1-6684-8117-2.ch022

Shahid, V., Nayyer, M. Z., & Ahmed, U. (2023). Trust-aware Cloudlet Federation Model for Secure Service Selection. *2023 International Conference on Energy, Power, Environment, Control, and Computing (ICEPECC)*, 1-5. 10.1109/ICEPECC57281.2023.10209493

Sharma, Sharma, Kumar, Kelkar, & Deshmukh. (2023). Cloud Top Management Role in Reducing Mobile Broadband Transmission Hazards and Offering Safety. *2023 3rd International Conference on Advance Computing and Innovative Technologies in Engineering (ICACITE)*, 1064-1068. 10.1109/ICACITE57410.2023.10182893

Shea Tally. (2023). *The Shared Responsibility Model in the Cloud.* Sonrai Security. https://sonraisecurity.com/blog/the-shared-responsibility-model-in-the-cloud/

Sheng, S., Holbrook, M., Kumaraguru, P., Cranor, L. F., & Downs, J. (2010, April). Who falls for phish? A demographic analysis of phishing susceptibility and effectiveness of interventions. In *Proceedings of the SIGCHI conference on human factors in computing systems* (pp. 373-382). 10.1145/1753326.1753383

Shukla, P., Muralidhar, A., Iliev, N., Tulabandhula, T., Fuller, S. B., & Trivedi, A. R. (2021). Ultralow-power localization of insect-scale drones: Interplay of probabilistic filtering and compute-in-memory. *IEEE Transactions on Very Large Scale Integration (VLSI) Systems*, *30*(1), 68–80.

Shukla, P., Nasrin, S., Darabi, N., Gomes, W., & Trivedi, A. R. (2022). MC-CIM: Compute-in-Memory With Monte-Carlo Dropouts for Bayesian Edge Intelligence. *IEEE Transactions on Circuits and Systems. I, Regular Papers*, *70*(2), 884–896. doi:10.1109/TCSI.2022.3224703

Sikeridis, Kampanakis, & Devetsikiotis. (2020). Post-quantum authentication in TLS 1.3: a performance study. *Cryptology ePrint Archive.*

Singh, R. (2021). Cloud computing and COVID-19. In *3rd International Conference on Signal Processing and Communication (ICPSC)* (pp. 552-557). IEEE.

Smith, J. (2018). Cloud Computing Security: Threats and Solutions. *International Journal of Computer Applications*, *181*(8), 17–21.

Smith, J., & Brown, A. (2021). Exploring Infrastructure as a Service (IaaS) in Cloud Computing. *Journal of Cloud Computing (Heidelberg, Germany)*, *5*(2), 123–145.

Spathoulas, P., Bravos, G., Samoladas, I., & Votis, K. (2016). Cloud litigation overview and key dimensions of cloud litigation preparation. *International Journal of Cloud Computing and Services Science (IJ-CLOSER)*, *5*(1), 38-55.

Subashini, S., & Kavitha, V. (2011). A survey of security issues in the cloud computing service delivery model. *Journal of Computer Networks and Applications*, *34*(1), 1–11. doi:10.1016/j.jnca.2010.07.006

Sultan, N. (2010). Cloud computing for education: A new dawn? *International Journal of Information Management*, *30*(2), 109–116. doi:10.1016/j.ijinfomgt.2009.09.004

Sun, L., Singh, J., & Hussain, O. K. (2012, December). Service level agreement (SLA) assurance for cloud services: A survey from a transactional risk perspective. In *Proceedings of the 10th International Conference on Advances in Mobile Computing & Multimedia* (pp. 263-266). Academic Press.

Suresh Babu, C.V. (n.d.). *Introduction to Cloud Computing.* Anniyappa Publications.

Suresh Babu, C.V., Akshayah, N. S., Maclin Vinola, P., & Janapriyan, R. (2023). IoT-Based Smart Accident Detection and Alert System. In P. Swarnalatha & S. Prabu (Eds.), Handbook of Research on Deep Learning Techniques for Cloud-Based Industrial IoT (pp. 322-337). IGI Global. doi:10.4018/978-1-6684-8098-4.ch019

Suresh Babu, C. V., Andrew Simon, P., & Barath Kumar, S. (2023). The Future of Cyber Security Starts Today, Not Tomorrow. In S. Shiva Darshan, M. Manoj Kumar, B. Prashanth, & Y. Vishnu Srinivasa Murthy (Eds.), *Malware Analysis and Intrusion Detection in Cyber-Physical Systems* (pp. 348–375). IGI Global. doi:10.4018/978-1-6684-8666-5.ch016

Svorobej, S., Bendechache, M., Griesinger, F., & Domaschka, J. (2020). Orchestration from the Cloud to the Edge. In T. Lynn, J. G. Mooney, B. Lee, & P. T. Endo (Eds.), *The Cloud-to-Thing Continuum: Opportunities and Challenges in Cloud, Fog and Edge Computing* (pp. 61–77). Springer International Publishing. doi:10.1007/978-3-030-41110-7_4

Syamala, M., Komala, C., Pramila, P., Dash, S., Meenakshi, S., & Boopathi, S. (2023). Machine Learning-Integrated IoT-Based Smart Home Energy Management System. In *Handbook of Research on Deep Learning Techniques for Cloud-Based Industrial IoT* (pp. 219–235). IGI Global. doi:10.4018/978-1-6684-8098-4.ch013

Syed, A. H. M., & Nawaf, Q. H. O. (2023). Yanlong Li1, Mohammed H. Alsharif, Muhammad Asghar Khan, Unmanned aerial vehicles (UAVs): Practical aspects, applications, open challenges, security issues, and future trends. *Intelligent Service Robotics*, *16*, 109–137. doi:10.100711370-022-00452-4 PMID:36687780

Tarahomi, S., Holz, R., & Sperotto, A. (2023). Quantifying Security Risks in Cloud Infrastructures: A Data-driven Approach. *2023 IEEE 9th International Conference on Network Softwarization (NetSoft),* 346-349. 10.1109/NetSoft57336.2023.10175501

Tomarchio, O., Calcaterra, D., & Modica, G. D. (2020). Cloud resource orchestration in the multi-cloud landscape: A systematic review of existing frameworks. *Journal of Cloud Computing (Heidelberg, Germany)*, *9*(1), 49. Advance online publication. doi:10.118613677-020-00194-7

Tony UcedaVelez & Marco M. Morana. (2015). *"Intro to Pasta," in Risk Centric Threat Modeling: Process for Attack Simulation and Threat Analysis.* Wiley. https://ieeexplore.ieee.org/document/9821030 doi:10.1002/9781118988374.ch6

Trivedi, J. Y. (2013). *A study on marketing strategies of small and medium sized enterprises. Research Journal of Management Sciences.*

Vaquero, L. M., Rodero-Merino, L., Caceres, J., & Lindner, M. (2011). Disruption in the Cloud: Towards a Cloud Definition. *ACM SIGCOMM Computer Communications Review*, *39*(1), 50–55. doi:10.1145/1496091.1496100

Veena, S., Mallikarjun, C. J. T., Adiga, S. V., Reddy, B. C. V., & Yogish, P. D. (2023). Cloud Security Using The Smart Contracts. *2023 International Conference on Computational Intelligence and Sustainable Engineering Solutions (CISES),* 312-316. 10.1109/CISES58720.2023.10183573

Veeranjaneyulu, R., Boopathi, S., Kumari, R. K., Vidyarthi, A., Isaac, J. S., & Jaiganesh, V. (2023). Air Quality Improvement and Optimisation Using Machine Learning Technique. *IEEE Explore*, 1–6.

Venkateswaran, N., Vidhya, K., Ayyannan, M., Chavan, S. M., Sekar, K., & Boopathi, S. (2023). A Study on Smart Energy Management Framework Using Cloud Computing. In 5G, Artificial Intelligence, and Next Generation Internet of Things: Digital Innovation for Green and Sustainable Economies (pp. 189–212). IGI Global. doi:10.4018/978-1-6684-8634-4.ch009

Venkateswaran, N., Kumar, S. S., Diwakar, G., Gnanasangeetha, D., & Boopathi, S. (2023). Synthetic Biology for Waste Water to Energy Conversion: IoT and AI Approaches. In M. Arshad (Ed.), (pp. 360–384). Advances in Bioinformatics and Biomedical Engineering. IGI Global. doi:10.4018/978-1-6684-6577-6.ch017

Venkateswaran, N., Vidhya, R., Naik, D. A., Raj, T. M., Munjal, N., & Boopathi, S. (2023). Study on Sentence and Question Formation Using Deep Learning Techniques. In *Digital Natives as a Disruptive Force in Asian Businesses and Societies* (pp. 252–273). IGI Global. doi:10.4018/978-1-6684-6782-4.ch015

Verma, S., & Shisodia, P. (2017). Security Threats, Connectivity and Countermeasures in IoT: A Survey. In *2017 International Conference on I-SMAC (IoT in Social, Mobile, Analytics and Cloud) (I-SMAC)* (pp. 790-794). IEEE.

Vincent, Van Leeuwen, Stout, & Lin. (2018). *Applying a Threat Model to Cloud Computing.* IEEE. https://www.osti.gov/servlets/purl/1594657

Vize, R., Coughlan, J., Kennedy, A., & Ellis-Chadwick, F. (2013). Technology readiness in a B2B online retail context: An examination of antecedents and outcomes. *Industrial Marketing Management*, *42*(6), 909–918. doi:10.1016/j.indmarman.2013.05.020

Vranken, H. (2017). Sustainability of bitcoin and blockchains. *Current Opinion in Environmental Sustainability*, *28*, 1–9. doi:10.1016/j.cosust.2017.04.011

Vyas, P., Bhavani, G. L., Gairola, N., Ranjith, D., Ibrahim, W. K., & Alazzam, M. B. (2023). Machine Learning Approaches for Security Detection in Cloud Web Applications. *2023 3rd International Conference on Advance Computing and Innovative Technologies in Engineering (ICACITE),* 1195-1199. 10.1109/ICACITE57410.2023.10183265

Wallace, R. J., & Loffi, J. M. (2015). Examining unmanned aerial system threats & defenses: A conceptual analysis. *International Journal of Aviation, Aeronautics, and Aerospace*, *2*(4), 1. doi:10.15394/ijaaa.2015.1084

Wang, C., Ren, K., Lou, W., & Li, J. (2010). Toward publicly auditable secure cloud data storage services. *IEEE Network*, *24*(4), 19–24. doi:10.1109/MNET.2010.5510914

Wang, J., Liu, Y., & Song, H. (2021). Counter-unmanned aircraft system (s)(C-UAS): State of the art, challenges, and future trends. *IEEE Aerospace and Electronic Systems Magazine*, *36*(3), 4–29. doi:10.1109/MAES.2020.3015537

Weaver, N., Paxson, V., Staniford, S., & Cunningham, R. (2003, October). A taxonomy of computer worms. In *Proceedings of the 2003 ACM workshop on Rapid Malcode* (pp. 11-18). 10.1145/948187.948190

Wegman, M. N., & Lawrence Carter, J. (1981). New hash functions and their use in authentication and set equality. *Journal of Computer and System Sciences*, *22*(3), 265–279. doi:10.1016/0022-0000(81)90033-7

Wei, P., Wang, D., Zhao, Y., Tyagi, S. K., & Kumar, N. (2020). Blockchain data-based cloud data integrity protection mechanism. *Future Generation Computer Systems*, *102*, 902–911. doi:10.1016/j.future.2019.09.028

Wilson, B. M. R., Khazaei, B., & Hirsch, L. (2015, November). Enablers and barriers of cloud adoption among Small and Medium Enterprises in Tamil Nadu. In *2015 IEEE International Conference on Cloud Computing in Emerging Markets (CCEM)* (pp. 140-145). IEEE. 10.1109/CCEM.2015.21

Wu, J., Mao, Z., Zhang, M., Li, J., & Li, J. (2010). Planning in cloud computing: Research challenges and opportunities. In *Proceedings of the 6th International Conference on Grid and Pervasive Computing (GPC'11)* (pp. 1-10). Springer.

Wu, S., Wang, J., Yan, Z., Song, G., Chen, Y., Ma, Q., Deng, M., Wu, Y., Zhao, Y., Guo, Z., Yuan, Z., Dai, G., Xu, X., Yang, X., Su, Y., Liu, L., & Wu, J. (2021). Monitoring tree-crown scale autumn leaf phenology in a temperate forest with an integration of PlanetScope and drone remote sensing observations. *ISPRS Journal of Photogrammetry and Remote Sensing*, *171*, 36–48. doi:10.1016/j.isprsjprs.2020.10.017

Yaacoub, J.-P., Noura, H., Salman, O., & Chehab, A. (2020, September). Security analysis of drones systems: Attacks, limitations, and recommendations. *Internet of Things : Engineering Cyber Physical Human Systems*, *11*, 100218. Advance online publication. doi:10.1016/j.iot.2020.100218

Yan, G., Wen, D., Olariu, S., & Weigle, M. C. (2013, March). Security challenges in vehicular cloud computing. *IEEE Transactions on Intelligent Transportation Systems*, *14*(1), 284–294. doi:10.1109/TITS.2012.2211870

Yazdinejad, A., Parizi, R. M., Dehghantanha, A., & Karimipour, H. (2021). Federated learning for drone authentication. *Ad Hoc Networks*, *120*, 102574. doi:10.1016/j.adhoc.2021.102574

Yerima, S. Y., & Alzaylaee, M. K. (2020, March). High accuracy phishing detection based on convolutional neural networks. In *2020 3rd International Conference on Computer Applications & Information Security (ICCAIS)* (pp. 1-6). IEEE. 10.1109/ICCAIS48893.2020.9096869

Young, R., & Jordan, E. (2008). Top management support: Mantra or necessity? *International Journal of Project Management*, *26*(7), 713–725. doi:10.1016/j.ijproman.2008.06.001

Zarrin, J., Wen Phang, H., Babu Saheer, L., & Zarrin, B. (2021). Blockchain for decentralization of internet: Prospects, trends, and challenges. *Cluster Computing*, *24*(4), 2841–2866. doi:10.100710586-021-03301-8 PMID:34025209

Zekrifa, D. M. S., Kulkarni, M., Bhagyalakshmi, A., Devireddy, N., Gupta, S., & Boopathi, S. (2023). Integrating Machine Learning and AI for Improved Hydrological Modeling and Water Resource Management. In *Artificial Intelligence Applications in Water Treatment and Water Resource Management* (pp. 46–70). IGI Global. doi:10.4018/978-1-6684-6791-6.ch003

Zeng, S., Li, Z., Yu, H., Zhang, Z., Luo, L., Li, B., & Niyato, D. (2023). Hfedms: Heterogeneous federated learning with memorable data semantics in industrial metaverse. *IEEE Transactions on Cloud Computing*, 1–15. doi:10.1109/TCC.2023.3254587

Zhang, J., Zhang, Y., Xiong, N. N., & Mao, Y. (2019). Internet of Things (IoT) Security: Current Status, Challenges, and Future Solutions. *IEEE Journal of Internet of Things*, *6*(2), 1993–2002.

Zheng, Z., Xie, S., Dai, H. N., Chen, X., & Wang, H. (2018). Blockchain challenges and opportunities: A survey. *International Journal of Web and Grid Services*, *14*(4), 352–375. doi:10.1504/IJWGS.2018.095647

Zhou, L., Wang, Q., Sun, X., Kulicki, P., & Castiglione, A. (2018). Quantum technique for access control in cloud computing II: Encryption and key distribution. *Journal of Network and Computer Applications*, *103*, 178–184. doi:10.1016/j.jnca.2017.11.012

About the Contributors

C. V. Suresh Babu is a pioneer in content development. A true entrepreneur, he founded Anniyappa Publications, a company that is highly active in publishing books related to Computer Science and Management. Dr. C.V. Suresh Babu has also ventured into SB Institute, a center for knowledge transfer. He holds a Ph.D. in Engineering Education from the National Institute of Technical Teachers Training & Research in Chennai, along with seven master's degrees in various disciplines such as Engineering, Computer Applications, Management, Commerce, Economics, Psychology, Law, and Education. Additionally, he has UGC-NET/SET qualifications in the fields of Computer Science, Management, Commerce, and Education. Currently, Dr. C.V. Suresh Babu is a Professor in the Department of Information Technology at the School of Computing Science, Hindustan Institute of Technology and Science (Hindustan University) in Padur, Chennai, Tamil Nadu, India. For more information, you can visit his personal blog at .

Sampath Boopathi completed his undergraduate in Mechanical Engineering and postgraduate in the field of Computer-Aided Design. He completed his Ph.D. from Anna University and his field of research includes Manufacturing and optimization. He published 100 more research articles in Internationally Peer-reviewed journals, one Patent grant, and three published patents. He has 16 more years of academic and research experiences in the various Engineering Colleges in Tamilnadu, India.

Selvan C. received the B.E. degree in Computer Science and Engineering in Manonmaniam Sundaranar University, India, in 2002, the M.E. degree in Computer Science and Engineering from Anna University, Chennai, India, in 2007 and the Ph.D. in Computer Science and Engineering from Anna University, Chennai, India in 2013. During his Ph.D degree he was a JRF, SRF under University Grant Commission (UGC, New Delhi) in Government College of Technology, Coimbatore. He had been working as a Software Engineer during 2002 to 2005. Further, he has been engaging in various responsibilities in the Engineering colleges, in Tamil Nadu since 2007. He was a Post-Doctoral Fellow in National Institute of Technology, Tiruchirappalli, under UGC, New Delhi, India from June 2017 to June 2022. In the year of 2022 June, he joined as a professor in New Horizon College of Engineering, Bangalore and worked up to January 2023. Currently he has been working as a Professor in the School of Computer Science and Engineering, REVA University, Bangalore since February 2023. His current research interests include Mobile Computing, Data Science and Artificial Intelligence. He is an IEEE senior member, an ACM member.

Eugene Berna I. is currently working as an Assistant Professor in the Department of Artificial Intelligence and Machine Learning, Bannari Amman Institute of Technology, Sathyamangalam. She completed her M.E in Computer Science and Engineering from Dhanalakshmi Srinivasan Engineering College, Anna University. She is pursuing her PhD from Anna University in Information and Communication Engineering and presently working in Machine Learning, Natural Language Processing and Deep Learning Projects. She has teaching experience of more than 10 years.

Jeyalakshmi J. has received B.Tech degree in Information Technology from Kamaraj College of Engineering and Technology affiliated to Anna University, Chennai, India in 2005, and M.Tech degree from Sathyabama University, Chennai, India in 2009. She has obtained Ph.D from Anna University, Chennai, India. She has published in several International Journals and Conferences. Her areas of interest include Data Analysis, Social Media Analysis. She is presently working as a Senior Assistant Professor at Department of Computer Science and Engineering, Amrita School of Computing, Amrita Vishwa Vidhyapeetham, Chennai, India.

Arnika Jain, a distinguished academician with a Ph.D. in Computer Science and Engineering (CSE), holds an impressive educational background, including a Master's degree in CSE, a Master of Computer Applications (MCA), and a Bachelor of Science in Physics, Chemistry, and Mathematics (PCM). Currently serving as an Assistant Professor in the esteemed Sharda School of Engineering and Technology at Sharda University, Greater Noida, Dr. Arnika brings to the institution nearly two decades of invaluable experience in academics. She earned her doctorate from Dr. A.P.J. Abdul Kalam Technical University, Lucknow, showcasing her commitment to advanced research in the field. Dr. Arnika's academic prowess is underscored by her achievements as a Gold Medalist in MCA with an outstanding 84.72% from Gurukul Kangri Vishwavidyalaya, Hardwar, and a Gold Medalist in M.Tech with an exceptional CGPA of 9.98.

Vijay K. is working as Assistant Professor (SG) in the department of Computer Science and Engineering, Rajalakshmi Engineering College, Chennai, Tamilnadu,

India. He is B.Tech., M.E., graduate and pursuing PhD in Anna University, Chennai in the area of Cloud Computing. Having 16+ years of experience in teaching. Received the award, "Active Participation Youth", under CSI Service Award at the CSI Annual Convention 2016. He was awarded with "Inspire Faculty Partnership Level award" in 2017 (Bronze Level) by Infosys. He is a life time member of Computer Society of India, IEI-India. He received Best Faculty Award many times. Presented/ published more than 30+ papers in various Conferences and Journals. His areas of interest include Cloud Computing, Image Processing, IOT and Machine Learning.

Muhammad Marakkoottathil has worked on data center switching, cloud offerings, routing, virtualization, WAN, Unified computing infrastructure, traditional to modern networking migration, software-defined solutions, hypervisor systems, and security product, building datacenter network strategy and road-map for many major enterprises including, standard chartered bank UK, KCB Kenya, AXA insurance Singapore, Saudi Telecom KSA, Ministry of Interior Abu Dhabi, Abu Dhabi Municipality, Abu Dhabi Police, Abu Dhabi Commercial Bank, Al Ain Hospital, Viva Bahrain, Du Telecom, Dubai Islamic Bank, Emaar & Emirates NBD bank in Dubai, NBK Kuwait, FAB Abu Dhabi, MOI AUH, CBO Oman, SINNAD Bahrain, etc. leading to his present assignment as Solution Architect- Sales, Muhammad Marakkoottathil have acquired skills in all phases of IT infrastructure domain including presales to improve technical selling through deep design, planning, review, auditing, architecting capabilities, Framework building and operation, consulting, leading and managing teams, enabling and managing project delivery. Muhammad Marakkoottathil has distinguished MBA degree from Birla Institute of Technology & Science, Dubai in 2022 and also carry more than 17 years of experience in working with customer on ICT space.

Prathibha Muraleedhara has a master's degree in information system security from the University of Houston, Texas, USA. Also has 10+ years of professional experience in the cyber security domain. She worked as a security architect where she performs cloud and on-prem threat modeling on a daily basis. She is currently working for Stanley Black & Decker as Manager security architecture where she is building and managing security architecture, threat modeling, SDLC, pentesting, secure coding and vulnerability disclosure programs. Below are some of her other achievements: Speaker at Grace Hopper Conference, WiCyS review committee member, Cyber Wyoming Member of the Board of Directors, ISSA North Colorado Chapter member, ISSA Women in Security Committee Member, and ISACA SheLeadsTech Ambassador.

Ambika N. is an MCA, MPhil, Ph.D. in computer science. She completed her Ph.D. from Bharathiar university in the year 2015. She has 16 years of teaching experience and presently working for St.Francis College, Bangalore. She has guided BCA, MCA and M.Tech students in their projects. Her expertise includes wireless sensor network, Internet of things, cybersecurity. She gives guest lectures in her expertise. She is a reviewer of books, conferences (national/international), encyclopaedia and journals. She is advisory committee member of some conferences. She has many publications in National & international conferences, international books, national and international journals and encyclopaedias. She has some patent publications (National) in computer science division.

Natraj N. A. is an Assistant Professor at SIDTM in Symbiosis International University, India. His academic chronicles include PhD in Electronics and Communication Engineering. He has 11 years of Academic experience in various Countries. His research interests include Wireless Sensor Networks, the Internet of Things, 5G and Communication Networks. He holds publications in reputed Journals and has published patents in the mentioned research fields. He has completed certifications in domains like 5G, IoT, Digital Forensics and Blockchain from various organizations like Stanford, Europe Open University, Qualcomm, University of London, etc.

Aravindhan Ragunthan has completed PhD in Computer Science and Engineering in Anna University, Chennai, currently he is working as an Associate Technical Architect, HCL Technologies Ltd. Chennai.

Manmohan Rauthan is working as Head of the department and professor in HNB Garhwal University in computer science and engineering department with 30 years of teaching experience. He has done M.Tech in 1987 from Roorkee University and has done his Ph.D. from Kumaon University in 2013. He has written a several research paper as well as 5 books in computer science. He is a core member of research committees, visiting committees.

Gnanavel S. is currently working as an Associate Professor in the department of Computing Technologies at SRM Institute of Science and Technology, Kattankulathur, Chennai, India. He Received the B.Tech (IT), M.E (CSE) and Ph.D. degree from Anna University Chennai, India. He has over 14 years of teaching and research experience. He works in the area of Multimedia transmission on Wireless Networks, Internet of Things and cloud security. His current research interests are in Machine Leaning, cyber security and cloud computing. He is a life time member of MISTE, ACM and MIANG. He published many papers in international refereed journals and conferences. He is serving as a reviewer for many journals and conferences.

Ramamurthy Venkatesh has obtained PhD from Faculty of Management, Symbiosis International (Deemed University), Pune, India. He is also engaged as International Adjunct Faculty at Symbiosis Institute of Telecom Management under Symbiosis International University. He has industry experience of about 30 yrs starting with his career as Indian Air Force officer as Flight Lieutenant. His previous engagements include Director – Learning & Development for eSquare Acamiea (2015-2017) and Senior Manager- Etisalat, Dubai (1999-2014), Manger -Projects at Tata Teleservices Ltd, India (1998-99), Technical Head at Usha Martin Telekom Limited, India(1994-98). He has also teaching experience as trainer /visiting teaching assignments in UAE @ Westford School of Management, Pacific Control Systems, SZABIST, Dubai Campus, UAE. His academic qualifications include MBA, Manchester Business School, UK , M.Tech (Computer Science), Banasthali University, India, B.E. (ECE), Bharathiyar University, India and certified PMP, ITIL V3 Foundation, eTOM, CGEIT. He currently lives and work in Dubai, UAE as Business Consultant for NETS International Communications.

Index

A

Access Control 1, 6-8, 12, 14, 17-19, 45, 65, 93, 100-101, 113, 119-120, 165, 167, 176, 199-200, 220-221
Adoption 8-9, 17-19, 26, 43, 56, 66-68, 70, 72-80, 83-90, 107, 193, 195, 198, 218, 239
Anomaly Detection 18, 43, 113, 116, 120-121, 124, 231
Artificial Intelligence 4, 18, 43, 46, 111-115, 120, 123-124, 212, 214-215, 229, 237-238, 240-242
Artificial Intelligence Drones 214, 229
Automation Security 24

B

Barriers 66, 72, 75, 87, 89, 129, 239
Blockchain 21, 91, 97-101, 108-110, 159, 211-212, 234, 239-240

C

Cloud 2-22, 24-56, 59-60, 63-80, 82-97, 100-103, 106-113, 115, 117-124, 159, 164-170, 177, 179-180, 182-187, 189-190, 192-213, 238, 242
Cloud Adoption 9, 19, 66-67, 70, 72-74, 76-80, 83-89, 195
Cloud Computing 1-9, 11, 15-22, 24-27, 31, 36-38, 40, 43, 45-56, 63-73, 75-77, 79-80, 87-92, 94-95, 97, 101, 106-110, 112, 122, 163-164, 180, 182-184, 186-187, 189-190, 192-194, 198, 201-202, 210-213, 238, 242
Cloud Infrastructure 7, 14, 16-17, 26-27, 34, 36-38, 42, 46, 52-53, 88, 96, 117, 195, 200, 203
Cloud Platforms 42, 163-164, 194, 206, 210
Cloud Providers 3, 5-7, 17, 32-33, 35, 38-40, 49-50, 69, 91, 95, 101, 106-108, 112-113, 115, 122-123, 163
Cloud Security 9-10, 12-14, 17-21, 25-27, 29-31, 36, 42, 47, 95, 97, 111-113, 117-121, 123-124, 163-164, 166-167, 179-180, 195-197, 205-208, 210-211, 213
Cloud Service Providers 6-8, 10, 14, 28, 30, 38, 87, 92, 112, 163-164, 183, 186-187, 203, 205, 207, 210
Conditional Random Field (CRF) 125, 132, 158
Cyber Threats 112, 124, 195, 212
Cybersecurity 7, 15, 56, 61, 72, 107, 109, 127, 133, 136-137, 209-210, 213, 236-238, 241

D

Data Breaches 1-2, 4, 7-10, 16-18, 25, 34, 38, 55, 75, 120, 190, 194, 196-198, 226
Data Protection 9, 14, 19, 34, 38, 99, 106, 120, 122, 188, 190, 199, 216, 223-224, 229, 231, 236-237
Data Protection and Privacy 120, 122, 224, 229
Decryption 58, 121, 194
Deep Learning 22, 114, 116-117, 130-132, 158-161, 240-242

Denial of Service 168, 171, 173-174, 176, 198, 201
Dubai 72

E

Emerging Technologies 108, 215, 233, 235, 237
Encryption 1, 6-9, 12, 14-18, 29, 34, 38, 45, 53, 55, 65, 91, 93, 96, 100-101, 107, 112, 120-122, 165-166, 170, 175-176, 179, 187, 194, 205, 207, 212, 220, 223-224, 231, 236
Exploit 112, 129, 139, 163, 166, 168, 170, 178, 197, 199, 203-204

H

Hashing 91, 98, 101
Hypervisors 48, 52-54, 63, 93

I

Insider Attacks 1-2, 4, 9-10, 15-18

L

Latent Dirichlet Allocation (LDA) 125, 130, 132, 142-143, 158

M

Machine Learning 4, 17-18, 21, 27-28, 43, 107-108, 111-117, 121-125, 127, 129-134, 137, 158-160, 204, 211, 213, 215, 234, 239, 242
Malware 10, 12, 22, 41, 113, 158, 167, 196, 200, 204-205, 207, 209, 219, 221

N

Neural Networks 114, 116-117, 159, 161-162

O

Orchestration 19, 24-25, 29-33, 41-43, 45-47, 52-54, 64, 108

P

Privacy 1, 7, 11-12, 19-21, 38, 45, 59, 63-64, 99, 101, 106, 108-109, 112, 120, 122-123, 155, 160, 187, 194-195, 198, 202-203, 211, 215-216, 218-220, 222-223, 225-232, 234-235, 237

Q

Quantum Key Distribution 48, 54, 56, 58-63

R

Regulations 38, 45, 72, 76-77, 101, 106, 112, 123, 126, 188, 190, 205, 210, 220, 223-225, 227-229, 235-237
Resource Pooling 2, 48-52, 64
Risk Assessment 1, 14, 118, 120, 170

S

Security 1-2, 4-23, 25-31, 33-38, 41-48, 51-63, 72, 75-76, 87, 93-97, 99, 101, 103, 105-109, 112-113, 117-121, 123-124, 126-129, 132-134, 139, 146, 155, 159-171, 173-181, 184, 186-188, 190, 192-213, 215-225, 229-232, 234-237, 240-241
Security Challenges SAO 24
Security Strategies 1, 45, 207
Service Level Agreement (SLA) 184-185, 193
Smart Cities 46, 107, 214-220, 222-223, 225, 227-228, 230, 232-235, 237-238, 240

T

Threat 10-13, 15, 17-19, 21, 27-28, 30, 35, 37, 43-45, 55, 111-113, 120, 123-124, 126, 128, 132, 163-165, 167-170, 173, 179-180, 194, 196, 198-199, 203-204, 206, 209, 213, 215-216, 219, 235
Threat Detection 10-13, 17-19, 28, 35, 43,

45, 111, 113, 124, 203
Threat Modeling 163, 168-170, 173, 179-180
Tracking 91, 98, 103, 108, 189, 234
Trust 17-18, 43, 98-101, 108-109, 158, 165, 177, 182-185, 190-193, 203, 209, 212, 214-216, 218, 223, 226-230, 232, 236-237

U

UAE 66-67, 71-73, 77-80, 84-88
UAE Public Cloud 66, 72

V

Virtualization 7, 50-53, 64, 93, 182
Vulnerability 15-16, 19, 30, 34, 42, 117-119, 126, 139, 163, 166, 169-170, 203, 215, 221

W

Web Ontology Language (OWL) 125, 158

www.ingramcontent.com/pod-product-compliance
Lightning Source LLC
LaVergne TN
LVHW080647011026
849160LV00014B/1344
* 9 7 9 8 3 6 9 3 4 4 9 0 3 *